LIVING HOPE

A Study of the New Testament Theme of Birth from Above

William Orr and William Guy

A Sundial Book from
Family Communications, Inc.
and

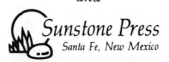

Sunstone Press
Santa Fe, New Mexico

Copyright © 1989 by William Orr and William Guy

All Rights Reserved.
No part of this book may be reproduced in any form or by any electronic or mechanical means including information storage and retrieval systems, without permission in writing from the publisher, except by a reviewer who may quote brief passages in a review.

First Edition

Printed in the United States of America

Library of Congress Cataloging in Publication Data:

Orr, William F. (William Fridell), 1907-
  Living hope, a study of the new testament theme of birth from Above.

  1. Regeneration (Theology)--Biblical teaching.   2. Bible. N.T.--Criticism, interpretation, etc. I. Guy, William, 1946-   . II. Title.
BS2545.R38077 1989   234'.£   88-34841
ISBN: 0-86534—132-X

Published in 1989 by SUNSTONE PRESS
Post Office Box 2321
Santa Fe, NM 87504-2321 / USA

The authors dedicate this book with gratitude to our friend Fred Rogers.
 o et praesidium et dulce decus noster

Contents

Preface / 5

Chapter 1. / 9
   Introduction to the Theme of Born from Above: Jesus Converses with Nicodemus.

Chapter 2. Two Women / 31
   i. The woman at the Well / 31
   ii. The woman who washed Jesus' feet (or anointed his head) / 40

Chapter 3. Peter's Painful Birth from Above / 48
   i. Basic personality traits in Peter / 48
   ii. Pause: assessment of Peter's progress in the new life / 58
   iii. Peter under stress during the last days of Jesus' life / 59
   iv. Peter and the early church / 71
   v. Peter's role in problems of the maturing church / 81
   vi. Peter's final phase: advances and relapses / 87

Chapter 4. Paul and the Stages of the New Life / 100
   i. The account in Acts / 100
   ii. Paul's letters: dying to one's sins and being born from above into the new life / 108
   iii. Maturity within the new life / 113
   iv. True glory and the refusal to flash credentials / 120

    v. Levels of service for all / 140
   vi. Love the true maturity / 148
  vii. Backslidings / 152
 viii. Paul himself as an example of someone born from above / 162
   ix. Paul's record of dealing with his opponents: an example of his growth / 172

Epilogue / 187

Footnotes / 193

Preface

This book began its life as a series of lectures given by Professor Orr in the Continuing Education program of Pittsburgh Theological Seminary. The lectures were given in the fall of 1984. One auditor of these lectures was Fred Rogers, a longtime student and friend of Professor Orr's. Fred was so moved and impressed by these lectures that he sought some way to see them into print. He spoke to an editor he knew. The editor proposed to Professor Orr that he turn his lectures into a book. Professor Orr did not want to undertake this writing project by himself. He agreed to do the book if his friend William Guy could be brought in on the project as writer. This arrangement was acceptable to all parties and work on the project began in January 1985 and continued, in its initial phase, for a year.

The world of publishing is an unpredictable environment these days. By the time the book was finished, the editor who had originally commissioned it was no longer interested, partly because of a change in the direction of his company. Other publishers also rejected the manuscript for various reasons. This series of rejections did not daunt Fred Rogers, whose belief in the project, a belief constantly communicated to the authors even (or especially) at their most discouraged moments, was unstinting. We would like to begin by thanking him for his generous support, both emotional and financial, of the writing of this book. One of the authors of this book lives in Pittsburgh, Pennsylvania. The other lives in Franconia, New Hampshire. Seven trips were necessary for the two of us to get together for work. Family Communications, Inc., which produces *Mr. Rogers' Neighborhood,* paid for all of these trips. Family Communications has now also paid for part of the costs of publication. It is hard sometimes to feel that one has deserved such grace, but it is never hard to feel grateful. We hope that the dedication of this book manages to convey some part, however inadaquate, of our boundless feelings of thanks.

The writing of a book of this kind required other kinds of help, and the authors would like to thank the people responsible for such help. When one author visits another author so that the two of them can work together, no matter who is traveling in which direction, hospitality is needed as some sort of sustaining element at the destination. The authors of this book (mostly Guy in his trips to Pittsburgh, which were the general rule) were both overwhelmed and buoyed up by such an element, and would like to thank Mildred Orr, Don and Sally Stone, and Vicki Guy for providing it. Without them our work could not even have been contemplated, much less begun or completed.

Vicki Guy has edited the most recent final and extensive revisions of this book, taking time from her own busy schedule of activities during the summer of 1988. It is very difficult to slip a sloppy sentence or an ill-thought-out paragraph past her. This book is no doubt shot through with faults still, but without her help it would have been shot through with many more.

Bill Isler of Family Communications Inc. has been another principal supporter of this project. One reads of people with worthy projects which they would like to attempt who have to scramble desperately for funds to carry them out and who sometimes never manage to find such funds. It has been nothing short of miraculous and a little bit dream-like for us to have had such unconditional encouragement from someone like Bill.

David Noel Freedman took time out from his truly impossible schedule to read the manuscript at an early stage for Guy. In addition to finding *every* small mechanical error, he offered his usual profound and sage counsel (not all of which we took, we must admit) on various Old Testament passages. He also obtained a reading for the manuscript by one commerical editor. And he kept up the spirits of the principal writer when those tended to flag and/or to droop, he told us to stick to our guns, not let anyone change the nature of *our* book. This advice was an oft-needed and much appreciated tonic.

Some discussion of our working method may be of interest and in order. For years before we began work on this book, the authors had been in the habit of reading works in Hebrew, Latin, and Greek together and of arguing over the meaning. This method was not really changed for the writing of this book, it was simply re-oriented a little. We analyzed passages in the Greek New Testament and the Hebrew Bible which could be applied to our topic. Guy would, after a day of these discussions, repair to the nearest word-processor and try to convert our discussions into written form. These attempts would be passed back to Orr for his suggestions, a process of negotiation over the written text was thus begun, a process which has never really stopped: we would probably go on fine-tuning our remarks for ever except that now someone is taking the manuscript out of our hands (after one last, rather massive re-writing). The experience of collaboration is an altogether surprising and gratifying one. The product is of course something more than what either contributor could have produced in isolation, but it seems also to be something more than merely the sum of two parts; a multiplication and a transformation of ideas tends to take place, perhaps something like the "grace upon grace" which we will be talking about in our text, or the "wonderful one times one" which E.E. Cummings coined as his term for talk about marriage. At any rate we have both grown in this encounter with each other and are grateful for the chance to have had it.

We have, in pursuit of our theme, used our own translations from both the Old and New Testaments. We issue this fact as a warning to save people the trouble and the frustration of trying to find our translation in *some* version of the Bible. Such a search would truly be endless.

CHAPTER 1.

INTRODUCTION TO THE THEME OF BORN FROM ABOVE:

JESUS CONVERSES WITH NICODEMUS.

We might begin with a question geared to contemporary religious discourse: what does the New Testament have to say about being born again? From the currency of the term "born again", and from the reported frequency of "born again" experiences, one would expect to find copious answers to such a question. There is one fairly obscure verse in Titus(3.5) where a noun meaning "again-birth" is employed. The first epistle of Peter(1.3, a passage which we will discuss later) refers to God's either begetting or bearing us again into a living hope through the resurrection of Jesus (the Greek verbal root *gennao* which is compounded in this passage with a prefix meaning "again" can mean either to bear or to beget). Otherwise, the New Testamant never actually mentions being "born again."

The text which, at least in one famous translation, seems to support the idea, and to describe the necessity of being born again occurs in the third chapter of the Gospel of John, where Jesus converses with Nicodemus, a Pharisee who has come to visit Jesus by night. Nicodemus has opened the conversation by acknowledging that Jesus has appeared as a teacher from God because, as Nicodemus puts it, "No one can do the signs which you do unless God be with him." (3.2). To this salutation Jesus replies "Truly truly I say to you, unless someone be generated from above, that person cannot catch sight of the kingdom of God."(3.3) This is the famous statement of Jesus the first part of which in the King James version is translated by the words "Except a man be born again . . . " The present writers are aware of how much our translation differs from this traditional one, and so it may be wise for us to begin by defending the English words which we have chosen. First of all, as stated above, the word *gennao*, which we have chosen to render from its passive Greek form as "generated", can mean either to beget or to bear a child, that is like its Hebrew counterpart (the verb *yaladh*), it can be applied either to a man or to a woman. At this stage of the discussion between Jesus and Nicodemus, we think that the sexual ambiguity inherent in this verb should remain unresolved, hence our choice of the English word "generated."

The next point to be considered is the Greek word *anothen* which we have translated as "from above." A study of the use of this Greek word shows that it almost always means one of two things, either "from above, from up there" or "from the beginning, from far back." Sometimes it can mean something like "again" or "afresh", but when it has this meaning, it is usually paired with another Greek word *palin*, which by itself means "again." If one examines all the New Testament appearances of the word *anothen* other than the one translated above, one finds that it always means "from above", except once (Luke 1.3) when it means "from the beginning" and once (Gal. 4.9) when it definitely does mean "again", but in this instance it is paired with the word *palin*. Thus in the present passage from John 3 the preferred translation is "from above." Jesus is talking about source of generation rather than repetition of it in time.

Having justified this much of our translation, and for the moment postponing a discussion of our phrase "catch sight of", we can now proceed to discuss the content of the conversation between Jesus and Nicodemus to see what it reveals about the process of being "generated from above." It is important to note first of all that Nicodemus comes to Jesus by night. On one level, of course, this is merely a detail of circumstance. Nicodemus may want to come stealthily to converse with Jesus, he may not want his fellow Pharisees to know what he is doing, and obviously nighttime conduces best with such a purpose of stealth. But even if he does not feel some need for secrecy in approaching Jesus, Nicodemus may have another reason for coming to him by night: the rabbis considered night the proper time for productive discussions of the Law, and the author may be suggesting that Nicodemus comes to Jesus with expectations of an orthodox legal discussion to follow. Owing to the fact, however, that many if not most details in the gospel of John's account of Jesus' life must be taken symbolically as well as literally, the writer of the Gospel may also be placing this visit at night to recall the general condition of darkness which threatens life/light in his cosmology (John 1.5). At this symbolic level of meaning Nicodemus may be evincing an instinct and a desire for the true light shining in the darkness, the unquenchable light which, according to this Gospel, Jesus is able to offer. On the other hand, it may be possible that while showing that he respects Jesus enough to take the trouble to achieve a difficult meeting with him, Nicodemus still may consider him only somewhat different in degree rather than in kind from the other rabbis he knows.

In other words, because of the multiple layers of meaning which one finds in the Gospel of John, it is hard to know just how to interpret Nicodemus's first words to Jesus referred to above, about his being a teacher sent from God and having God with him. They could imply recognition of Jesus as something more than just an ordinary rabbi, but they would also be fitting as a respectful greeting from one ordinary rabbi to another, his colleague and peer. Whatever these words are meant to convey, it is the last part of them that prompts Jesus' reply about being generated from above. Nicodemus has mentioned Jesus' being a teacher sent from God, perhaps as a mere pious compliment, perhaps as more. Jesus' answer is tantamount to saying "It's necessary to be from God all right, but not in any way that you might be thinking of." Jesus seems to assume that Nicodemus wants to belong to the group that Jesus is trying to create around himself, but he warns him that "Unless someone be generated from above, that person cannot catch sight of the Kingdom of God." (3.3) Our English phrase "catch sight of" translates the infinitive of the Greek verb *horao* in its aorist aspect of *idein*. The aorist aspect of Greek verbs can express various ideas, but here, as our translation shows, it conveys the idea of inception, of beginning to see, of catching a first glimpse. Jesus is saying that unless a person has been generated from above, he or she cannot gain even a rudimentary vision of the Kingdom of God, or if Jesus is using the verb "see" to mean "experience" as it sometimes does in the Old Testament, than again the idea is that without generation from above one cannot even begin to have an experience of the Kingdom, one cannot even achieve the status of novice in the Kingdom. Also, "begin to see" or "catch sight of" would include the act of perceiving. Without the birth from "up there", one cannot form even a rudimentary notion of the manifestation of God, much less enter into the kingdom which constitutes that manifestation.

Just as Jesus had focused on and been prompted to reply by a certain phrase of Nicodemus's, the one about being a teacher sent from God, so Nicodemus now focuses on a certain word in Jesus' speech. He is usually thought to be focussing on the word *anothen,* wrongly interpreting it to mean "again", but as Strack and Billerbeck show in their commentary on this passage, it is more likely that he has ears only for the passive infinitive form of the verb *gennao*, the female application of which Nicodemus shows that he has in mind: "How can a person be born when he is old?" he asks Jesus. "He can't enter into his mother's womb a second time and be born, can he?" (3.4)[1] What has bothered Nicodemus and what he is cryptically and even huffily responding to is the suggestion to be inferred from Jesus' remarks that he has no more standing in the Kingdom of God than a Gentile would or does. The Jews spoke of proselytes as being like new-born babies, as receiving their true birth by becoming members of Israel. Nicodemus is rejecting the notion that he, a Jew, should have to undergo such a process since he has standing by natural birth in the Kingdom of God. In this respect Nicodemus is like a later group depicted in this Gospel: "Jesus was speaking to the Jews who had believed in him. 'If you remain in my word, you will truly be my disciples, and you will know the truth, and the truth will free you'" (John 8.31-2) Like Nicodemus, the crowd hears only one of Jesus' words, namely the word "free," and angrily responds to it: "We are Abraham's seed and have never served anyone". (John 8.33) So it is with Nicodemus, who is perhaps on the brink of believing in Jesus: he hears one word and is upset at what he thinks it suggests about him.

But Jesus continues to press his point about the need for a new life: "Truly truly I say to you, unless a person be generated from water and spirit, that person cannot enter into the Kingdom of God." (3.5) The phrase "water and spirit" is being used by Jesus to expand and clarify his idea about being generated from above. In this passage "water" and "spirit" mean the same thing. This statement can be made with some confidence because in a later passage, when the Gospel writer depicts Jesus at the feast of Tabernacles in chapter 7, water and spirit are equated. In that passage the writer quotes Jesus himself: "In the last great day of the feast Jesus took his stand and began to cry out saying, 'If anyone is thirsty, let that person come to me and drink. The one who puts trust in me, as the scripture said, rivers of living water shall flow from his insides.'" (7.37-8) Then the Gospel writer explains: "He said this concerning the spirit which those who had put their trust in him would receive. For there was no spirit yet, because Jesus had not been glorified." (7.39) Water *is* spirit then, but there can be no spirit until the son of man is glorified. Of course to understand this equation, one needs to know how the word "glorified" is being used. The Gospel of John presents the paradoxical notion (although, as we shall see, it is a notion rooted in the Old Testament) that Jesus' glorification consists of his being crucified. Jesus himself is shown to be the source of this idea, for after Judas has gone out to betray him and thus set in motion the machinery of crucifixion, Jesus says "Now the son of Man has been glorified and by him God has been glorified." (John 13.31). Therefore, if the writer of the Gospel were going to be consistent with his own symbolic system, one would expect to find some manifestation of the spirit in his depiction of the crucifixion. It is exactly this sort of manifestation which one does find when one of the soldiers stabs Jesus in the side with a spear while he is hanging on the cross (John 19.34). The passage from chapter 7 tells us that the water flowing out from Jesus' side is spirit and as Raymond Brown and other scholars have shown, this flowing out of water/spirit probably stands proleptically for the bestowal of the holy spirit upon the disciples which takes place after the resurrection of Jesus (John 20.22-3).[2] The crucifixion releases, sets in motion, stands as the source of the water/spirit by which one needs to be generated in order to enter into the Kingdom of God.

If we return then to chapter 3, we can see that within the metaphoric system of the Gospel of John, albeit in rather veiled language, Jesus is telling Nicodemus that to be generated from above a person has to be involved with, and somehow to identify with the crucifixion of the Son of Man, a crucifixion which, in the Gospel of John, Jesus seems to anticipate from a point very early in his career, if not from the beginning.[3] As we will see later on in this study, it is not always so easy to put one's trust in such a reprobated figure, such an outcast from society who represents the persecuted failures of the world. Peter, for instance, will flee from the condemned Jesus, convinced that his mission has been a failure. Interestingly enough, Nicodemus eventually satisfies Jesus' requirements for generation from above and admission to the kingdom by coming to anoint Jesus' dead body. Nicodemus that is throws his lot in with that of the disgraced, the despised and rejected leader (John 19.39). But back at the time of his first conversation with Jesus, he continues to find Jesus' words hard to understand.

Jesus of course does very little to soften them or make them more accessible. He persists in fact along the same obscure line of presentation with which he has started. He admits that there are two kinds of birth: "That which has been generated from the flesh is flesh, and that which has been generated from the spirit is spirit." (3.6) Then he seems to corroborate the basic soundness of Nicodemus's understanding that he was talking about the need on the part of a Jew to experience a generation other than the merely natural one, about the insufficiency of mere pedigree as qualification for the Kingdom. He says "Don't be amazed that I said to you [singular] that you [plural=Jews] must be born from above. The wind blows where it wills, and you hear the sound of it, but you do not know where it comes from and where it is going. It's this way with everyone who has been generated from the spirit" (3.7-8) This statement by Jesus seems to be repeating a point that the writer of the Gospel had already made in his prologue, namely that generation from above, i.e. from water and the spirit, is not according to blood lines or along any of the cherished family channels which the Jews have always set such store by (John 1.12-3, a passage which we will examine later in some detail).

But Nicodemus remains baffled by these additional remarks of Jesus. He again asks "How can these things be?" (3.9) Jesus answers with ironical amazement: "You're the teacher of Israel and you don't know these things? Truly truly I say to you, that we speak what we know and bear witness to what we have seen, and you do not receive our testimony." (3.10-11) He then warns Nicodemus that his next remarks may be even harder to understand: "If I spoke earthly things and you do not believe, how will you believe if I speak heavenly things?" (3.12) The "heavenly things" do not really constitute a wholly new subject in Jesus' remarks. What Jesus means is that if Nicodemus did not understand what Jesus was talking about when Jesus spoke in terms of wind and water (=earthly things), then how will Nicodemus understand when he draws an apocalyptic picture which includes heavenly things in its imagery. Not waiting for an answer from Nicodemus, Jesus inaugurates this new apocalyptic/"heavenly" strain in his remarks: "And no one has gone up into heaven except the one who came down from heaven, the Son of Man. And just as Moses lifted up the serpent in the wilderness, so must the Son of Man be lifted up so that everyone who trusts in him might have eternal life." (John 3.13-15)

Again Jesus seems to be stressing the need for some sort of solidarity with himself as an outcast figure. The lifting up of the Son of Man refers to his crucifixion: when Jesus refers on another occasion to being lifted up, the writer of the Gospel of John records that "He said this to signify by what sort of death he was going to die." (12.33) Thus the thrust of Jesus' remarks to Nicodemus really has not changed: the one who is to be born from above has somehow to come to terms with Jesus' crucifixion. The real question that needs to be answered at this point, though, is why or how Jesus is using the term "Son of Man" to refer to his suffering role.

In the seventh chapter of the Book of Daniel the term "Son of Man" refers to the group of the righteous saints of Israel who, after experiencing persecutions, appear before the Ancient of Days and are given a kingdom which supplants the kingdoms of the four beasts which, in the historical allegory of Daniel, represent the Babylonians, Medes, Persians, and Greeks. In the first chapter of the Gospel of John we learn that Jesus already, at the beginning of his ministry seems to prefer to designate himself by this name. The latter part of this first chapter (vv.35 ff.) can in fact almost be seen as a rehearsal of various names for Jesus until the right one, the one Jesus prefers, can be hit upon. Andrew, for instance, tells his brother Simon that they have found the Messiah (name 1) (1.41). Phillip tells Nathanael that they have found the one whom Moses in the law and the prophets spoke of (name 2) (1.45). When Nathanael is astonished by the telepathic powers of Jesus, he calls Jesus son of God and King of Israel (names 3 and 4) (1.49). In answering Nathanael, though, Jesus reveals the name which he prefers to be known by: "Do you believe because I said to you I saw you under the fig tree? You shall see greater things than these. Truly truly I say to you, you shall see heaven open up and the angels of God ascending and descending on the Son of Man." (John 1.50-1) Coming at the end of such a sequence of other highly significant names, the name "Son of Man" receives a very strong emphasis here, and from the beginning it seems to identify suffering as a keynote to Jesus' career.

But what kind of suffering? The seventh chapter of Daniel does not specify what travails the saints of Israel must pass through. The passage quoted above, about the Son of Man's being lifted up so that all who put their trust in him might have eternal life (3.14), suggests a redemptive or a salvific dimension to Jesus' understanding of the career of the Son of Man. This element seems to be Jesus' addition, Jesus' own contribution to understanding the Son of Man passage from Daniel. The passage which we have just quoted from the first chapter of John may offer some clue as to where Jesus derived this extra salvific dimension. Jesus' statement in that passage combines mention of the Son of Man with an allusion to the story of Jacob's dream in chapter 28 of Genesis (in his dream Jacob sees a stairway leading up to heaven and angels going up and down upon it). Some connection seems to exist here between the Son of Man and God's servant Jacob in the mind of Jesus. But then the question arises who is God's servant Jacob, and more specifically does his name refer to only one figure, the Biblical patriarch with the twelve (male) children, or is it somehow more representative? Jacob was never simply one character, he always stood in some way not just for himself but for a whole nation. In this representative role he could be put to varying uses, depending on the perspective of the Biblical writer who wanted to use him as an exemplar.[4]

One Old Testament book that Jesus evidently felt profoundly influenced by was what we now call Second Isaiah (chapters 40-66). Second Isaiah is particularly interesting for the gamut of illustrative uses to which it puts the representative figure of God's servant Jacob, and for the variety of prospects, from the most triumphal to the most abysmally gloomy, which it projects for this same figure. One surmise that can be made about the career of Jesus, about any development that may have taken place within that career (assuming that is that Jesus did not have everything all mapped out from the beginning, despite what the Gospel of John seems to suggest, assuming that Jesus had to come up against various obstacles and thereby grow through disappointment) is that at various times he was attuned to different strains within Second Isaiah, for instance he at first envisioned converting Israel to the task of enlightener to all the nations which Second Isaiah seems to map out for it upon its return from Babylonian exile. Jesus' first preaching experience, as depicted by Luke (4.16-30), when he preaches release for captives and sight for the blind from Second Isaiah, would show what sort of program Jesus may have hoped originally to put into motion. The reaction of his auditors on this occasion also shows with what sort of resistance he met. At some point in his career, Jesus would have had to decide what he was going to do about such resistance, which did not grow more tame; he could have tamed his message of course, thereby perhaps reducing the resistance, but such a course does not seem to have appealed to Jesus even to the extent that the idea of a political messiahship must have appealed to him for him to have been "tempted" to it by Satan. At some point Jesus must have reached the conclusion that to be resisted, to be rejected, rather than to succeed in converting Israel was the real purpose of his career. This would not have been an easy conclusion to reach, in fact the epistle to the Hebrews states that Jesus was able to reach it only at the expense of "mighty wailings and tears" (Hebrews 5.7). Moreover the document that would have helped him in this revision of his agenda would have been the fifty-third chapter of Isaiah, with its gruesome picture of what God's servant Jacob needed to undergo.

The fifty-third chapter of Isaiah presents many problems for interpreters. Although it follows hard upon a great celebratory hymn (Isaiah 52.7-9), it presents a picture of utter desolation and rejection. It is hard to know whether the prophet means to say that the throes and pangs which he shows the servant passing through in chapter 53 have all been completed, in which case the servant would stand for Israel while it was in exile, an Israel that was in a position to sing a hymn of celebration at being released, or whether such throes and pangs are still to come, in which case the rejected servant might represent some sort of death's head at the banquet or some sort of Poesque cautionary Red Death-figure, a reminder that times of seeming triumph, especially for nations, are really times of incipient peril.

Whatever the writer of Second Isaiah intended this figure to stand for, what Jesus evidently saw in the figure of the servant was a rationale for the rejection which he had started to undergo already. The figure of the servant as depicted in Isaiah suggested that redemption could arise from rejection, and not just redemption for Israel: in Isaiah it is certain Gentile kings who are telling the servant's story and who are also deriving benefit from the servant's suffering. They describe the servant as despised and forsaken of men, a man of sorrows and "pain's familiar", as one who had slunk with his face turned away from them and as one whom they did not esteem. (53.3) They perceive that he has carried off their pains and borne their wounds, the servant is one whom they had considered plagued and smitten of God (53.4) They now see that he was pierced by their transgressions (not "for their trangressions" as many translations would have it — the idea is that the kings as transgressors are actually doing the stabbing), pulverized by their crimes, they see him as one who has upon him the discipline of their prosperity and as one by whose stripes healing has devolved upon them (53.5) The kings announce a paradoxical fact: although it is each one of them who has wandered and strayed away like sheep, God has caused their iniquity to fall on the servant, and yet the servant says nothing: harassed and bowed down, he does not open his mouth, he is led like a sheep to the slaughter and as a sheep in the presence of those who shear him he is mute. (53.6-7)

It is a ghastly picture of suffering and yet there is more. The servant is taken from constraint and justice (i.e. he is taken outside whatever protection the legal system may afford), there is no one to consider his generation, his life is excluded from the earth, from the transgression of someone's people[5] a plague is upon him. (53.8) He makes his grave with the wicked and yet he himself has not done wickedness. (53.9) God has been pleased to pulverize him and has made him sick. Finally at this point the purpose of all this abuse begins to manifest itself: the text mention's the possibility of God's having appointed his life as a sin-offering, i.e. the servant's sufferings would cleanse some people somehow. Furthermore, the text says that if God has appointed his life as a sin-offering, the servant will nonetheless see seed and prolong days; the text also says that it is the pleasure of God for the servant to thrive by God's hand. (53.10) Here one can see a connection with the idea later expressed by Daniel that the suffering saints of Israel would in the end be recompensed. From the labor of his soul, the Isaiah text goes on to say, the servant will see and be satisfied, and by his knowledge God will justify his righteous servant to the many and he will bear their iniquities (53.11). Therefore someone (another person unidentified in the text) will make a lot for him among the many and with the mighty the servant will inherit spoil in exchange for having poured out his soul to death — but then there is one last summarizing statement of the work the servant has to do as an outcast: he will be assigned a place with the wicked and he will carry the sins of many and interpose on behalf of transgressors. (53.12)

If we return to the discussion between Jesus and Nicodemus, we now may be in a position better to understand what Jesus means when he says "And just as Moses lifted up the serpent in the wilderness, so must the Son of Man be lifted up so that everyone who trusts in him might have eternal life." (John 3.14-5) Or at least we may have some better idea of what Jesus means here by the term "Son of Man." We have still not dealt with what it means to put one's trust in the Son of Man and thereby gain eternal life. To do so, it may be best to turn back again to the first chapter of the Gospel of John for help.

In his prologue, the writer of the Gospel of John describes a family which is brought into existence in a way other than the ordinary way of nature: "As many as received him [or it, i.e. the Word] he gave to them the authority to become children of God, to those who are putting their trust in his name, the ones who are generated not from bloods or from the desire of the flesh or from the desire of a husband but from God." (John 1.12-13) If trust in the son of Man results in one's becoming part of this divine family in one passage, and if it results in eternal life in another, then it is probably not too much of a leap to say that becoming part of this divine family, being generated from God or from above, is the same thing as having eternal life. Thus in describing to Nicodemus what the benefit to humankind (or to that subset of humanity which puts its trust in him) of his "lifting up" will be, Jesus is still taking about being born from above. Using different figures of speech, he repeats the same ideas to Nicodemus over and over again.

The key to becoming part of this divine family envisioned by Jesus is putting one's trust in the name of the Word, which name, as we have just seen, is Son of Man with the Suffering Servant included as an element of that name. A person puts his or her trust in this name in order to receive the authority to become one of "the natural children of God" (the literal rendering of the Greek phrase). The author of the Gospel here presents a puzzling concept: how or why does one receive the authority to become what one already is supposedly by nature? The answer to this question arises in part from the context in which the writer of the Gospel makes his assertion. In verse three of chapter one we learn that the Word is the source of all life: "All things came into being through him [or it] and without him [or it] not one thing which has come into being came into being." This idea is restated in verse four ("In him [or it] was life"), another idea is added to it ("and the life was the light of human beings"), and then yet another, namely that "the light is shining in the darkness, and the darkness did not overcome it." (verse 5)[6] No origin of this darkness is ever proposed; the writer of the Gospel simply implies that it exists wherever and whenever the light exists.

But to return to statements that the writer makes about the Word: as light the Word is available to all: "It was the true light which illumines every person who comes into the world." (1.9) The fact is, though, that the Word often goes unrecognized: "It was in the world, and the world came into being through it, but the world did not know it." (1.10) In other words this verse describes the threat to the light which the darkness constitutes, a threat which Paul describes in the first chapter of Romans as the general failure of human creatures to recognize their creator and give thanks to him or her for the world in which they all live. (Romans 1.18-23) Furthermore, the history of Israel represents a special subset of this general failure of the entire human race to recognize and give thanks: "He [the Word] came to his own home and his own people did not receive him" (John 1.11) This verse probably refers to successive failures on the part of Israel to respond to successive manifestations of God's word among them, to the entire span of Israel's history and the Biblical process.

But even amid the failure to recognize the Word — and here we come back to the verses under consideration, to the subject of the divine family — the human race may receive the authority to become what they in fact could and should have been by nature: "As many as received him he gave to them the authority to become children of God, to those who are putting trust in his name . . ." (John 1.12). The Gospel writer's use of the word "authority" in this passage suggests that he may have in mind, as part of being generated from above, the idea of restoring the image of God. The concept of the image of God appears in Genesis 1.27, which is usually translated into English as "And God created the human creature in his image", the phrase "in his image" being used to translate the Hebrew phrase *besalemo* which might better be translated by "as his image", meaning as his representative or as some sort of concentrated symbol of his power. The *selem* was an image or totem which the king left behind to symbolize his authority when he could not be physically present in some place. When the writer of the P-source of the Pentateuch says that human beings are created as the *selem* of God, he is talking about their being given the authority on earth to somehow stand in for God (this meaning is made explicit in verse 26 of Genesis 1 where the writer has God say "let us make the human creature as our *selem* and likeness [translating Hebrew *kidmutenu*], and they will exercise dominion over the fish of the sea and over the birds of heaven and over the beasts of all the earth and over all things that creep on the earth." The human creatures whom God made received a grant of authority. Thus when the Word gives authority to those who put their trust in his name to become the natural children of God, he restores them to their original state of being related to God, of having authority delegated to them by Him.

Those who put their trust in the name of the Word which God has sent are "generated" from God. Such generation implies entry into the divine family which God intends to bring into existence. This family stands in contrast to the sort of family at which "the desire of a husband" aims. A Hebrew male begot children so as to insure his own immortality by the survival of his particular family line. This sort of interest in a limited group of those whom a man could identify as his blood descendants was therefore selfishly motivated and tended to separate the human race into various rival factions all warring for their share of the same limited global turf whereas the family which God wants to beget would have as its members those who could think of and who wanted to care for *all* human beings as their brothers and sisters. As we will see in connection with several of the characters whom we study, this universalist outlook, this ability to think of all human beings as one's fellow family members is a true sign that one has been generated from God.

The suffering of the Son of Man is aimed at establishing this divine family. It is sin that has heretofore prevented this family from coming into existence, sin defined as a missing of one's ethical mark, as a kind of existential failure. Sin separates human beings into entities at war with and resentful of the God whom they consider to be the judge bent on condemning them for such failure. Sin or rather the guilt engendered by sin also isolates them from their fellow human beings: one person keeps distant from another out of a feeling of worthlessness and at the same time, maybe a little perversely, resents that other person for not showing love even when that other person is not being given the chance to show love — sin sets a whole vicious circle of interpersonal dodges and evasions in motion. Furthermore, under the shadow of the eternal death-threat, people feel driven to squeeze as many satisfactions as possible from their limited life-spans, which is understandable and might in some ways even be good except that thus driven, they begin to see other humans as competitors for a limited turf of existential gratifications. They may resort to illusory stopgaps (power, money) to convince themselves that they are really achieving the satisfactions to which they feel entitled, these stopgaps may be achieved at the expense of other people — the Epistle to the Hebrews describes this kind of strategy as being subject to slavery all one's life from fear of death. (2.15)

Isaiah 53, with its figure of the Suffering Servant, suggests a program by which such a state of general enmity among humans and between humans and God might be abolished if only the right person to carry the program out can be found: first of all the Suffering Servant would expose sin, draw it out of all the respectable, even splendid places in which it hides (e.g. behind the golden robes of kings), allow it to express its hostility against the God who is ultimately held accountable for the whole human situation of guilt, and then, by some mystery, some divine alchemy, convert the most heinous evil (the attempted obliteration of the one who offers release from sins, the one who represents the God who loves and does not judge) into the greatest good (the bestowal of eternal life, i.e. acceptance by God, upon anyone who will put his or her trust in the name and therefore in the function of the Son of Man). It is this sort of alteration of the nature of reality which has been described by the writer of 1 Peter when he says: "Blessed be the God and father of our Lord Jesus Christ, who according to his great mercy has given us new birth [or begotten us again] into living hope through the resurrection of Jesus Christ from the dead . . . " (1 Peter 1.3) Hope based on anything other than Jesus' resurrection is dead or under the power of death, motivated (even if subconsciously) by the vain desire of circumventing death as Hebrews 2.15 suggests, shot through with the angst which Kierkegaard and other existential philosophers and also Freud have depicted with their intense power of scrutinizing intuitions and motives. The Christian message as summed up here in 1 Peter is that the resurrection of Jesus has changed the human condition by giving it an option of hope that is alive, not dead, an option of hope that is alive because it is pointed toward life, not death.

It is this sort of renewal of the human race which Jesus seems to have in mind when he talks about eternal life or being born from above, which is really an invitation put out by God to human beings that they should re-become his children, it is an offer of God's acceptance, it is this sort of renewal which he talks about, for instance, when he mentions the benefits that will derive from the Son of Man's being "lifted up." The discussion of this subject continues in the third chapter of John, even though, when we reach the seventeenth verse of that chapter, we may have left Jesus' own words behind and passed over into commentary on those words made by the writer of the Gospel.[7] One might say that if Nicodemus at the time of his conversation with Jesus had read the words of the writer (perhaps vss. 15-21), he would have found them puzzling in the same way he found the words of Jesus puzzling, mainly because of the unorthodox picture of the function of the Son of Man which they present. In Daniel, the function of the Son of Man had included judging, or a bequest of the power of judging from the Ancient of Days, but according to the writer of the Gospel of John, "God did not sent the Son into the world in order that he might judge [or perhaps condemn] the world but in order that the world might be saved through him." (3.17) Not that the world's individual entities are being saved or have been saved willy-nilly. The element of personal choice remains, but again the crux is whether or not one can put one's trust in the Son or in the name of the Son: "The one who puts his trust in him is not being judged. The one who does not put his trust has been judged already, because he has not put his trust in the name of God's unique son." (3.18)

Here the putting or the not putting of one's trust seems to involve a slightly new aspect of the Son of Man. In these remarks by the writer of the Gospel the implicit question seems to be "Can one accept the fact that one is accepted by God?" Judgment results not from any disposition on God's part but rather from an inability on the part of humans to accept the fact of God's desire to accept them. The function of the Son of Man as light is to embody and to reveal that desire, but then there are different kinds of reaction to the light, and it is these reactions that the Gospel writer refers to as judgment, i.e.: "This is the judgment, that the light has come into the world and people preferred the darkness to the light for their works were evil. Everyone who does paltry things hates the light and does not come toward the light, in order that his works not be shown up for what they are" (3.20-1)

On the surface, these two verses could appear to be propounding a sort of punitive outlook, with evildoers relegated to a world of outer darkness, although if this were the case, it would be hard to reconcile them to the statement which stands close by them, namely that God did not send his son into the world in order to judge or to condemn the world. The present writers would like to hazard two novel interpretations, which we feel are crucial to an interpreation of this passage. First of all we believe that the phrase "for their works were evil" has a subjective reference, i.e. that it refers to an inner self-judgement on the part of the doers of the deeds rather than to any objective valuation — people shrink from the light of love with which the life of Jesus' penetrates the ordinary human darkness because they think that their deeds are evil and that they are not worthy to bask in such illumination; they therefore love darkness, and in them we see the effect of sin which we discussed above, namely the isolation of guilt-stricken individuals. Secondly, we believe that careful attention should be paid to the meaning of the Greek word *phaula*, which we have translated "paltry" but which according to Liddell and Scott in their Greek-English Lexicon can also mean shabby, second-rate, or base. The group whose works are paltry is not the same group as those who think that their works are evil (another word, *ponera* in Greek). The group whose works are paltry might be the strict keepers of the Jewish legal ordinances; their work is second-rate when compared with the higher work of keeping the commandment of Love which Jesus assigns to his followers later in this Gospel. One might expect the keepers of the law to shun the light of God's acceptance and love out of pride, i.e. because they feel that they do not need the help which it offers, because they can stand on their own, but interestingly enough, in this passage the writer of the Gospel seems to suggest a different idea, namely that this group secretly doubts its own high accomplishments; he suggests that the keepers of the law hate the light and do not come to the light for fear that their works will be shown for the second-rate things which they are in the eyes of God, they fear that they are imposters.

Neither of these two groups then, the one who thinks that its works are evil or the one whose works are shabby, can put their trust in the name of Son as the one who does not judge. They consign themselves to what the Synoptics call the outer darkness. Their judgment is self-inflicted.

Having described these two groups, the writer of the Gospel describes once more the kind of person that *can* come to the light: "The one who does the truth is coming to the light, in order that it might be revealed that his works have been done in God." (3.21) In a work that is rooted in Hebrew ideas the way the Gospel of John is, the word "truth" does not denote some sort of abstract standard by which ideas must be measured. It is more an ethical term involving fidelity, reliability — in this sense the exemplar of Hebrew truth par excellence and the source of truth is God who, in the Old Testament, shows that he can be relied upon and called upon in every human situation. The one who "does the truth" enters with confidence upon the life which God, who is reliable, has made possible through the agency of the Son of Man/Suffering Servant, enters upon the new life in the family of God where all the old barriers to communication which had been created by sin have been broken down. In this new life, because one is not jealously and suspiciously defending one's own eternal status, because that status has been assured, it is possible to be open to and loyal to the interests of God and open to and loyal to the interests of one's fellow human beings; to "do the truth" is to enact this sort of openness and loyalty. In this passage from the Gospel of John, in contrast to those whose works are evil or whose works are second rate, the people who do the truth are not preoccupied with themselves, they come to the light in order that works which have been done in God or by God might be revealed. The model for this behavior of theirs is Jesus as he is portrayed in the Gospel of John always disclaiming personal credit, power, or glory, and ascribing all his wisdom and prowess to the Father who works through him.

It should be pointed out that to come to the light in this way is not the same thing as to glory in Jesus as *my* personal saviour, with an emphasis on the "my", with an emphasis on what God has done for *me*. As long as the standing of one's particular ego remains up front, as long as one continues tallying one's own personal score vis-à-vis the prize of salvation, then one is not doing the truth or even ready to do the truth as the writer of the Gospel of John conceives of that quality. During the last five years one of the writers of this book (Guy) has had the privilege of belonging to the Community Church of Christ of Franconia, New Hampshire and of coming under the influence of William Briggs, the pastor of that church and the author of *Faith through Works,* a book on church mission which is Johannine in its outlook, especially if one takes as one's clue to the Gospel of John the invitation that Jesus extends to Andrew in the first chapter, namely "Be coming along and begin to see." One needs to render this verse in exaggerated English in order to show the difference in aspect between the two verbs in Greek (the verb "come" is linear, denoting some sort of continuous action, a process, whereas the verb "see" is aorist, denoting inception), a difference in aspect which suggests that revelation begins after a process has been entered into, after some (perhaps new) form of experience has been tried out. "Do and ye shall know," a formula coined by John Ruskin, seems to be making the same sort of promise as the one made by Jesus to Andrew, to be pointing to the same sort of process of personal growth. But to return to William Briggs: if one were to attempt to summarize his prophetic witness to the Gospel, one would say that it consists of an invitation to act on behalf of those who have need, but then this sort of description would still fall short of the essence of the new experience being offered and promised — one would say that the invitation consists almost of the promise of a party, which promise one tends to react to with extreme scepticism before the fact, i.e. "It might be interesting, illuminating, sobering, harrowing to go down to work in an extremely poor village in Honduras, but how could it really be fun?", but then fun is exactly what such an experience turns out to be, the essence of this new life entered into is *hilaritas* or joy, and joy of such a sort that one can hardly think that one is piling up merit for oneself. The fact is, though, that one's own personal merit soon stops even being an issue.

What the example of Reverend Briggs makes one aware of is that by hammering away constantly at the individual, by attempting to extort some sort of concession from the stubbon prideful individual soul, by placing stress on the tidying up of one's personal peccadilloes, Christianity has in effect really been slamming shut the portals of real birth from above, making it impossible to achieve the state of "doing the truth," of getting beyond self which constitutes the real essence of being born from above, which equals coming to the light. Paul seems to be talking about the same sort of achieved spiritual state when he writes about its no longer being he that lives but rather Christ in him (Gal. 2.20), even though in the world of contemporary Christianity one sees and hears this verse more often than not being used as a sort of yardstick to measure or to demonstrate one's own personal self-surrender and therefore one's own personal progress toward salvation — one sees and hears this verse being used as such a yardstick when it is not being turned into a sort of cudgel wherewith to castigate all those who have not replaced themselves with a somehow indwelling Jesus. To use the verse in this way, to ascribe any merit to oneself is to fall unawares into the category of those who perform the shabby, second rate legalistic-type deeds in an attempt to distance themselves from the world of unclean sinners, this despite the fact that in context, Paul's statement about Christ living in him is connected with statements about being dead to the works of the law!

At this point, it will be helpful to look at certain passages in the First Epistle of John, which was written by the author of the Gospel — in these passages some of the ideas which we have just been looking at in the Gospel of John are treated more fully or less cryptically. Examination of certain passages in the First Epistle will act as a check on the interpretation of the passage from chapter 3 of the Gospel which we have now hazarded above. The Epistle does discuss the idea of generation from above, as in the following passage, which also talks about coming openly to the light: "And now, children, remain in him so that when he appears, we might have openness and not shrink from him when he appears beside us. If you understand that he is righteous, you know that everyone who does righteousness has been generated from him." (1 John 2.28-9) Grammatically in Greek "everyone who does righteousness" is the same sort of participial phrase as "the one who does the truth." It is important to understand that in Greek the participles are present linear and therefore convey the idea of continuous action, or the idea of set policy. With this passage from the Epistle, the question presents itself as to what sort of policy one is carrying out when one is "doing righteousness", just as the question as to what sort of policy one is carrying out when one is "doing the truth" arose in connection with the passage from the third chapter of the Gospel of John.

Again, we have to be aware of Hebrew ideas, and again, as with the Hebrew idea of truth, we encounter not some sort of abstract standard of righteousness which has to be upheld as we do in the basically Roman legal tradition which we are the heirs of but rather an idea, a dynamic of ethical action. Righteousness among the Hebrews has to do with the righting of wrongs in society, of vindicating the victims and correcting imbalances, of restoring the oppressed to what they have coming.[8] Righteousness is active and personal so that when the author of this epistle describes Jesus as righteous he is not talking about some awesome, stern, and upright upholder of a legal standard but rather about one whose concern it is to restore human beings oppressed by sin to the status of God's children which is theirs by nature and by right. This conception of Jesus is stated more explicitly at another place in this epistle: "If we confess our sins, he is faithful and righteous so as to forgive our sins and cleanse us from every evil." (1.9) The faithfulness ascribed to Jesus might almost in the Hebrew sense be called truth; it means that human beings can count on him, that he will be loyal to their eternal interests. The righteousness that leads him to forgive the sins of humans is that vindicating Hebrew kind which corrects social evils and relieves oppression, the oppression in this case being that of human creatures under the load of sins with which the Accuser (Satan) is persistent to charge them. According to the writer of the Epistle to the Hebrews Jesus leads his earthly life so that "he might nullify the one who has the power of death, that is the devil, and set free those who by the fear of death have been enslaved all their lives" (Hebrews 2.14-15) This is the sort of action which is envisioned by the writer of the first epistle of John when he describes Jesus as righteous. The writer of First John also seems to be alluding to the idea of the Suffering Servant when he describes Jesus as cleansing us from every sin — here again we have the idea of that divine alchemy, that mystery by which the servant absorbs the mephitic element of sin and transforms it into something sweet and beneficial.

This cleansing is another function of Jesus' righteousness. What the writer of First John is saying is that if a person identifies with this aspect of Jesus, that is makes righteousness his or her policy, then that person is showing that he or she has been generated from above. This doing of righteousness is contrasted with another kind of doing farther along in the Epistle: "Children, don't let anyone lead you astray. The one who is doing righteousness is righteous. The one who is doing sin is from the accuser, because the accuser sins from the beginning. The son of God appeared for this reason, that he might loosen the works of the accuser." (3.7-8) Here again we have a participial clause, namely "doing sin", which is like "doing the truth" and "doing righteousness" grammatically. To do sin is to subscribe to and carry out the accuser's policy, which is the opposite of righteous Jesus' policy. "Sin" destroys by judging, accusing, and belittling people so that they become incapable of realizing their potential as people or as children of God. Jesus wants to loose us from sin's oppression by restoring us to a sense of our own self-worth, the accuser wants to tighten such oppression's chains by devaluing persons, by making them feel worthless, unloveable, and therefore, as we have said above, unable to love. Accordingly, when the writer of this epistle goes on to say that "Everyone who has been generated from God is not doing sin" (3.9), he does not mean that such a person never commits a sin but that he or she is not committed to the accuser's policy of judgement. In another place the writer says "all unrighteousness is sin" (5.17). An English translation cannot really convey the idea which this verse contains in Greek, namely that the absence of the righteous disposition makes for sin. Furthermore, one needs to keep in mind here that at its root the word "sin" in Greek means missing the mark. Absence of a righteous disposition misses the mark: it certainly misses the mark of God's will, which is that the barriers between people should be broken down and the divine family come into existence; it may also miss the mark, any mark one may be thinking of because ultimately it is futile, God's aim being, as Paul says, to reconcile all things to himself. (Colossian 1.20)

Continuing the discussion of these ideas, the writer of 1 John introduces an "earthly" metaphor for the birth process: "Everyone who has been generated from God is not doing sin, because His seed remains in him and he is not able to sin, because he has been generated from God. In this the children of God and the children of the devil are made manifest. Everyone who does not do righteousness and the one who does not love his brother is not from God." (3.9-10) Conversely then, according to this logic, the one who does love his brother must be from God. But this raises the (eternal) question of what it means to love one's brother.

The schism which the writer of this epistle is having to deal with involves this very question. The splinter group which the writer criticizes evidently thinks that one's only obligation is to the spiritual salvation of one's brother or sister, that one can neglect the baser bodily needs which come from the realm of unclean matter. The writer of the epistle vehemently challenges such a position: "Whenever one has the life of the world [=property] and sees his brother in need and closes up compassion from him, how does God's love remain in him?" (3.17) Love then has to do with opening up to the immediate needs of real people in one's environment, their needs as people in this world, which needs may of course be psychological, not just physical or financial. What the writer is trying to say is that we must help each other with our real needs in this life if we are to manifest the love of God. We cannot wish away this world in favor of some imagined spiritual realm in which we suppose God is more likely to dwell.

But one can never be open to the needs of others in this way if one is still isolated from them by the guilt which sin engenders. Generation from God manifesting itself in love of brothers and sisters derives from a knowledge of God as the one who accepts us in spite of our sins: "Beloved, let us love one another, because love is from God, and everyone who loves has been generated from God and knows God. The one who does not love has not known God, because God is love. By this the love of God has been made known among us, that God sent his unique son into the world in order that we might live through him" (4.7-9) Here again the need for the suffering servant who carries off sin and nullifies it is stated. We are under a sentence of death and we know it; the accuser, "who from the beginning has been a slayer of persons and who does not stand in the truth" (Gospel of John 8.44) has brought charges against us and we are alienated from God, whom we have regarded in our own minds as the judge who will pronounce sentence, but the sevant carries our sins off and converts them as we are committing them, in effect he leaves the Satan nothing to charge us with if we will rightly recognize his action ("the one generated from God holds on to Him and the evil one does not touch him" — 5.18). He reveals that the disposition of God toward persons is one of love even when the utmost in heinous hostility is being directed against God's servant. "Love is in this, not that we love God [quite the contrary in that we afflicted his representative] but that God loved us and sent his son as a means by which sins are forgiven." (3.10) The last phrase in this quotation ("as a means . . .") is an accurate enough literal translation of a phrase containing the Greek word *hilasmon,* but it leaves unexpressed all that word's important connotations. *Hilasmon* refers to the means by which a reconciliation is achieved between two warring parties and by which a state of joyous celebration can be entered into. It is therefore the perfect word for describing the function of the Suffering Servant/Son of Man, who makes possible a reconciliation between humans and God and humans and humans and who allows the joyous life of "truth" to be entered into.

Taken together then, these passages in the First Epistle of John seem to support the interpretation of doing the truth and coming to the light which we advanced above. The possibility of there being any truth to do at all depends on God's redemptive action, which, as the light of God's forgiving love, aims to free humans from anxious preoccupation with self and aims to let them be open to the needs of others. The keynote of the new life, when entered into, the new life of addressing others' needs, ought to be joy, the sense of an "abounding, glittering jet".

At this point, though, rather than examine any more passages that talk from above or from the outside about birth from above, or from a theological standpoint, it will probably be more useful to look at case histories of people in the New Testament who actually went through the process of "birth." Everything is abstract after all, as Keats said, until it is felt on the pulses of a real person.

CHAPTER 2.

TWO WOMEN

Two women provide our first examples of birth from above. These women present us with one significant problem in that they walk on and walk off rather quickly in the drama of Jesus' life. Thus they do not seem to conduce with any systematic or sustained treatment. Nevertheless, their cases do seem to make up in depth for what they lack in breadth, they offer certain profound slants and insights into the theme we are treating, and they also furnish perspectives from which to judge our two more fully documented cases, Peter and Paul. Therefore we start with these two women.

i. THE WOMAN AT THE WELL.

Near the beginning of his fourth chapter, the writer of the Gospel of John tells us that for Jesus to go from Judea to Galilee, "it was necessary for him to go through Samaria" (4.4) — necessary that is if he did not want to take the long way around through Transjordan, even though most Jews took that long way around in order to avoid the risk of contamination which a trip through Samaria was thought to pose, or we could ask what the nature of the necessity was, i.e. metaphysical or merely geographical. We could speculate about why it was necessary for Jesus to take the shorter route, perhaps the necessity derives from hindsight on the part of the writer of the Gospel. Jesus himself might not exactly have been able to foresee what the result of this excursion through Samaria would be. At any rate, the trip first induces in him exhaustion of body so that when he comes near the Samaritan city of Sychar, Jesus stops at the well of Jacob to gain some much-needed rest while his disciples go into the town to buy food. The text tells us that it was about the sixth hour — twelve noon in our time. (4.6) There is a point to this detail of time: a Samaritan woman aproaches to draw water from the well. There were various customary hours for women to come and draw water but twelve noon was not one of them. The implication may therefore be that this woman has a reason for wanting to come to the well when she can be alone, i.e. that she is some sort of social misfit.

Jesus startles her by asking her to give him a drink from the water of the well. She demurs on the ground that "Jews and Samaritans don't use objects in common" (4.9), meaning that she can't believe that Jesus would think of touching the pot she would have to use to draw up water from the well. At issue here is a complicated tension between Jews and Samaritans concerning ritual purity of women after menstruation. According to the Jews, the Samaritans did not correctly calculate the interval through which a woman had to pass before she was then ready to be made clean again after her menstrual period. Samaritan women therefore and through them the whole Samritan land and people were constantly being infected by a contagion of uncleanness. Jesus ignores this objection and replies "If you had known the gift of God and who the one is saying 'give me something to drink', you would have asked him and he would have given you living water." (4.10) Somewhat like Nicodemus in her limited understanding of Jesus' words, the woman takes him to be talking about living water in the natural sense of fresh (not salt) water, running (not stagnant), pure (not polluted). She also wonders what kind of shaman or worker of tricks Jesus might be pretending to be since he does not have a bucket. Not even Jacob who gave them the well could have produced this living water without a bucket. Again Jesus does not seem to be answering the woman's question, for he says "Everyone who keeps on drinking from this water will thirst again. Whoever takes a drink of the water which I will give him will never thirst, but the water which I will give him will become in him a spring of water leaping up into eternal life." (4.13-14) This translation tries to convey a distinction which different tenses of the verb "to drink" make clear in the original Greek, namely that one could go on drinking from the well of Jacob continuously and never slake one's thirst whereas one drink from the water which Jesus gives will turn into a never-ending, seemingly self-generating or at least self-renewing source. Thus on a deeper level Jesus has answered her question: yes he is greater than Jacob or any other human well-digger.

But still, what does Jesus mean by drinking of the water which he has to offer and by his claim that it will turn into an endless supply coming out of the drinker? The answer to this question can be found in a later scene from the Gospel of John when Jesus says "if anyone thirsts let him come toward me and drink. The one who puts his trust in me, as the scripture said, rivers of living water will flow from his insides." (7.37-38)[1] In the light of this later passage one may equate drinking of the water which Jesus has to offer with putting one's trust in him, since both are said to have the same result, namely the flow of some kind of water from within the person. But then there is more. As we have shown in our introduction, the writer explains that this whole later statement by Jesus about water in chapter seven is really about the spirit: "He said this concerning the spirit which those who put their trust in him would receive." (7.39) Since, in talking with Nicodemus, Jesus had connected water and spirit together as an explanation of how one is born from above, now in telling the Samaritan woman about a mystical kind of water which she can have within herself, he is really telling her about being born from above, from the spirit. The source of the water is trust in Jesus, which, as we also showed in our introduction, results in being born into the divine family, which is the same as eternal life. These terms exist as an interrelated complex within the Gospel of John.

The woman's reply to Jesus at this point suggest that she still doesn't quite understand the level of reality which Jesus is referring to. She says "Sir, give me this water, so that I may never thirst or come here to draw," (4.15) that is she sees Jesus' offer as a possible release from an irksome daily task: to furnish water for her home she would have been compelled to carry each day a heavy earthen pot full of water on her head at least a mile.

But Jesus again veers off onto another subject, apparently an irrelevant one at this point. He says to her "Go call your husband and come here." (4.16) The point of this directive to her becomes clear when she replies, "I don't have a husband." (4.17) Jesus, having evidently intuited that this woman was in some sort of emotional trouble, means to draw her out on this topic. This determination on his part suggests something about the process of being born from above, namely that it cannot be thrust in upon a person's life like some sort of theological juggernaut, that it has to be connected with the facts of a person's real life in the real world. Birth from above is not an invitation to super-mundane euphoria or some sort of free-floating theological state. Furthermore, somewhat along the lines of the statement that Jesus makes in the synoptic gospel (Mark 2.17 and parallels) about those who are well not being in need of a physician, Jesus seems to want to let the woman know that the regeneration of which he speaks does not depend upon a person's life being in perfect order beforehand. He says to her "When you say 'I don't have a husband', you put it beautifully. For you had five husbands and the one whom you now have is not your husband. This you have said truly." (4.17-18) He does not make this statement out of any desire to judge her. His statement of the facts, however uncannily he may seem to have come by them,[2] reflects the normative reading of her marital situation in that day: two or three divorces were tolerated, a greater number was considered beyond the pale; living with a man without the formality of marriage was even worse. In offering simply to know her and to accept her as she truly is, without any pretense of her being respectable, Jesus is enacting the verses about the light of love coming into the world in order to save the world in the third chapter of John, verses which we have discussed in our introduction to the subject of birth from above. He is offering the woman the chance to bask, i.e. to put trust in this light.

Actually, she has already evinced her total willingness to do so by telling Jesus that she has no husband. Jesus had shown himself to be a scorner of taboos in even talking to her, first of all because she was a Samaritan, second of all and even worse, because she was a woman (it is the fact that Jesus is talking to a woman which most amazes his disciples, as we will see shortly). His unconventionality may have encouraged a like unconventionality on her part, may have led her to believe that she had nothing to hide from this man, who would not be likely to subscribe to any of the verdicts which society had rendered against her with her suspect sexual life. One can posit her willingness to bask in the light of Jesus' non-judgemental love in spite of or perhaps because of the fact that she now appears to be changing the subject. Some critics have opined that because she now appears to be asking Jesus his opinion concerning an old theological dispute between Samaritans and Jews ("Our fathers worshipped God upon this mountain while you say that Jerusalem is the place where one ought to worship" — 4.20), she is dodging the more personal issues which Jesus has broached, that these issues are becoming too intense, that she is introducing a more pleasant topic than her own poor hapless self to talk about.

Such a bail-out would not be totally implausible although in this case there would appear to be another explanation, an explanation which almost seems to introduce something of a comic note into this conversation. It seems possible that, having come up against a prophet, the woman decides, so as not to let such a rare opportunity pass, that she should trundle out all the questions she has that a prophet might answer, and in particular she thinks: why not get this prophet to settle the age-old dispute about which is the holy place, i.e. Mt. Gerizim (as the Samaritans think), or Jerusalem (as the Jews think). In her own way of course the woman is raising a question which has always plagued religious groups, the question whether there is any one sacred spot in which God prefers or even needs to be worshipped, whether God needs to dwell in a temple or at any kind of site made by human hands. It plagued the Jews after they had settled in the land of Canaan and had to decide whether to consolidate the sacrificial system under one roof, so to speak, or let the local shrines keep thriving. It has plagued the Christian church ever since Stephen was stoned to death over it (Acts 6-7). In our time, when people cling to a particular church building as the one and only spot where they can ever imagine themselves having a satisfactory religious experience, they are coming down on a particular side of this question.

Jesus rejects the kind of parochialism implied by the woman's question. He offers her instead a vision of a far more enlightened form of worship. "The hour is coming and now is when the true worshippers will worship the Father by spirit and truth. For the Father is seeking such kinds to worship him." (4.23) As we have seen both in our discussion of this passage thus far and in our discussion of chapter 3 of the Gospel of John, "spirit" and "truth" are terms which, in Jesus' mind, are connected with the birth from above. Spirit is what results from putting one's trust in the name of Jesus. Truth denotes the kind of life which one's coming to the light, which one's accepting the fact that one is accepted by God enables a person to lead. In the light of these two terms, Mt. Gerizim and Jerusalem would both stand as relics of an old religious system in which and by which one's own standing before God (either personal or corporate as assured by proper sacrificial offerings) was of paramount concern. What Jesus is calling for is a new life based on concern for the needs and the interests of others, a life that can grow out of the fact that one no longer needs to be anxious about one's standing before God.

The woman demonstrates that she has been born into this new life, that she has "caught a glimpse of the Kingdom of God," both by her actions and by her words. It is hard to decide which of her two kinds of demonstration is the more forcible. She goes back into the town, leaving Jesus at the well. Significantly, she has left her water jar behind, as if she no longer needs such a receptacle of the old way of only temporarily slaking her thirst.[3] She has gone back into a town which she had left as an outcast probably moments before and started boldly preaching the good news of which Jesus has made her aware, she has been empowered to cast off the designation of her which society has made, from being some sort of victim of it she has been transformed into a would-be benefactress of that same society, as if in fulfillment of Mary's prophecy that God "has raised the shameful on high" (Luke 1.52).

This in itself would be a sufficient sign of the power of birth from above, but in addition she makes a remarkably clear translation of the code which Nicodemus was simply unable to crack, the hard doctrine of the third chapter: "Come and see a man who told all the things I did, might not this one be the Messiah?" (4.29) She offers this translation despite the fact that in her time, in terms of the religion of Israel, her logic would not have been conceded to be self-evident: there were other notions than hers of what the messiah ought to be, mostly nationalistic and militaristic notions, expectations involving a restorer of the *imperium* of Israel and a caster-out of the Romans. The Samaritans had cultivated their own expectations of a sort of alternate messiah known as the *taheb;* it may be that the woman was in part evoking this expected Samaritan figure, who was expected to restore their ancient religion. Nevertheless, as a formulation of what Jesus had been trying to communicate to Nicodemus, her words reveal a remarkable grasp of the essential message. In their simplifying power they are a little bit like Karl Barth's famous reduction of the whole message of the New Testament down to the words "Jesus loves me, this I know." She is testifying to her experience of having come to the light, of having been accepted just as she is. For her this experience has had the force of revelation, she has apparently seen God and lived, or rather gained new life.

The behavior of Jesus' disciples offers proof that a transformation like that of the woman is not something that simply happens automatically when one is exposed to the person of Jesus. The disciples returning in this story with the food which Jesus has sent them off to buy reveal just how radical a notion for his time and for his place Jesus has just been proposing both by his words and by his example. By talking to the woman, Jesus has evinced confidence in a God other than a fault-finding, fence-constructing one. By so doing, he has perplexed his followers. They evidently have managed to screw their courage up to the point of crossing Samaria with Jesus, they have also been willing to go off to town and handle things in common with Samaritans to the point of buying food from them, but it has been too much for them to come back and find Jesus talking with a woman. Their behavior almost seems to illustrate a statement of Paul's about the Gospel, namely that God has chosen the insignificant ones of the world, the ones without pedigree, the ones treated with contempt, the things which are not, in order to deprive the things which are of their force. (1 Cor. 1.28) Not that Jesus had chosen his disciples from any lofty social station, but at lease they had minimal status, some source of minimal self-esteem as true Israelites and as men, status which they evidently had expected their teacher to confirm them in, but he has descended even below them in the pecking order. They by their behavior reveal an aspect of birth from above which we will be commenting on again in other places, namely that it presents problems to those who have something, even a rather small something already, it is a threat to the established social order.

The story suggests that it threatens other orders too, or that volatility is one of the characteristics of the new life which being born from above institutes, that the new life is like the new wine uncontainable by old skins which Jesus speaks of in the synoptic gospels (Mark 2.22 and parallels), that consequences are unforeseeable or even paradoxical within the new life. The writer of the Gospel implies such changes within the new life first of all when he depicts Jesus as no longer hungry when his disciples come back from Sychar. To receive the full impact of this apparent restoration of Jesus one has to remember that he was physically exhausted when he arrived at the village, so exhausted that he had to sit down on the edge of the well and let his disciples go off in search of food. It could of course be that Jesus simply recovered spontaneosusly by the time his disciples come back, that his crisis of hunger had passed, but as we stated when dealing with the nocturnal setting in the third chapter of the Gospel of John, the writer of this Gospel has a tendency to charge physical details with metaphysical meanings. Nor does Jesus himself seem to speak of his recovery in merely physical terms. "Eat, rabbi," his disciples have said to him when they come back with their provisions, but Jesus says to them "I have food to eat which you do not know." His disciples infer from this statement that someone else must have brought him something to eat, but Jesus corrects them: "My food is that I do the will of the one who sent me and that I bring his work to completion." (4.31-4) In one sense, this is an understandable statement, or at least most people could corroborate it from some comparable experience in their own lives, some experience of transcending merely physical needs, of being too caught up in some exciting work to need or even to think about food for example, but given Jesus' penchant for making puzzling remarks, one suspects that there is something more in this remark than merely an appeal to the kinds of peak moments that all people sooner or later experience. The mingling of incommensurables in this statement is like a similar mingling in a passage from the Sermon on the Mount: "Do not then be anxious saying, what are we going to eat or what are we going to drink or what are we going to wear. For the gentiles are out to get all these things. For your heavenly father knows that you need all these things. But seek first the kingdom of God and his righteousness, and all these things will be added unto you." (Matt. 6.31-33)

Both statements seem to be implying that something strange happens once one commits oneself to the kind of new life that is possible to those who have been born from above. The statement in Matthew is a little bit clearer, especially if we remember the Hebrew meaning of righteousness which was discussed in our previous chapter. Correct the wrongs of society, and there will be food, drink and clothing enough for all might be a rough paraphrase of this directive which Jesus has issued, you won't have to be looking out for your own petty concerns all the time because everyone will be looking out for everyone else and therefore you (among all the others) will be taken care of. The feeding of the five thousand is a practical application of this same directive, Jesus having told his anxious disciples that they should start feeding the crowd themselves (Mark 6.37 and parallels) . The results are amazing.

One suspects that Jesus' statement quoted above from the Gospel of John about his alternative food source is pointing to the same sort of dynamic, the same unimpeded flow of benefits, "grace upon grace," (John 1.16) that can be set in motion within the Kingdom of God by people who will dare to let go of their own limited outlooks and stakes. One gets back as much as or maybe even more than one has given out. Jesus has helped the woman at the well to satisfy her thirst permanently, Jesus has been "fed" in return.

Nor is it just Jesus who has been fed in this way or who is capable of being fed. Having described his own satisfaction (physical and/or metaphysical) to his disciples, he then points out that there is also "food" for them to go out and pick for themselves: "Do you not say that it is the fourth month and the harvest is coming; behold I say to you lift up your eyes and begin to see the fields that they are white toward harvest already." (4.35) The statement about the fourth month and the harvest is evidently some sort of proverb,[4] a proverb which for Jesus seems to summarize somehow the way his disciples think. The situation here is again somewhat like that which one can see in the feeding of the five thousand, when the disciples come to Jesus asking what *he* is going to do about the crowd and Jesus tells them to fed the crowd themselves. Their thought near Sychar (interpreted by Jesus) is that something might happen someday off in a future which they don't have to think about and toward which they can be passive. Jesus might be saying to them here that although the hour is coming, it also now is and they are responsible for it. From having talked with one Samaritan woman, Jesus (and through him his disciples) are now in the position of the apple-picker in Frost's poem who keeps "hearing from the cellar bin/The rumbling sound/Of load on load of apples coming in," they have almost too much to deal with, i.e. a whole town of Samaritan converts (4.42) whom the woman has caused to "sprout", just as there were baskets full of leftovers to be picked up after the feeding of the five thousand. (John 6.13; Mark 6.43 and parallels) The rules of precedence and hierarchy are all upset by this ferment that the new birth prompts: "I have sent you to reap what you have not worked". (4.38) Jesus here resembles the master of the house in the parable (Matt. 20.16) paying the laborers hired late in the day what they had not earned, i.e. that same wage which those who have worked in the sun all day have received; in one sense, in terms of what we tend to think of as justice, the all-day workers are being cheated, but again the point may be that the volatile new life of the Kingdom makes all such categories, i.e. of "just" recompense, irrelevant, a new kind of abundance available to all is being sketched out. So is it with the harvest near Sychar which, in this story, Jesus tells his disciples to go out and pick. The old expectations no longer obtain, a new form of life has begun. Thus, in the glimpse of it which we seem to receive from this story of the woman at the well, the birth from above seems to be a means of transforming society, of unsettling the world as it is. This inference will have to be tested by further examples.

ii. THE WOMAN WHO WASHED JESUS' FEET
(or anointed his head)

In the seventh chapter of his gospel (verses 36-50) Luke tells the story of a dinner Jesus has been asked to attend at the house of a certain Pharisee whose name is Simon. Luke recounts that a woman in the city (unnamed in Luke) who is a sinner knows that Jesus is in the Pharisee's house and so she comes there bringing an alabaster jar of ointment. Entering the house, she stands "behind, beside the feet" of Jesus — Luke gives an accurate picture here: the heads of the people reclining on couches at a dinner like this one would be next to the table, facing in on the center of the room; their feet would be facing away from the table, so that standing more or less outside the circle of diners, the woman is both behind Jesus and beside his feet. Luke also tells us that the woman is weeping, or perhaps wailing, as the Greek word may be construed. She wails and begins to wet his feet with her tears and to dry them with her hair and then to kiss his feet and to anoint them with the ointment she has brought. (7.36-8) Jesus' host is discomfited by this action of hers or rather by the way Jesus does not seem to be bothered by it. The Pharisee, we are told, says to himself "If this one [meaning Jesus] were a prophet, he would know who and what sort of woman this is who is touching him, that she is a sinner." (7.39) It is interesting to note that the Pharisee, like the Samaritan woman, believes that psychological intuition or telepathy forms part of the normal equipment of a prophet. The Pharisee is certainly not wrong to expect Jesus to have such a capacity — where he is wrong is in expecting Jesus to have a predictable reaction to a "sinful" character-type when he comes upon it.

As a matter of fact, Jesus now demonstrates that he *can* search hearts for he seems to know what the Pharisee has been thinking to himself. He says "Simon, I have something to tell you." Simon says "Say it teacher, speak," (7.40) and Jesus then proceeds to relate the story of two people who were in debt to the same creditor, one for the sum of five hundred denarii, the other for the sum of fifty. Neither one is able to pay and so the creditor forgives both of them. Which debtor, Jesus asks, will love his former creditor more? Simon says that he supposes the one to whom more was forgiven will love his creditor more. Jesus agrees with Simon's interpretation. "You judged correctly," he says. (7.41-3)

Turning to the "sinful" woman, Jesus now proceeds to make

application from this parable. "Do you see this woman?" he asks Simon. "I came to your house. You did not give me water for my feet. She, on the other hand, began to wet my feet with tears and with her hair she dried them. You did not give me a kiss. She on the other hand from the time I came in did not leave off kissing my feet. You did not anoint my head with oil, but she with ointment anointed my feet. Because of which I tell you, her many sins have been forgiven for she loved much. The person to whom little is forgiven loves only a little." (7.44-7) In the face of grumbling objections by some of his fellow recliners-at-table along the lines of "Who is this that he forgives sins?" Jesus again tells the woman that her sins have been forgiven and also, perhaps somewhat surprisingly, that her faith (which according to New Testament usage would mean something like her trusting attitude) has saved her. (7.48-50)

The above passage contains various exegetical difficulties. Many critics, scholars, and readers have seen a conflict in Jesus' saying, on the one hand, that the woman's sins have been forgiven because she loved much and, on the other hand, saying that her faith has saved her, thereby implying that she loved much because her sins had been forgiven already, through her faith: for instance, Rudolf Bultmann, the famous Twentieth Century New Testament scholar, felt that in the remark about the woman's faith having saved her, a second supplemental source including the parable of the two creditors had been spliced on to an original main story. Furthermore, although in an ancient setting a host's neglect of the laws and the rituals of hospitality would have been considered a grievous failing, one can wonder why Jesus, who stressed forgiveness so much, on this occasion felt he had to be so severe with Simon for his apparent negligence as a host. Also, the question arises about how one ought to apply Jesus' parable to Simon: Simon is being contrasted to the woman; the woman is explicitly related to the more grateful debtor, the one who had owed more in the story; is Simon therefore to be considered the less grateful debtor and if so, how is he in debt to Jesus?

Although these problems with the story and especially the contradiction between sins being forgiven because one loves much and being forgiven by a pure gift of grace can perhaps be resolved without recourse to any other parts of the Bible, at this point it will help to look at the other New Testament stories about a woman administering some kind of unguent to Jesus. The interesting fact is that each of the other three gospels contains a story of this kind. (Matthew 26.6-13; Mark 14.3-9; John 12.1-8) As the stories have been handed down, they differ in various details, but at the same time they display enough details in common to suggest that they may all derive from one original story. Some of the details in Luke will become clearer after we have tried to recover the form and content of this orginal story.

Matthew and Mark give closely similar accounts of an anointing which according to them takes place in Bethany at the house of a man named Simon, identified as a leper, by which designation they probably mean that he is a former leper, one who has been cured and restored to society by going through all the formal steps that we see Jesus recommending to the leper he cures in a story told by the three Synoptic writers. (Matthew 8.1-3; Mark 1.40-5; Luke 5.12-16)

In Matthew and Mark a dinner is in progress and again a woman comes to Jesus at the dinner with an alabaster jar full of something — Matthew and Mark differ concerning what the alabaster jar contains: Matthew (26.7) says that it contains "very expensive ointment", Mark (14.3) that it contains "very precious genuine oil-of-nard ointment". Whatever the jar contains, the woman pours it out on Jesus' head (not on his feet as in Luke), at which action some of Jesus' fellow-diners become indignant — Matthew is rather significantly specific about who these grumblers are; he says that they are "the disciples". (26.8) Whoever they are, they base their complaint upon the presumed fact that the ointment could have been sold — Matthew (26.9) says "for a lot", Mark (14.5) says "for more than three hundred denarii" — and given to the poor.

Jesus asks them why they are bothering the woman who has done a good deed in him (Mark 14.6) or for him (Matthew 26.10). Jesus points out that they will always have the poor in their midst (Matth. 26.11) — to do what good deeds for them they wish, Jesus says in Mark (14.7) — but that they will not always have him. Jesus then explains the woman's action to them. "She did what she could" he says in Mark. "She did the job of anointing my body for burial ahead of time." (14.8) The explanation in Matthew (26.12) is similar. Both gospel writers also have Jesus saying that wherever the gospel is preached in the whole world, what the woman has done will be related as a memorial to her. (Matth. 26.13; Mark 14.9)

This conection of the woman's good work with Jesus' upcoming passion and death points to a chronological difference between the Matthew/Mark version and the version in Luke. Luke places his story about the sinful woman early in Jesus' career and makes it one of the occasions for a strong initial resistance to Jesus and his message. Luke stresses opposition to Jesus from the very first time he preaches in a Galilean synagogue. (4.16-30) Jesus' treatment of the sinful woman in the house of Simon elicits further opposition over the matter of Jesus, "presumption" of the power to forgive sins, hence the difference between what the grumblers single out as Jesus' offense in dealing with the sinful woman in Luke ("Who is this that he forgives sins?") and what they single out in the Matthew/Mark account (why this waste?). If the four Gospel accounts are all thought to be reflecting only a single story, then it may not be possible to decide absolutely, beyond a doubt, just where this story belongs in the career of Jesus, although as we will see later, in placing this story near the end of Jesus' career, the writer of the Gospel of John may connect it to that period in a way which decides the chronological issue. Apart from the chronological discrepancy which their versions introduce, however, it is important now to see whether any details which Matthew and Mark include in their accounts of the anointing at Bethany may help us better to understand the dealings between Jesus and this "sinful" woman as these have been represented by Luke.

One first notices that like Luke, Matthew and Mark mention someone named Simon as the host of the meal. Could this possibly be the same Simon in all three places even though in Luke he is described as one of the Pharisees whereas in Matthew/Mark he is described as a leper? He could be the same person if one assumes that he was both a Pharisee and a leper, or rather restored leper. His having been a leper might help to explain Jesus' dissatisfaction with him in Luke, especially if one were to make the further assumption that he had been cured by Jesus. If he had been cured by Jesus, one might almost say that he and the sinful woman were in the same position in relation to sin, given the ordinary idea that leprosy bespoke uncleanness and pollution, and its cure required a cleansing as in the case of sins; one could thus say that he is the other debtor whom we need to complete the parallelism within the parable Jesus has told in Luke, and yet Simon doesn't seem to want to show any gratitude toward Jesus the way the woman does, and Jesus rather emphatically points this fact out, not only by telling the parable but also by reprimanding Simon for his lack of hospitality.

It is at this point that one can begin talking about the woman as someone who has been born from above and in this way perhaps clear up the possible confusions in her status which were discussed earlier, i.e. have her sins been forgiven because she loved much or rather did she love because she had been saved through her faith? The usual New Testament idea, set forth both by Jesus and by Paul, is that the forgiveness of sins somehow empowers or frees a person to love, that a new ethical era can begin when the presumption of one's guilt before God is removed. The New Testament idea is that forgiveness usually has to precede love. Does Jesus' statement about the woman in Luke really contradict such an idea? Jesus says "Her many sins [which by the way are never specified in any of the versions — it has often been assumed, perhaps rightly, that her sins were those of a prostitute] have been forgiven because she loved much". As has been granted already, he could mean that her loving much became a cause by which her sins could be forgiven, but he could also just as well be saying to Simon "You may assume that her sins have been forgiven previously because you can see the fruits of this forgiveness in the amount of love she is displaying now." Jesus could be saying that the love which she shows is a demonstration of a prior change in her status from sinner to one whose sins have been forgiven and of course then it would not be contradictory to say that her faith, that is her attitude of trust, had saved her because such faith, such trust, such coming to the light, such willingness to stand in the light of the Redeemer's non-judgmental love is what loosens the fetters of a person's slavery to sin and then allows the person to love. The story in Luke does not show us the first stages of someone being born from above explicitly the way the story of the Samaritan woman at the well seems to do, a reader has to infer such stages from the sinful woman's past, but in their way those stages can be said to shine through Luke's account, by the Lucan woman's fruits one seems to know what she must have been through before.

The woman's tears then are probably tears of gratitude, a release of pent-up emotion, tears of appreciation for the restoration to a sense of self-worth, to a sense of acceptance which Jesus has bestowed on her (and which he continues to bestow: for instance, his parting words to her convey no exhortations to amend her ways but rather say simply "Go in peace" — Luke 7.50). Again, as with the case of the Samaritan woman, although without necessarily having had such a motive in mind from the start, Jesus gets something back from having given back her sense of self to this woman. This at least would be one way to understand the remarks about her helping to prepare him for burial which Jesus makes in the Matthew/Mark version of the story (having tried to give our reasons for doing so, we will now take the liberty of assuming that all these versions reflect the same original episode in the life of Jesus, and therefore we will move around among them rather freely): Jesus seems to be crediting her with some kind of prophetic insight into his true redemptive task of having to die on the cross and therefore with doing all that she can to assist him in that task, i.e. anointing him. At a time when his supposed disciples are getting ready to desert him and when they are all still more or less resistant to the idea that the Son of Man must suffer, Jesus finds a least one true follower in this woman. We remember that although Nicodemus found the birth-from-above doctrine, and especially its grounding in the idea of a suffering servant, difficult to fathom at first, he eventually came to understand and to identify with it in that he helped with the burial of Jesus. The woman in this story seems to have been an even apter pupil of the doctrine and of its demands: she helps with Jesus' burial beforehand, she does whatever she can. Jesus certainly assigns her an ineradicable place in the true gospel history which he proleptically alludes to.

But in some sense, at least in the Gospel of John's account, she is more than just a pupil, she even becomes a sort of teacher to Jesus. It is at this point, in connection with this aspect of her contribution, that we need to look at that account.

Some of the details in the Gospel of John's version of this story (John 12.1-8) appear to dissipate the clear picture that has been emerging so far from the versions in Matthew, Mark and Luke. The Gospel of John does agree with Matthew and Mark that the dinner occurred at Bethany, but it fails to name the host or to identify him as a Pharisee or as a leper. In naming people who were present, the author of the Gospel of John may be substituting for Simon an even more famous beneficiary of Jesus' powers, namely Lazarus, celebrated for being raised by Jesus from the dead — unless one wants to assume of course that both celebrities, Simon *and* Lazarus, could have been present at this same dinner, with the writer of John just leaving out the name of Simon.

At any rate, if this Gospel tends to complicate anew what had almost become plain from the Synoptic versions by omitting Simon's name, it also seems, finally, to provide the identity of the elusive "sinful" woman: she is Mary, Lazarus's sister, who uses the same kind of expensive substance (here "a pound of genuine very precious ointment of nard") as in Mark to anoint a part of Jesus' body (here, as in Luke, it is his feet which she anoints). The writer of the Gospel of John relates that the house was filled with the smell of the ointment when she applied it. (12.3)

Now we come back to the grumbling reaction which her action of anointing elicits in every account. In Matthew and Mark it was an interesting although perhaps coincidental fact that the anointing of Jesus by the woman and the grumbling by some of Jesus' fellow diners and/or disciples were placed immediately before Judas's going out to betray Jesus (Matt. 26.14-16; Mark 14.10-11) In the Gospel of John a similar placement seems to be explicit and intentional. The writer of this Gospel tells us that there was only one grumbler, namely Judas himself, who asks "Why wasn't this ointment sold for three hundred denarii [the same proposed amount as in Mark] and given to the poor?" (12.5) The Gospel writer also offers an analysis of Judas's motives: "He said this not because the poor were any concern of his but because he was a thief and, having the money bag, he was filching what was thrown in it." (12.6) Judas assumes that if the ointment had been sold for a sum to be given to the poor, then as treasurer for the group he would have been able to filch this amount too, thereby increasing the profit from his peculations. He will end up later having to settle instead for the far paltrier sum of thirty pieces of silver which according to Matthew (26.15) is what the head money for Jesus amount to. The writer of the Gospel of John does not say specifically that disgust with the woman's gesture of love and with the loss which this gesture causes him is what finally set Judas in motion toward betraying his teacher, but he implies such a connection, and thus in this respect would seem almost to anchor the story in a setting near the end of Jesus' career.

There is in this Gospel, however, an even more important connection made between what the woman does and what Jesus is starting to undergo, a connection to his beginning passion which is made by Jesus himself. As in the versions of Matthew and Mark, Jesus here in John defends the woman from the attack in this case of her sole detractor, using the same arguments and almost the same words that had appeared in those other two versions. As in Mark he says "Leave her alone". As in both Mark and Matthew he defends her action as an anticipatory burial observance, and talks about the poor always being with them after he himself will no longer be present. (John 12.7-8) Of even greater importance, though, is the way Jesus in this Gospel then takes up and applies what Mary has done to him as if to magnify its meaning. Not long after the episode in Bethany, Jesus himself washes his followers' feet (abeit without the expensive ointment) (John 13.1-20). By this act he should be seen hopefully to be preparing them for their burials just as he by Mary had been prepared for his. In other words, at this stage Jesus is still hoping that the Son of Man/Suffering Servant will be a group, just as in the seventh chapter of Daniel the Son of Man is a group of the righteous saints, and he imitates Mary's action as his means of expressing this hope that he will have companions in his ordeal. [5]

By so doing he is also "lowering" himself to the level of mere woman's work or servant's work. One suspects that this departure from dignity by Jesus is part of what contributes to Peter's discomfort: he dislikes having the master minister to *him*. Peter does not like seeing his leader so demean himself, and so he says that he is not going to submit to having Jesus act as his lackey, thus underscoring the point of Jesus' gesture even as he, Peter, is missing that point. (13.6)

The full implication of this woman's gesture, as it has been adopted, therefore ratified as an example (13.5) by Jesus will not be clear until we have looked at the cases of Peter and Paul, our two most fully documented examples of birth from above. In some ways, one could say that footwashing or various kinds of equivalents to it will remain as a sort of standard by which disciples all must be measured, this action points to the strait gate, the birth canal through which disciples must pass to begin with and maybe keep on passing. It is our natural human resistance to the idea that "when I am weak [i.e. down on my knees like a servant or a woman or even worse, hung on a cross], then I am strong" (2. Cor. 12.10) which those who would be born from above must deal with each in his or her own sphere. We will next examine Peter and Paul as they try to deal with that radical idea.

CHAPTER 3.

PETER'S PAINFUL BIRTH FROM ABOVE

i. BASIC PERSONALITY TRAITS IN PETER.

We begin with one advantage in trying to understand how Peter comes to be born from above: the Gospels show something of his life and character before the acutal birth process begins. In the case of the two women whose encounters with Jesus we have just examined, we had to make guesses from only a few hints about what they were like before they had been born from above. Not so with Peter: with him some essential features of his pre-birth life are visible.

It seems, at least from Luke's account of Peter's call to follow Jesus, that we should group Peter with the two women under the category of "sinner" — in fact Peter puts himself in this group.

Luke's account of Peter's call to follow Jesus involves a version of the story of the miraculous draught of fishes. The writer (or one of the writers) of the gospel of John places a similar story at the very end of his gospel, in a post-resurrection setting, so that one cannot be sure where this story really belongs. We will examine John's version of this story later, in connection with how Peter must carry on after he no longer has Jesus present as his teacher and guide. Here, by laying aside the critical problems and using the Lucan story merely as a means to gain some initial glimpses of Peter, one is struck by his own characterization of himself as a sinful man.

Luke says that a crowd has been pressing in on Jesus and hearing the word of God. As Jesus stands beside the Lake of Gennesaret, he sees two boats standing beside the lake. The fishermen who operate these boats have stepped away from them and are cleaning their nets. Jesus goes into one of these boats, the one which belongs to Simon, and asks him to put out from the shore. Here, presumably at a somewhat more comfortable distance from his audience, Jesus goes on with his teaching. (Luke 5.1-3)

After he stops teaching, Jesus tells Simon to put out into the deep and to lower his net for a catch. Although Simon is obviously skeptical about this piece of advice from a non-fisherman ("Teacher, we worked all night and didn't catch a thing"), nevertheless something, perhaps something in Jesus' way of offering it, leads him to follow this advice: he says he will lower the nets "at Jesus' word". The result of course is that the nets enclose a great multitude of fish and do not break; the catch is so great that those in Peter's boats have to signal to their colleagues in the other boat to help them come and take in the haul; it is also so great that it makes the two boats sink down in the water. (5.4-7)

At this point Peter reveals an interesting part of himself. Having seen what has happened with the catch, he falls on his knees before Jesus, saying "Depart from me, sir, for I am a sinful man." (5.8) This may be the remark of a sinful man who is also superstitious. We may surmise that Peter's idea of sinful behavior includes such superficial violations of the law as failure to honor seasonal observances, rough language in the presence of religious teachers, perhaps even the general lack of a civilized veneer. One hazards such guesses about Peter's use of the word sinful because of a tendency to identify with an orthodox scheme of values which he manifests all through his appearances in the New Testament. As a superstitious man he imagines powerful forces at work in the cosmos, forces always primed for retaliation against people whenever they take those forces for granted. The conception of God which such a mind usually encompasses is at the opposite extreme from that conception of God as caring parent which Jesus has come to encourage.

What also makes Peter interesting is that he shows other tendencies too, not just this tendency toward a legalistic, orthodox viewpoint. The first chapter of the Gospel of John shows Jesus intuiting the essential nature of several persons on first meeting them. Peter has been brought to meet Jesus by his brother Andrew, a former disciple of John the Baptist who believes he has now found in Jesus the Messiah. The Gospel tells us that Jesus really scrutinizes Peter (literally "looks in" him) and then says "You are Simon the son of John, you shall be called Cephas" — the text then says that "Cephas" means "Peter". (John 1.42) Jesus thus posits or at least implies two personae in Peter that vacillate back and forth and will often display themselves in the future. One persona is the Galilean fisherman that he has been up till now, the other a character of great strength and endurance as implied by his new name of "Rock" (or perhaps something closer to "Rocky" as Raymond Brown suggests in his Anchor Bible commentary on the Gospel of John)[1]

The aptness of Jesus' reading of Peter's character can be tested in an episode from the Gospel of Matthew, one of the versions of Jesus' walking on the water. Jesus has just finished feeding the five thousand men (the number five thousand does not include the women and children, as Matthew is careful to note — why they were not counted Matthew does not say). He immediately compels the disciples to enter the boat and go before him to the other side, until he releases the crowds. Then Jesus goes up into the mountain by himself to pray and when evening comes he is there alone. (Matt. 14.13-23)

Meanwhile the boat containing the disciples has already gone many "stades" or furlongs distant from the shore and is being tossed about by the waves and by the contrary wind. Eerily then, without any introduction (although Matthew tells his readers that it is the fourth watch of the night,) Jesus comes toward the disciples in the boat, walking on the sea. The disciples decide that what they are seeing must be an apparition (in Greek a "phantasm") and they cry out from fear. Jesus immediately tries to reassure them: "Cheer up, it's me. Don't be afraid." (14.24-7)

Resembling the intrepid Hamlet who does not hesitate to confront his father's ghost at the beginning of Shakespeare's play, Peter now shows something of his "Rocky"/courageous side by daring to speak to this putative ghost which the disciples have seen: "Lord, if it's you, command me to come to you on the water." Jesus complies with this request by saying "Come". Peter than gets down from the boat and begins to walk upon the water and comes toward Jesus, but seeing the strong wind, he starts to be afraid and to sink. He cries out, saying "Save me, Lord." Immediately Jesus extends his hand, takes hold of him and says, "Oh one of little faith, what were you afraid of?" After they both have gone up into the boat, the wind ceases. Like Peter at the time of the miraculous draught of fishes in Luke 5, those in this boat get down on their knees in front of Jesus and say "You truly are the son of God." (14.28-33)

If one just looks at the psychology of Peter in this story, without trying to settle the difficult question as to what really was going on out on the sea that night, one can say that in a surge of confidence he did not fear the force of gravity that would pull him down through the water, nor was he afraid of launching himself into a previously unknown experience. It was only when he saw the strong wind, a force which was all too familiar to fishermen, that he lost courage. In other words, this story discloses a Peter ready to grapple with the completely unknown yet with a countervailing cowardice in the face of familiar bugbears, a cowardice which cancels the other fine forthcoming readiness.

Peter's readiness to grapple with the unknown, to take risks, to launch himself in feats of daring also involves perhaps a certain adolescent desire to be the star pupil, a desire to make the remark that the teacher will appreciate and always remember. Such an impulse probably lies behind Peter's confession at Caesarea Philippi, especially in Matthew's version of this confession, but probably to a certain extent in the other versions too. (Matt. 16.23-28; Mark 8.27-9.1; Luke 9.18-27)

The basic story, at least in Matthew and Mark, is of Jesus and his disciples out walking in the region of Caesarea Philippi. Jesus first asks the disciples to tell him who people say that he is. They give him a list of names by which people have identified him: John the Baptist, Elijah, Jeremiah, one of the prophets. Jesus then asks the disciples who *they* say he is. In all three gospels it is Peter who serves as spokesman in giving an answer although in all three gospels the answer he gives is different. In Mark (8.29) he says "You are the Messiah"; in Luke (9.20) "The Messiah of God"; in Matthew (16.6) "You are the Messiah, the son of the living God."

The Matthew version diverges significantly from those of the other two gospels when it reports Jesus' response. Although all three gospels end with Jesus charging the disciples in more or less strong language not to tell anyone about what they have just observed, Matthew alone inserts a passage in which Jesus praises Peter for his insights and assigns him a future role which is commensurate with those insights: "Blessed are you, Simon son of John, because flesh and blood did not reveal it to you but my heavenly father. And I say to you that you are a rock, and I will build the church upon this rock, and the gates of hell shall not prevail over it. I will give you the keys of the heavenly kingdom and whatever you shall bind on earth shall have been bound in heaven and whatever you loose on earth shall have been loosed in heaven." (Matt. 16.18-19)

We have already pointed out that there is a question whether the story of the miraculous draught of fishes belonged early in Jesus' career where Luke put it or after Jesus' resurrection, where the Gospel of John placed it. The same sort of critical question might be asked about this response by Jesus to the confession at Caeserea

Philippi. Though there is no version of Jesus' congratulation of Peter other than the one in Matthew and no other setting suggested in any report of pre- or post-crucifixion episodes, Oscar Cullman has concluded that this exchange between Jesus and Peter really belongs to a time after Jesus has been raised from the dead. At any rate, unless it can be removed from its present setting, Jesus' response to Peter in Matthew confuses the rest of the story. The whole event as Mark, Luke, and even Matthew (if one omits the passage just quoted) depict it does not culminate in any fervid congratulation of Peter: all three gospel versions show that Jesus rebukes Peter (and by extension all the rest of the disciples with him since Mark and Luke actually say that he rebuked "them") and in Mark (8.33) and Matthew (16.23) he is soon even calling Peter Satan.

The Greek word *epitimao*, which Mark (8.30) and Luke (9.31) use to describe Jesus' reaction to Peter's answer, shows just how strongly he disapproved. In certain contexts this word can mean "command", "order", or "warn", but in a series of important earlier passages in all three gospels it has the much stronger meaning of "rebuke" or "scold". When Jesus stills the tempest, all three gospels use the verb *epitimao* to show Jesus rebuking the storm (Mt. 8.26; Mk. 4.39; Lk. 8.25). In a scene from Matthew (12.15-16), Jesus either rebukes or strongly warns (same verb) a crowd not to make known the healings he has performed. In Mark 3.11 the context is even more noteworthy: some unclean spirits, having seen him, fall down before him and confess him as the son of God, but Jesus greatly rebukes then, or warns them, that they not make him manifest. Similarly, in a Lucan healing story (4.41) demons were coming out of many crying aloud and saying "You are the son of God" and Jesus rebuked them and would not allow them to speak because they knew him to be the Messiah.

What kind of Messiah, though? Having himself overcome the temptation to become the political Messiah that many in Israel longed for, having overcome this temptation in a protracted battle with Satan in the wilderness, as Matthew (4.1-11) and Luke (4.1-12) show, Jesus is not anxious to have the expectations of a political Messiah which are always ready to erupt into fiery enthusiasm among the Jews of his time whipped up by the loose lips of any evil spirits. In that Luke and Mark have Jesus rebuke the wind and certain indiscreet and hostile unclean spirits, one is led to conclude that, far from welcoming Peter's confession that he was the Messiah or the Messiah of God or the Messiah, the son of the living

God, Jesus looked upon such a confession as Satanic and wanted to make sure that it was not circulated among the volatile Jewish crowds where it might incite some to calamitous action. Matthew has Jesus strictly enjoining his disciples not to tell anyone that he is the Messiah — Matthew (16.20) uses *diastellomai*, a weaker word than *epitimao* — the overall effect of Matthew is to blunt the point that Luke, and especially Mark, make quite directly. The Matthew version also seems to make Jesus terribly capricious or self-contradictory: one can wonder why Jesus is calling Peter Satan so soon after he has praised him as the divinely inspired confessor, but the contradiction disappears, and the rebuke of Peter then makes sense when the encomium of Peter is transferred to a post-resurrection setting, to a time after Peter has denied and deserted Jesus and has then come back, and when one sees his confession at Caesarea as Satanic rather than divinely inspired.

In all the Caesarea Philippi passages Jesus then starts to teach the disciples that he is Son of Man rather than the Messiah, that he must go away into Jerusalem, suffering many things from the elders and priests and scribes and be killed and on the third day be raised from the dead (the wording of this passage is quite similar in all three gospels). Now interestingly enough in terms of word choice, it is Peter who takes Jesus aside and rebukes *him* for having made such horrible statements — Luke does not contain this passage, but in Matthew (16.22) and Mark (8.32) the verb used to describe what Peter does to Jesus is *epitimao* again. Then in Matthew Peter says "May God have mercy on your soul, sir." He is here evincing again that superstitious streak which came out in the Lucan version of the miraculous draught of fishes. He thinks Jesus has uttered some kind of blasphemy for which he is liable to be struck down by the divine anger. He then says "This will never happen to you" (16.22) perhaps trying to cancel what Jesus has said about the suffering he must endure.

Now Jesus in his turn has to re-rebuke Peter. He then makes explicit what the verb *epitimao* has been implying all along when he says to Peter "Go behind me Satan". Matthew alone (16.23) has Jesus saying to Peter "You are my stumbling block", then both Matthew (16.23) and Mark (8.33) have Jesus saying "because you don't think the way God does but the way human beings do." God's way of thinking as expressed in part by the prophets and as embodied in the insights of Jesus includes the need for a Suffering Servant. Human ways of thinking are focused on the hope for a triumphant political

Messiah who will drive the Romans out and restore Isreal to its former prosperity, power, and importance.

Jesus now goes on to elaborate his revolutionary notions of the true value of a human life. First of all, those who wish to really follow him will have to elect the path of crucifixion because to want to gain one's life is in essence to lose it, just as the decision to lose one's life is in essence to gain it (here Jesus is being paradoxical in the same way he is paradoxical when in the Beatitudes he tells his listeners that true happiness consists of being poor and hungry and persecuted — everything is reversed). He ask what good all earthly success can be if it entails the loss of one's real life and reminds the disciples that there is nothing, no pledge by which to redeem a forfeited life. He then warns that whoever is ashamed of him and of his words, ashamed that is to identify with the apparent loser/outcast-image of the Suffering Servant, is one of whom the Son of Man will be ashamed when he comes in the glory of his father with the holy angels. (Mark 8.34-8; Matt. 16.24-8; Luke 9.21-7)

It is important to understand that the term Son of Man, as Jesus uses it here, includes the idea of a group and not necessarily only one person. The Son of Man whom Jesus is thinking of is the Son of Man who goes up to heaven in Daniel 7.13 — in Daniel the term Son of Man refers to the true children of Israel who remain faithful through a succession of tribulations. What Jesus is saying is that if a person is ashamed to identify with him and with his words (which would probably comprise Jesus' actions as well as his sayings), then that person will have no part in the eventual glorification in heaven of the group that persevered through suffering. Jesus tells his disciples that some of them standing there with him will not taste of death until they see the Kingdom of God coming in power — what the disciples and in particular Peter, who is their spokesman, cannot grasp is that the power of the Kingdom of God is manifested in the apparent weakness of the suffering servant, the one who is despised and rejected, who will be nailed to a cross.

It seems that Peter's mind is blocked to what Jesus is saying. He is like a person who does not want to hear any bad news and therefore tries to work up ways of denying the bad news when he is actually presented with it. Jesus has now made it very clear to his followers what it means to be a true disciple, to be in the retinue of the Son of Man, but then when he takes his inner circle, which consists of Peter, James, and John, up onto a high mountain alone in order to give them a premonition of his glory, Peter repeats the mistake he has already made in his confession and pretends that everything that he envisions for his leader has already been accomplished, that the time for collecting, for reaping the benefits of discipleship has already arrived and that a time of triumphant prosperity lies ahead.

What this small group has been taken up to witness is Jesus' transfiguration, which the writers of the three synoptic gospels all describe in different ways. Mark (9.3) says that Jesus was transformed in front of them and that his garments became glistening, exceeding white, such that no fuller on earth could whiten them thus. Matthew (17.2) adds the detail that his face shone as the sun which is probably meant to recall the skin of the face of Moses sending forth rays as he came down from Mt. Sinai. (Exodus 34.29-34) Luke (9.29) says that the form (appearance) of his face became different and flashed white as lightning.

In the next phase of the transfiguration Elijah appears to Jesus' disciples along with Moses. Luke (9.31) is more detailed about the conversation which Jesus holds with these two Old Testament luminaries. He says that Elijah and Moses and Jesus appeared in glory and were discussing his departure (in Greek the word is *exodon,* which obviously has important scriptural associations) which he was going to fulfill in Jerusalem. Luke then adds the strange detail that Peter and those with him were weighted down with sleep. It is hard to know whether or not they missed the talk of Jesus' departure: their falling asleep is listed after the subject of the conversation, but Luke does not say whether the talk and the sleep were simultaneous or successive. (9.32)

Luke says that Elijah and Moses had already gone away before Peter next spoke. In Mark and Matthew they are evidently still there when he speaks. At any rate they all agree almost totally as to the content of what he says: in Mark's version (9.5) he says "Lord, it is good for us to be here, and let us make three tents, one for you and one for Moses and one for Elijah." It is only Mark (9.6) and Luke (9.33), however, who add the comment that Peter "did not know what he answered" (or "what he said" in Luke). Mark adds that "they had become afraid", evidently trying to excuse Peter's remarks because of the nervousness which he and his comrades must have been feeling. But the fact that Mark seems to feel that he has to make excuses for Peter shows that the inappropriateness of Peter's remark must be evident to him. Matthew, significantly, does not comment upon Peter's remark, nor should we expect him to since he characterized what one ought to understand as Peter's Satanic confession as one of the most glorious breakthrough moments of Jesus' career.

Mark and Luke seem to imply that Peter shows again how wide of the mark his understanding of the Messiah's true role is: he thinks that it is time for them all to celebrate some kind of joyous milestone whereas what Jesus has been trying to tell him is that the real tribulations are only beginning and that his true followers will be discriminated from the false by how they react in the face of such tribulations. As an indication that Jesus has truly been representing "the way God thinks" as opposed to "the way human beings think" a voice from heaven now speaks, "This is my beloved son" (Mark 7.6) or "This is my beloved son in whom I am well pleased" (Matthew 17.5) or "This is my son who has been chosen" (Luke 9.35). All three Gospels record the voice as then saying "Hear him", a command which may show that although Moses and Elijah were both major figures in the history of Israel (and were sometimes associated as in Malachi 3.21-3), the real prophet toward whom that history had been moving is the one who is now left with the disciples after Moses and Elijah have departed, for as Moses himself had said. "Yahweh your God will cause a prophet like me to arise from among you, from your brothers; listen to him." (Deut. 18.15)

Peter may have been able to listen to this new prophet every day, but the gospels contain many further instances of how he did not seem to understand the prophet's outlook. In one such instance even Jesus is amazed when Peter has to ask him to explain a certain statement. Jesus had been telling the Pharisees why his disciples did not, according to the tradition of the elders, wash their hands when they ate bread. Afterwards, conversing alone with his disciples, and having been told that those who had heard his words about not washing had been shocked, Jesus makes some rather stinging remarks about false religious leaders: "Every plant which my heavenly father has not planted shall be uprooted. Let them go. They are blind guides of the blind. If a blind one leads a blind one, they shall fall into a pit." (15.13-14) Peter then asks Jesus to interpret "this parable," by which Jesus evidently understands him to mean not the remark about the blind guides but rather his "shocking" earlier remark that "It is not what goes into the mouth that makes the person unclean, but what comes out of the mouth, this makes the person unclean" (Matthew 15.11). At any rate, Jesus now speaks again, even more emphatically, about food and sanitation: "Do you not know that everything that goes into the mouth proceeds into the stomach and is thrown out into the latrine;

the things which go out of the mouth come forth from the heart; those things defile the person. For out of the heart come arguments, evil things, murders, adulteries, sexual immoralities, thefts, false witnesses, slanders. It is these which defile the person; to eat with unwashed hands does not defile the person." (Matthew 15.17-20)

This is an interesting statement in its own right. The point here, though, for our examination of Peter is that Jesus has been amazed, perhaps even exasperated by Peter's having asked the question that prompted this statement: Jesus seems to think that Peter should have understood this matter already, because to Peter's request that he explain the parable, Jesus' first comment had been "And are you still without understanding?" (15.16) The "still" in Jesus' question implies that there had been some problem before or even all along with Peter's understanding of Jesus.

It does seem true that Peter tends to want to have statements by Jesus applied to him personally, as when he asks "Lord, how many times will my brother sin against me and I forgive him? Up to seven times?" (Matt. 18.21) Jesus has been talking about ways to win one's brother back after he has sinned against one; he has described a disciplinary process which should be carried out among those who already belong to a community of believers. (18.15-20) Peter evidently wants to know how many times the process has to be before one can simply give up on one's brother. Jesus says that there is no limit to the persistent forgiving love one has to show a repentant brother (18.22): this is what his answer to Peter of "Seventy times seven" means.

The desire to know how Jesus' remarks apply to him (or how he ought to apply them to himself) would not necessarily be a bad trait on Peter's part, but if we try to bring this trait into slightly clearer focus, we might tend to conclude that "What's in it for me?" is how this desire to know on Peter's part is often slanted. Not that Jesus' answers to the question "What's in it for me?" are always pleasing to Peter. For instance, after Jesus has had his discussion with the rich young ruler, one of the points of that story being how hard it is for a rich man to part with his possessions, Peter makes the following rather expansive observation: "Behold, we have left everything and followed you". All three synoptic gospels (Matt. 19.27; Mk. 10.28; Lk. 18.28) report this statement almost identically. Matthew, however, has Peter ask a further revealing question of Jesus: "What will we than get?" Matthew (19.28-30) then goes on to show Jesus promising that they will "get" plenty: first of all, in the new age they will sit upon thrones judging the twelve tribes of Israel and in that age everyone who has left house or brother or sisters or father or mother or children or fields on account of Jesus' name will receive a hundredfold and will inherit eternal life. In Matthew's version Jesus seems simply to be confirming Peter's shallow expectation, Peter's belief that the payoff time for Jesus' inner group has arrived (like his belief on the mount of Transfiguration). We have to turn to Luke and Mark to have Jesus' answer brought into clearer focus. In Luke the disciples have earned in a particular way the right to sit on thrones and do the judging: "You are the ones who have remained with me in my trials and I will make a will for you just as the Father has willed me my kingdom, in order that you may eat and drink at my table in my kingdom and sit upon thrones to judge the twelve tribes of Israel." (Luke 22.28-30) This payoff is not automatic in other words, nor is the other payoff that Matthew has Jesus promise without its hidden sting, as Mark makes clear in his version of the same promise: "Truly I say to you, there is no one who has left house or brothers or sisters or mother or father or fields for my sake and for the gospels's sake who will not receive a hundredfold now in this season houses and brothers and mothers and children and fields with persecutions, and life eternal in the coming age." (10-30) Jesus is here trying to give Peter a true notion of the staggering cost of discipleship, but Peter does not want to know it or is not able to hear.

ii. PAUSE: ASSESSMENT OF PETER'S PROGRESS IN THE NEW LIFE.

At this point, having reviewed this many of the revealing episodes of Peter's career, having made note of Peter's uncertain progress, one might be tempted to ask in what sense, if any, Peter has been born from above. It would seem that in comparison with the two women whose births from above have already been discussed, Peter is certainly having a difficult time of it. It would be hazardous to generalize from only three cases, especially since the data from two of them are so limited, but it does seem that inasmuch as they are less committed to (because they have less to gain from?) the established male system of religious values, women in the New Testament, especially women who have been judged culpable by that system, have an easier time passing through the spiritual birth canal (a process which includes tribulations) into the new life offered by Jesus, whereas for men that birth canal is as narrow as a needle's eye and they are somewhat like camels trying to pass through it. One only has to think of how the Mary who washed Jesus' feet, whatever she herself might have wanted for Jesus, nevertheless does her best to help him in the dire career he has elected rather than, like Peter, refusing even to understand it. But to return to Peter in particular: if one were to develop more fully the idea of birth so as to apply it to his career, one would probably have to say that up till now all we have really witnessed is his spiritual conception and somewhat stunted gestation. With the onset of Jesus' passion he may be said to have at last passed into the birth canal, but even then he seems to be positioned in its sideways, not passing easily through it or perhaps not passing through it at all. It is only with the resurrection of Jesus that Peter will pass out into the light and air of the new life, but even then, although his energies will be organized and oriented differently, in a fundamental sense he will remain the same old Peter. In other words, birth from above in the New Testament, when one carefully examines certain key instances of it, does not magically deliver a person from the tensions which his or her personality has heretofore entailed. In the new life one may have to work with many or even most of the elements of one's old personality.

iii. PETER UNDER STRESS DURING THE LAST DAYS OF JESUS' LIFE.

There is an abundance of material on Peter during this passing-through-the-canal-phase of his birth from above, one certainly does not have to go scouring the gospel texts for it, and yet it is tempting to begin with a doubtfully Petrine episode simply because it so well exemplifies the type of difficulty which Peter will be having all through the period of the passion. This episode occurs at the beginning of the so-called Synoptic Apocalypse when Jesus is asked to catalogue the signs of what apparently he alone has sensed as the coming woe. We are told in Mark that it is Peter, James, John, and Andrew alone who are presented with this catalogue. Although there is some doubt as to how one ought to relate the sequence of their names to the singular verb "asked" (13.3), it would still appear that it is Peter who initiates the topic of the sign of things to come. For Peter seems, as always, to be acting as spokesman and the statement which is made just before he asks Jesus about the time and sign of the coming woe seems of a piece with some of his earlier fatuities. One suspects that Peter is that "one of his disciples" who, coming out of the temple, in a burst of civic and patriotic pride, says "See what wonderful stones and what wonderful buildings!" (13.1) It is as if this disciple were saying, perhaps with an eye to having some power and influence in the new order which the political messiah will establish, "Isn't it a great thing that we have here?" The answer of Jesus is certainly not calculated to endorse such complacency or to confirm such satisfaction: "Do you see these great buildings? Not one stone which has not been torn down shall be left upon stone". (13.2)

This exchange seems to reflect the same theological battle that Peter and Jesus have constantly been waging up to this time. It is not necessary to discuss here the entire ensuing speech of Jesus, since it does not apply obviously or primarily to Peter. It is significant, though, that at the culmination of this speech (Mk. 13.23-27) Jesus again introduces the figure of the Son of Man from Daniel, thus reminding his disciples and especially Peter of one of the alternative paradigms in terms of which he now intends to continue what is left of his career: no political Messiah but rather the Suffering Servant who after passing through trials will go up to God as the Son of Man.

This dichotomy is also depicted in the Gospel of John's account of Jesus' last days. It is probably in hopes of gathering together that group which according to Daniel is supposed to constitute the Son of Man that Jesus washes the disciples' feet in the thirteenth chapter of John. This interpretation has already been suggested in the discussion of the woman who washes Jesus' feet with ointment, i.e that Jeus is repeating the woman's gesture and thus revealing his hope that there will indeed be a faithful group to go with him to suffer. He does not seem to expect here that Peter will understand what he is doing because he says "what I am doing you don't know now, but you will know after these things". (John 13.7) Nevertheless he does warn Peter that unless Peter submits to being prepared in this way for burial, Peter will have no part with him (13.8), presumably in the rule which is the Son of Man's reward as depicted by Daniel.

In typical extravagant fashion, probably because he has in mind a share in another kind of kingdom, Peter asks for an even more extensive wash ("Not my feet only, Lord, but also my hands and my head" — 13.9), but Jesus tells him that "The one who has been bathed has no need except to have his feet washed, but is clean completely". (13.10) Jesus later explains what he means here by cleanliness: "You are clean already on account of the word which I have spoken to you" (15.3) The word that he has spoken is that they are his siblings and friends in the divine family which has God as its parent — this is what has made them completely clean, but they still need to be prepared for burial, i.e. prepared for the trial through which it is necessary for them to pass as constituent members of the Son of Man.

The author of the Gospel of John now makes Jesus stress that aspect of his mission which all among has caused someone like Peter to stumble. When Judas goes out to betray Jesus, the author of this Gospel has Jesus say "Now the Son of Man has been glorified and God has been glorified in him" (13.31) — in the kingdom Jesus is inaugurating, as in the Beatitudes, all the normal categories have been reversed, what seems like the nadir is actually the zenith. Shortly afterwards in this Gospel there begins an extraordinary series of exchanges between Jesus and his obviously troubled disciples. Jesus has said "Children, I am with you yet a little while. You will look for me and just as I said to the Jews that where I am going you cannot come, so also I am saying now to you.". (13.33) Peter takes this theme up and asks Jesus "Lord, where are you going?" (13.36) Jesus answers: "Where I am going you cannot now begin to follow me, but you will follow later" (13.36) (this is a prediction which Jesus will make more explicit in John 21 and which will be discussed in connection with that chapter). Peter keeps pressing Jesus: "Lord, why can't I begin to follow you now? I will lay down my life for you." (13.37) There are two ways to punctuate the first part of Jesus response to this boast of Peter's (13.38): it could be a question ("Will you lay down your life for me?") or it could simply be a statement ("You will lay down your life for me"), but Jesus then definitely does make a prediction: "Truly, truly I say to you, the rooster will not crow until you deny me three times."

At this point, the traditional chapter break in the Gospel does a serious disservice to Jesus' remarks; he should not be thought of as starting a new topic but rather should be seen as going right on from what he has just said to Peter even though, as the pronouns in the Greek show, he is now talking not just to Peter but to the whole group: "Let not your heart be troubled. You believe in God, believe also in me. There are many rooms in my father's house. If not, would I have said [or I would have said — again two kinds of punctuation are possible] that I go to prepare a place for you. And if I go and prepare a place for you, I am coming again and will receive you to myself in order that where I am you also might be" (14.1-3) The many rooms refer to the various opportunities that the disciples will have in the future to accept the office of suffering servant.

It seems that by now Jesus is beginning to doubt whether he will have many companions in performing that office. In Luke, just as in John, he predicts that Peter will at some point fall away, but he also wants Peter to realize that falling away, even at such a culminating moment of Jesus' career, is not the same as being rejected forever for service in Jesus' cause. "Simon, Simon, behold the Satan has asked permission to sift you like wheat. But I have prayed for you that your faith not fail. And when you return, strengthen your brothers." (Luke 22.31-2) Two points are noteworthy here. The first is that Jesus can make a prayer and have the answer to it be "No", i.e. Simon's faith *does* later fail. The second is that in Jesus' mind the return of Peter is, if not a certainty inasmuch as Peter does have free will in despair to stay away permanently if he wants to, then at least an option to which there is no obstacle from Jesus' point of view. Failures will be welcomed back.

Here in Luke Peter now makes the same sort of boast he made in John about how he will never desert Jesus and about how he will defend Jesus to the death, and Jesus again predicts that Peter will deny him three times. (22.33-4) It is important to understand that in terms of his own limited understanding Peter does keep his pledge. This is why Jesus in John may first agree to Peter's pledge that he will lay down his life for Jesus, and then nevertheless predict that Peter will deny him. The denial comes after the attempt to fulfill the pledge, because Jesus, in a final demonstration that he is not the political Messiah and that he will offer no resistance to the enemies who surround him, has rejected Peter's heroic offer to lay down his life.

It is true that before making good on this offer, Peter first falls asleep as Jesus is praying in Gethsemane (Matt. 26-40; Mark 14.37; Luke 22.45-6) and thus fails to receive the spiritual strengthening which Jesus receives as the fruit of a great inner struggle, but when the crowd finally does come out to arrest Jesus, Peter draws his sword and cuts off the ear of the high priest's servant. We are dependent upon the Gospel of John (18.10) for the identification of Peter as the one who performs this action; the synoptic gospels say simply that it was one of Jesus' diciples (Matt. 26.51; Mark 14.47; Luke 22.50). Given the fact that it is Peter, though, Jesus' rebuke of Peter is of great significance; in Matthew (26.52-4) Jesus gives a long speech about why he doesn't need to be protected by the swords of his disciples; one suspects the the simplicity of Jesus' words and gesture in Luke (22.51) may be closer to what actually happened: "Jesus answered and said, That's enough. And touching the ear, he healed it." Whichever version is more accurate, it is at this point that Peter collapses. He lingers a little while longer, mere flotsam in Jesus' wake, but since the utmost loyalty he had to offer has now been rejected (Jesus might have been saying here, as he did on another occasion, "And are you still without understanding?"), he is left feeling utterly bereft of any faith in the Master's mission.

The scene in which Peter finally does deny Jesus is one of the dramatic masterpieces of world literature, even if it does happen to be splintered into four different versions (the version in John being extremely compressed and of less interest than the other three). Peter has followed Jesus at a distance as far as the courtyard of the high priest, where he stands and warms himself beside a fire that is lit. The trial of Jesus then gets underway. Meanwhile Peter is subjected to a series of questions about himself. In all three synoptic accounts the first question comes from a maid or slave-girl. She asks if Peter was with Jesus, who in Mark (14.67) is called the Nazarene and in Matthew (26.69) the Galilean. Peter says no in various ways in the three Gospels and then in Mark and Matthew he changes his position, moving either to the forecourt (Mark 14.68) or to the gateway (Matt. 26.71). In Matthew (26.71) and Luke (22.58) he is then accused by another person of being one of Jesus' band and he again denies. In Mark (14.69) it is the slave-girl who persists and makes her accusation not to Peter but to those standing beside her. An interval passes before Peter is accused for the third time. In Matthew (26.73) and Mark (14.70) it is a group that confronts him, in Luke (22.59) it is an insistent individual. In Luke and Mark this third accusation is based on his being an apparent Galilean, in Matthew it is his speech that gives him away.

In Mark (14.71) and Matthew (26.74) Peter invokes a curse on himself as part of this third denial, in Luke (22.60) he simply says that he does not know Jesus. It is at this point that the rooster crows and at this point also that Luke contributes a searing detail when he says that "the Lord turned and looked straight at Peter" (22.61). Evidently a door is open and Jesus is able to look out from the inner place to the courtyard which in Luke Peter has never left. Luke does not elaborate on this look Jesus gives, and one can only speculate as to the quality of it. It is the kind of encounter the intense emotions of which would require the genius of a Piero della Francesca or a Tintoretto or a Rembrandt to capture. It would also conduce with vivid cinematic treatment, the lens at this point zooming in on Jesus.

At any rate in all three gospels Peter now remembers what Jesus had said about how Peter would deny him. Luke (22.61-2) and Matthew (26.75) have Peter rush out and weep bitterly. Mark (14.72) uses an obscure phrase which probably means something like "he began to weep" or even "he broke down and wept" although there is some small ancient evidence for what would be the most remarkable picture of all: "he covered his head and wept." Whatever the exact picture of Peter's despair may be, he now drops out of the Passion story, his progress toward being born from above apparently stalled permanently.

Where does Peter go now? The answer to this question has to be excavated from the details of the various Resurrection stories in the gospels. In Mark (16.1), when the sabbath is over, Mary Magdalene, Mary the wife of James, and Salome buy aromatic spices in order to anoint the body of Jesus. They go to the tomb early, at sunrise on the first day of the week, i.e. the Sunday after Good Friday (16.2). As they approach, they wonder who will roll back the stone from the door of the tomb for them (16.3), but then when they look, they see that the stone, which was very great, has been removed and so they enter the tomb (16.4). There they are confronted with a young man seated to the right, clothed in a white robe (16.5). They are amazed, but he tells them not be be (16.5-6). He tells them that Jesus the Nazarene, whom they seek, has been raised and is not there (16.6). He then gives them some instruction: "Go tell his disciples and Peter that he is going before you into Galilee. There you will see him as he told you." (16.7)

There is only one more verse in the true text of Mark: "And they came out and fled from the tomb, for fear and amazement possessed them, and they said nothing to anyone for they were afraid. (16.8)" There would be a certain literary awesomeness to ending a gospel in such suspended fashion, but if it seems more logical to assume that Mark did originally contains some account of the Galilean appearance which Jesus had promised his disciples (Mark 14.28), this account was lost in the process of transmission, then it is to Matthew that one turns to gain some idea of what such an appearance must have been like in Mark.

There are some discrepancies between the early part of Matthew's

Easter Sunday account and the early part of Mark's. Matthew has an earthquake accompanying the arrival of an angel of the Lord. This angel then rolls the stone back from the door of the tomb and somehow perches upon it (28.2) His appearance is as lightning and his clothing white as snow (28.3). He stuns those guarding the tomb so that they are as dead ones (28.4). But then aside from these supernatural trappings, he talks to the women (this time there are only two, namely Mary Magdalene and "the other Mary" — 28.1) in much the same way as the young man in Mark did (28.5.7). This similarity suggests that Matthew and Mark are dealing with the same basic version of Easter Sunday events.

At this point Matthew tells us that "they went out quickly from the tomb with fear and great joy and ran to announce to his disciples", (28.8) but then they meet Jesus instead. He greets them, they fall down and worship him (28.9). Then Jesus says to them "Don't be afraid. Go and announce to my brothers that they go into Galilee, there they will see me." (28.10) This version raises two questions: first, in running to tell the disciples, were the women sure that they would find them and second, were the brothers whom Jesus directs the women toward the same as the disciples, or could Jesus literally have meant that the women go and tell his siblings?

There is a reason for asking these questions. If one skips over the bribing of the soldiers (28.11-15), which seems like an insertion in Matthew, and proceeds directly to the appearance of Jesus to the disciples in Galilee, one finds (28.16) that the disciples "had gone into Galilee" (this is a reading strongly to be preferred of the tense of the Greek verb), i.e. had already left Jerusalem, one assumes out of a conviction that the great enterprise for which they had entertained such great hopes has by now been totally smashed, or maybe they retained some faint glimmer of hope, since they had gone to the mountain at which Jesus had commanded them to regather, and here, Matthew relates, they saw him and worshipped, although some began to doubt. (28.16-7) At any rate, in reference to the first question asked above, the important point to notice here is that they could not have been found around Jerusalem by the women who had gone to Jesus' tomb, because they were already in Galilee.

The details of Jesus' charge to the disciples on this occasion do not pertain to the study of Peter which is being conducted here, and besides, it is probable that the twenty-first chapter of the Gospel of John contains a more interesting version of this same Galilee appearance even though that appearance is chronologically out of place where it now stands in that Gospel. We will be returning to the twenty-first chapter of John since it contains the final word on Peter's rehabilitation after he has denied Jesus. In the meantime, though, it is important to continue trying to re-establish a viable chronology of the events surrounding Jesus' resurrection. An argument is here being made for a sequence in which Peter and the rest of the inner band, out of deep discouragement, fled toward Galilee from Jerusalem, probably on Good Friday. The risen Jesus first appeared to some women near what had been his tomb on what we call Easter Sunday, then to his disciples sometime shortly thereafter in Galilee. Commissioned by Jesus, they must have returned immediately to Jerusalem — vigorous walkers, they would have been able to complete the round-trip posited here within a week's time.

Which brings us to Luke's resurrection account, which is decidedly different from that of Matthew and Mark. In Luke, the women who had come with Jesus from Galilee follow the body of Jesus to its burial place, see where the tomb is, then return and prepare spices. (Luke 23.55-6) They remain quiet on the sabbath according to the commandment (23.56), then on the first day of the week, when dawn is still deep, they go to the tomb carrying the spices which they had prepared (24.1). All this suggests that we are dealing with events of the first Easter weekend, but then, as will be seen, the events which Luke goes on to relate are so different as to require that what Luke is mistakenly telling as a story of the first Easter weekend is actually a story from a subsequent, probably the next weekend. The women (unnamed at this point) go into the tomb in Luke's account, having found the stone removed, but they do not find Jesus' body (24.2-3). They are at a loss concerning this fact, then two men in dazzling apparel are standing by them (24.4) The women become afraid and incline their faces toward the earth (24.5). The angels say to them "Why do you seek the living among the dead? He is not here but has been raised. Remember what he said to you while he was yet in Galilee, saying that the Son of Man had to be given over into the hands of sinful men and on the third day rise up." (24.5-7)

At this point it is important to note the difference between the wording in Luke and that in Matthew and Mark. Matthew and Mark talk about Jesus going before some group of his followers into Galilee (Matth. 26.32; Mark 14.28). Luke omits this detail, he only has the angel talking about what Jesus has said while he was yet in

Galilee, while he was still alive. According to the material he had gathered the disciples were back in Jerusalem very soon after the resurrection of Jesus — Luke evidently did not see how they could have gone up to Galilee and gotten back so quickly to Jerusalem, therefore he omits having anyone mention the promise Jesus made to meet his disciples there. Luke is dealing with resurrection events after the return of the disciples to Jerusalem. What he does not realize is that they are not the first resurrection events.

In his account the two angels now recall other more generalized prophecies of Jesus, the women remembering these depart (Luke 24.7-8). We are now told that the women on this occasion are the ever-present Mary Magdalene and Joanna and Mary the wife of James, plus others. These women now tell what has happened to them to the apostles, i.e. to the group of the eleven, which had despairingly retreated to Galilee, been met there by Jesus, then returned to Jerusalem to take up their Master's mission with renewed fervor (24.10 — in verse 9 Luke also mentions "all the others" to whom they announced these things). Then Luke makes the rather amazing remark that these things appeared before the apostles as nonsense and that the apostles were not believing the women (24.11). This reaction is partly orthodox male chauvinism, reflecting Jewish rejection of the testimony of females except in the most restricted spheres, but then it also grows out of the fact that for them to have had a post-crucifixion vision of Jesus did not necessarily suggest to them that his body would be missing from the tomb — they disbelieve the remarks of the women because they simply assume that Jesus' body must still be in the tomb.

There is one rather significant exception to this derisive reaction of the disciples: Luke tells us that Peter got up and ran to the tomb and bent over and saw the linen cloths by themselves and went away by himself amazed at what had happened (24.12). This action of his helps to locate John 20 chronologically because although in that chapter it is only Mary Magdalene who comes to the tomb and who then runs away when she finds the stone rolled back (20.1-2), still there is an episode involving Peter much like the one which Luke describes, only in John the one who bends over and sees is not Peter but rather his companion, the disciple whom Jesus loved. In the Gospel of John's version, Mary runs away from the tomb and tells these two that they have taken her Lord and she does not know where to find him (20.2). These two then go to the tomb, the beloved disciple runs ahead more quickly than Peter and goes into the tomb first, or at least into what must have been a kind of entryway for the tomb because he now stoops down and sees the linen cloths lying there but then we are told that he does not go in (20.4-5). Coming up behind him, Peter is less reluctant: he goes into the tomb, sees the linen cloths lying there and also the sweat cloth that was on Jesus' head, although this is not lying with the linen cloths but is by itself, wrapped up separately in one place (20.6-7). The beloved disciple now enters the tomb and according to the text he sees and starts to believe (20.8).

There is something of that aspect of Peter that was noted at the beginning of his career in his bolting into the tomb on this occasion: he still shows himself ready to launch off into the unknown without much concern for any possible consequences, but it may be that he is not really doing so with any great degree of insight. It is that beloved disciple who, standing back a little, seems better to understand what both he and Peter are now becoming witnesses to. A similar difference between their forms of behavior comes out also in chapter 21 which, although it follows chapter 20 in the Johannine sequence as handed down, should actually come before chapter 20 since it deals with that time of discouragement up in Galilee on "Easter Sunday" when to the remnant of the inner group around Jesus everything that they had worked for must have looked lost. We are told that they are together beside the Sea of Tiberias (i.e. Galilee) (John 21.1). The gospel of John gives us some of the names of those who constituted this remant: Simon Peter and Thomas the one called twin and Nathanael from Cana of Galilee and the sons of Zebedee and also two other disciples (21.2). Peter still seems to be the leader of the group: he announces that he is going fishing and the other disciples follow (21.3). In other words, Peter and his comrades have gone back to their old occupation with no more hope of being fishers of human beings.

At this point the Johannine version of the miraculous draught of fishes, the story which Luke had used in discussing the call of Peter to be Jesus' disciple, begins — in John it is the story of Peter's recalling rather than the story of his first calling.

The men are still fishing as day is breaking. Jesus is standing on the shore although the disciples do not know that it is Jesus (21.4). Jesus says to them, "Children, you don't have any fish, do you?" They tell him no. (21.5) He than says "Throw the net onto the right side of the boat and you shall find." They throw with the same result as in the Lucan story: a bulging net-full of fishes which they cannot pull in. (21.6) At this point the beloved disciple is granted another one of his insights: he says to Peter "It is the Lord". (21.7) Peter then performs a preliminary action which it is somewhat difficult to gain a clear conception of. He seems to have been lightly clad (one meaning of the Greek word which is usually translated "naked" in this passage), wearing some kind of loose-fitting fisherman's smock, which he now proceeds to tuck in for easier swimming. He then throws himself into the sea and presumably thrashes his way to the shore. (21.7) The other disciples come in by boat (21.8). Again it has been Peter who acts, the beloved disciple who hangs back a little and sees.

Peter next asserts himself when the group is on the shore. Arriving there, they have seen a charcoal fire lit (almost as if, having betrayed Jesus around one charcoal fire — the same word is used in Greek — Peter were going to be given a chance to re-state his loyalty beside another one), and a fish being roasted upon it and bread (21.9). Jesus says "Bring from the fish which you have caught now" (21.10). At this point Peter, again apparently in his role of leader of the group, his role as the one who always responds first to any orders, goes up into the boat and drags the net onto the land (21.11). A breakfast now begins among Jesus and his extremely diffident disciples.

After breakfast Peter and Jesus conduct a conversation in which and by which Peter's difficult birth from above seems at last to be effected. Jesus begins this conversation by asking "Simon, son of John, do you love me more than these?" (21.15) It is important to notice two facts about this question of Jesus': first of all he reverts to calling Peter Simon, son of John, that name by which he had addressed him at their first meeting back in chapter one (v.42) — by employing this form of address Jesus might almost be sayings that it is time for Peter to go back to the beginning and start all over again. The second fact to notice is that the word of Jesus which is here translated as "love" is *agapao* in Greek. Whole books have been written on whether or not, in the New Testament period, there is any difference either in denotation or in connotation between the Greek verbs *agapao* and *phileo*, which both have to be translated into English as "love" (English, which is usually so rich in words, being in this case quite poor). Without being able to settle the controversy, which has vast scholarly armies amassed on either side of it, or to make a real decision, we might suggest that in using the verb *agapao* here, Jesus is trying to find whether Peter will claim still, as in his earlier promise to lay down his life for Jesus, to have an unconditional commitment toward the cause of Jesus, a commitment which needs no motive cause and which will admit of no obstacles, which will not alter when it alteration finds or bend with the remover to remove, an ever-fixed mark of a commitment. If so, then it is highly significant that in answering Jesus' twice-asked question "Do you love me (*agapao*)?", Peter insists on the verb *phileo* in his affirmative answers: *phileo* might suggest a personal commitment to Jesus based on qualities which appeal to Peter but no longer some kind of extravagant commitment which is beyond or somehow prior to relationship; it is significant that Peter would use the verb *phileo* in his answers and perhaps even more significant that Jesus would seem finally to settle for such a response, would even adopt the verb *phileo*, switching over from *agapao* when for the third time he asks Peter "Do you love me?", but then it has already been somewhat clear that Jesus is settling for this response even before he switches over to Peter's verb because each time Peter answers, Jesus gives him some directive — it is as if Jesus were saying "All right, that's good enough" and then, certainly without stopping to commend Peter, proceeding nonetheless to give him his instructions: first "Feed my lambs" (21.15), i.e. my little ones (perhaps with the milk that Paul says beginning disciples need?), then "Be a shepherd to my sheep" (21.16), i.e. show those who already belong to the flock which way they must go, then finally "Feed my sheep" (21.17) (using the same verb as in the case of the lambs), i.e. give this same group the spiritual message that they need.

It is striking that at this juncture we are presented with a saddened, sober Peter who hardly seems to resemble that Peter who used almost to gloat in the rewards he thought would be coming to him in the new Messianic kingdom. There is no discussion of any rewards here, the discussion is all of difficult tasks that will need to be performed. In addition to being told that he will have tasks to perform, Peter is also told with what kind of death he is to glorify God, i.e. he is given some cryptic idea of what room awaits him in his heavenly father's house: "Truly truly I say to you, when you were younger, you girded yourself about and walked wherever you wanted. But when you grow older, you will stretch out your arms and another will gird you about and bring you where you do not want to go." (21.18) This may be the most difficult task of all those awaiting Peter.

Interestingly enough, lest we forget, the birth from above as Peter has finally experienced it does not mean that all his old personality traits just magically fall away like the skins of a snake. Peter shows a little of the same self-interest that has been noted in him before. He shows that he is still somewhat interested in the question "What's in it for me?" or more precisely on this occasion "What's in it for other people as well as for me?" He sees his companion, the disciple whom Jesus loved, and fearing that that one will perhaps get off with a much lighter sentence than the one he himself has just received, Peter asks Jesus "Lord, what about this one?" (21.21) Jesus tells him that the fate of the beloved disciple is not his concern and then identifies Peter's real concern in one succinct order: "You follow me." (21.22)

In Acts and in some other parts of the New Testament we have material which allows us to watch Peter trying to carry this order out.

iv. PETER AND THE EARLY CHURCH.

In the first glimpse which we receive of Peter in Acts, he seems to have suffered something of a relapse into old attitudes and expectations, if we can assume that in the days leading up to Pentecost he remains the spokesman for the apostolic band. In the first chapter of Acts Luke states that "during forty days" Jesus "presented himself alive with many decisive proofs" to the apostles. (Acts 1.3) This time span of forty days has often been thought to be some kind of round or symbolic number (like that of the time span for Jesus' temptation), but in fact it may help to corroborate the chronology of Resurrection appearances which has been posited above. Pentecost, by Jewish law, had to come seven weeks plus one day after the Sabbath which followed the Passover. If, when they are all sorted out and harmonized, the Resurrection appearances require two Sundays with one week (six days) intervening, then there would still be six weeks or about forty days left before Pentecost. In other words, what Luke may be saying in Acts (although without clearing up the discrepancy of why he has already shown Jesus being taken up to heaven at the end of his gospel) is that Jesus continued to be some sort of living presence among his disciples after the first Resurrection appearances which the Gospels depict, that he in fact presented himself from time to time throughout the period from

Easter until Pentecost.

Whether or not Luke is actually trying to make such a point, he does seem to show that in this interim period, the disciples remain as obtuse about some of the larger purposes of Jesus after his resurrection as they were before he was crucified, and in particular they seem completely to misunderstand his promise (in Acts 1.5) that they will be baptised by a holy spirit. They assume that Jesus is alluding to an inauguration of the last days of Jewish expectation and that those last days will above all feature some kind of exclusive reward for Israel ("Lord will you in that time restore the kingdom to Israel?" — Acts 1.6). Once again Jesus has to try to re-orient their understandings. He tells them first of all that even if he is going to restore the kingdom to Israel, it is not for them to know either the times or the season which the father has placed in his own power, but then he tells them that he is talking about a kind of power other than a merely political power anyway: he tells them that they will receive a power coming from the holy spirit and that they will be his witnesses in Jerusalem and all Judea and Samaria and "as far as the last part of the earth." (Acts 1.7-8) The book of Acts of course will in part be an account of how the apostles manage to ignore or to bicker about this directive which would seem to have been straightforward, even unmistakable, but to return to the subject of Peter: since he is pictured throughout the gospels as the spokesman for the apostolic band in almost every situation, one assumes that he asked Jesus the question about the restoration of the kingdom. Luke says that "they" asked Jesus, but one doubts that he meant for that pronoun to be taken literally. Someone must have been speaking for the group, and even if Peter was not the actual spokesman on this occasion, he must have shared the atavistic expectation that the political kingdom might be restored since Luke mentions no objectors from within the apostlic band. Even in the presence of the Risen Lord, Peter could relapse to a Jewish parochial position.

The disciples are cautioned about a further failure to understand what Jesus' resurrection means for them in the next episode of this first chapter of Acts. Jesus is taken rather suddenly up into heaven and the disciples are shown looking fixedly into that region after he has gone. At this point, according to Luke, two men stood beside them in white garments and said "Galilean men, why do you stand looking into heaven? This Jesus who was taken up in this way from you into heaven will come in the way you saw him going into heaven." (Acts 1.11) This passage is usually taken to foretell a second coming, a coming back by Jesus as the glorious judging Son of Man at some time.[2] There might, however, be another way to interpret it, especially if one remembers that the direction in which the Son of Man moves toward the Ancient of Days in Daniel is up. The two men in white might then be saying to Jesus' followers that the earth will be the staging area for all further comings of the Son of Man toward God — Jesus is the first-fruits, the first born of many brothers and sisters, but the Son Of Man is ultimately to consist of many who stand the test of suffering, who are confirmed for presentation to God. The Son of Man will continue to come as the disciples have just seen Jesus going, but he as a collective entity will not be coming down from heaven but rather coming up from earth. So again, by wistfully looking up as if waiting for Jesus to return, Peter along with his fellow disciples seems to have misunderstood some fundamental aspect of the new dispensation which Jesus has inaugurated.

Further misunderstandings on Peter's part emerge. In the next episode in Acts a replacement for Judas is being chosen. It is not just that according to Peter, the replacement must have been an eyewitness and a follower of Jesus from the time of his baptism up until the time of his assumption, a requirement that even Peter could not have met, since according to Luke he was not present for Jesus' baptism — in retrospect, given all the squabbling that takes place over the subject of who or what an authentic apostle is, this requirement in its narrowness almost seems designed to provoke the squabbling, but what is perhaps more disturbing about Peter at this gathering is that he addresses a group that includes women (cf. verses 13-14) as "Men, brothers", i.e. he ignores the women in these deliberations, forgetting the example of how Jesus had acted toward women. It is one of the strange facts of church history (especially in recent interpretations of it) that Paul has gained a reputation as the arch male-chauvinist when Peter may be much more deserving of the title. From the evidence both of Acts and of his letters, Paul would seem to have treated women as equals and as colleagues in the new divine society.

It is possible then to show Peter still finding it difficult to be a child born from above at the beginning of the book of Acts, but at the same time one must not ignore the obvious signs that he has become some kind of new person. First of all, the one who had manifested a certain martial courage in an impulsive burst by drawing his sword and preparing to fight for Jesus in Gethsemane but who had then collapsed when Jesus rebuked him for such a course, the one who had denied Jesus and then in the wake of Jesus' trial before the high priest had skulked in total despair away to Galilee, is now back declaring Jesus' name in the midst of the same city in which, only seven weeks before, the name of Jesus had been anathema to both the Jewish and the Roman ruling groups. However one wants to account for this change in his behavior, Peter now manifests a fearlessness which apparently cannot be shaken. Furthermore his preaching is of a kind to "stab" hearts (Acts 2.37) and convert great numbers of listeners at Pentecost (Acts 2) and in the stoa of Solomon in the temple after he has cured the crippled beggar (Acts 3). And then of course the ability to effect such a cure in itself indicates that Peter has received startling new power from some source (although at this point whether he will always use such power in keeping with the mind of Christ remains to be seen). As one final piece of evidence that Peter has undergone some kind of character transformation there is the fact that in the new Christian group of which he is evidently the leader all things are shared in common, possessions are sold and the proceeds are divided according as each has need (Acts 2.44-5). It is as if the group were implementing the words of Jesus that whoever would leave father, mother, brothers, sisters, and belongings for his sake and for the sake of the gospel would receive those things back one hundredfold (with persecutions) in this life, it as if those words had indelibly impressed Peter although some time had to elapse before he could put them into effect. At any rate, at this point one sees very little of that tendency once evinced by Peter to ask how he personally or how his own little group might benefit from a given activity. At least in respect of their material resouces both he and the group which he now leads have received some kind of birth which is from the spirit, i.e. birth from above; Peter in fact at the end of his Pentecost speech (Acts 2.38) specifically promises such a receipt of the spirit, such a birth from above to those who will repent and be baptized on the basis of the name of Jesus Christ.

The above positive aspects of the behavior of Peter in the early chapters of Acts are somewhat general. If one looks more closely at some of the positions Peter advances in these chapters, one sees that for all his admirable ardor Peter still may not have understood the full meaning of the resurrection of Jesus. At least such a failure on Peter's part is evident from the way he preaches by the stoa of Solomon after he has healed the crippled beggar. Some scholars have seen this speech as preserving an extremely primitive Christology. Its Christology certainly differs from that of the Pentecost sermon in which Peter declares Jesus to have come already into his full Messianic office: "Let all the house of Israel know for certain that God made both Lord and Messiah, this Jesus whom you crucified (Acts 2.36)". In the speech at the stoa of Solomon, by contrast, Peter seems to doubt whether Jesus is the Messiah yet: it is true that at one point Peter says that "God in this way fulfilled the things which he promised before through the mouth of all the prophets that his anointed one would suffer" (Acts 3.18), as if Jesus had suffered as the Messiah, but then later Peter suggests that the Messiah has not yet been sent and that certain things have to happen before he can be: "Repent then and turn around to have your sins wiped off, so that from the presence of God the times of refreshment might come and he might send to you the appointed Messiah Jesus whom heaven must receive until the time of the restoration of all things which God spoke through the mouth of his holy prophets from of old" (Acts 3.19-21) In this sort of exhortation Peter can be seen repeating the error of the disciples when the two men in white found them gazing up to heaven after Jesus had ascended, that is he is looking to the wrong quarter for the next phase of the salvation process, he fails to understand how decisive an event the resurrection of Jesus has been, how it has already inaugurated the new age. In looking up to heaven he is also perhaps still filled with the traditional Jewish expectation of some kind of conquering military hero, some kind of warrior-lord who will descend.

Peter, however, always comprises a strange and interesting mixture of the obtuse and the insightful and even in this speech, when he may be misinterpreting the meaning of the earthly career which Jesus has now completed, he is at the same time speaking of Jesus in certain terms which may look back to Jesus' own way of talking about himself. Twice in this speech at the stoa of Solomon (vv. 13,26) Peter uses the Greek word *pais* which appears in the Septuagint version of the fifty-third chapter of Isaiah as the designation of the despised and rejected servant of Yahweh. From Peter's use of this word here one may be able to conclude that he has taken his cue from Jesus' rejection of the Messianic title at Caesarea Phillipi, that he has at last understood and adopted one of Jesus' preferred designations of himself as the suffering servant of God, but in so doing Peter has also gone too far in reducing the status of the earthly career of Jesus, he has failed to see that the suffering servant was already at the same time the Messiah.

Whatever one may want to say about its Christology, this speech does have two results: it produce many more believers (Acts 4.4) and it also earns Peter and John a night of confinement in prison prior to their being examined the next day by the rulers, the elders, and the scribes. (Acts 4.2-22) During this examination Peter manifests more of the unstinting boldness that has already been mentioned as one of his new characteristics. Noting the openness with which Peter speaks, and furthermore realizing that he and John are "illiterate" and "untrained", their examiners are amazed: no Jewish lay person is expected to challenge or to confront the religious authorities as Peter and John have done. The leaders confer with Peter and John outside the room. They decide to warn them not to speak anymore on the basis of the name of Jesus. It is in response to this warning that Peter and John raise what the rabbis would no doubt have thought to be an absolutely settled issue: "Judge for yourselves whether it is just before God to listen more to you than to God". (4.19) For the average pious Jew it *was* just to listen to their leaders more than to God because only their leaders were qualified to understand what the word of God was, but Peter and John claim to have the right to bypass those who were supposed to mediate the word of God to them: "For we cannot not speak what we know and have heard". (4.20) They are in fact claiming a new kind of authority for themselves and a considerable part of the interest of the next section of Acts will derive from watching whether they avoid any or even some of the pitfalls which confront the possessors of such authority.

The release of Peter and John is celebrated by a great raising of the church's collective voice in a request to God that he will enable his servants to continue speaking with the same kind of openness that Peter and John have displayed. (Acts 4.23-31) The situation of sharing all things in common is again described. (Acts 4.432-35) One might almost describe this period as a sort of honeymoon or idyll for the church. If so, then that propitious atmosphere is soon disrupted. Even before it is disrupted, as people like Barnabas are handing over the proceeds from the sale of property which they own to the communal treasury, a little detail may tend to disturb: the method for handing these proceeds over is to lay them by or before the feet of the apostles as if in some sort of act of obeisance (Acts 4.37); in the light of one of Jesus' most solemn injunctions to these same disciples ("You know that those who think to rule the Gentiles lord it over them and that their great ones exercise authority over them. Let it not be that way with you, but whoever would like to become great among you shall be your servant" — Mark 10.42-3), one would tend to question the appropriateness of such an insistence by the apostles on an acknowledgement of their sublime or lordly position. That there is something ominous in this kind of behavior on their part is soon confirmed by the story of Ananias and Sapphira (Acts 5.1-11).

The behavior of this couple is immediately set in contrast to that of Barnabas who has handed over all the proceeds from the sale of a field that he owned; Ananias sells his property, but then with the knowledge and consent of his wife he holds back some of the proceeds, and brings only a portion of them to lay by the feet of the apostles. (5.1-2) At this point Peter who, as another aspect of his birth (or of his partial birth) from above seems to have acquired some of those powers to read minds which Jesus displays in certain Gospel stories, confronts Ananias with his crime: "Ananias, why did the Satan fill your heart for you to lie to the holy spirit and to hold back from the price of the field? Did it not remain to you while it remained and being sold, was it not in your power? Why is it that you put this deed in your heart? You didn't lie to human beings but to God." (5.3-4) What this speech of Peter's seems to suggest first of all is that although most of the Christians were turning the full proceeds from the sale of their property over to the group, nevertheless each individual did have a choice whether to do so or not. It suggests further that Ananias would have been within his rights to retain some of the proceeds from the sale of his land for himself, that the impropriety of his action consisted not in the holding anything back but rather in claiming to hand it *all* over and thus attempting to deceive the Holy Spirit. Some in fact have gone so far as to assert that Peter is here accusing Ananias of that very sin against the holy spirit which Jesus had pronounced to be unforgivable, i.e. Ananias expressing contempt for the holy spirit by assuming that he could dupe it; if this interpretation is correct, it would show Peter as having strayed rather far from Jesus' definition of the sin against the Holy Spirit; Jesus had said that the sin against the holy spirit consists of saying that someone who was doing good had been empowered by Satan. (Matt. 12.22-32) But then the sin of Ananias is also said by Peter to be against God and here one notes a possible alarming shift in Peter's thinking: when he had been examined by the authorities he had claimed to be able to hear God directly, now he seems to be claiming to be able to stand in for God., i.e. to deceive him is to deceive God. It is hard to be sure here about the real extent of Peter's claim. It is also hard to be sure about his exact intention in confronting Ananias: although his words do seem to cause the immediate death of Ananias, Peter may not have meant for them to do so, he may just have been trying to scare him.

At this point, that is, one can still give a charitable coloring to Peter's actions, even though he never expresses remorse at the death of Ananias that now follows. One has no such option, however, in interpreting what Peter does after an interval of three hours when Sapphira appears not knowing that her husband has died and been buried. In a way Peter entraps her by asking "Were you given back so much for the field?", to which Sapphira answers "Yes, so much," (5.8) but the harshness of this mode of treating her is insignificant when compared to how he treats her next by saying "Why did you agree to test the holy spirit? Behold, the feet of those who buried your husband are at the door and they will carry you out." (5.9) One who was extremely determined to exonerate Peter here might say that he meant these words as nothing more than a prediction, but it seems far more likely that he meant to bring about a result rather than simply to predict it, that he intended to smite Sapphira with some kind of telepathic force. At any rate Sapphira dies immediately, she is buried with her husband, and "a great fear comes upon the whole church and upon all who were hearing these things" (5.10-11) so that the respect which the apostles had been garnering when the people were laying proceeds from the sale of property at their feet was as nothing next to the holy awe which Peter after the manner of some kind of *Jupiter tonans* now inspires.

The question must be asked of course whether Peter has used this power in consonance with what Paul calls the mind of Christ. We know from a story told in the gospel of Luke that when James and John had manifested a penchant toward the punitive use of supernatural power, Jesus had strongly disapproved. Some messengers had gone into a Samaritan village as advance agents for Jesus but had not been received there. When James and John saw this, they said "Lord, do you want us to tell fire to come down from heaven and destroy them." (Luke 9.54) In response Jesus turns around and rebukes them (Luke 9.55 — the word used is *epitimao* the connotations of which we have discussed above in connection with Peter's "Satanic" confession at Caesarea Philippi). Peter, who must have been aware of this response of Jesus, has certainly not been deterred by it here in bringing down death upon Ananias and Sapphira.

Furthermore, in evaluating Peter's behavior, one also has to try to guess what Jesus himself might have done in such a situation. One can only guess since there are no exact analogies to the Ananias-Sapphira story in any of the Gospels. The closest one comes to such an analogy is in the story of Jesus' betrayal by Judas and here when the affront is far more personal than the affront was to Peter in what Ananias and Sapphira did, Jesus responds with a kind of equanimity, most startlingly so in Matthew (26.50) where, as Judas is betraying him, Jesus addresses him as "friend", and in general Jesus always treats those categorized as sinners with so much tolerance and compassion, is so concerned to rehabilitate rather than to annihilate them that one can only feel that Peter's behavior on this occasion would sorely have disappointed or probably even grieved his teacher.

It is a great mystery of the religious life of the human race that what must be most grievous to God or to his anointed servant often has a very different kind of effect on the multitude of human beings. The fear produced by Peter's action toward Ananias and Sapphira has already been noted above. Luke goes on to tell more in a sort of summarizing paragraph (Acts 5.12—16) "Through the hands of the apostles," he says, "many signs and wonders arose among the people, and they were all of one mind in Solomon's stoa", the "all" here probably referring to the apostles, "but of the rest no one dared adhere to them, but the people were magnifying them." "The rest" probably refer to some larger group within the church who were now afraid to draw close to the awful apostle after having seen what sort of destructive power they could wield, but the people, i.e. the interested bystanders who only had a vague notion of what was going on inside the church still continued to consider the apostles as men of extraordinary power and worth. So much for the ideal of a Jesus who could say "Come unto me all ye who labor and I will refresh you" — the practice now seems to be one of putting the "fear of God" into potential believers. Nevertheless, as Luke now tells us, many new believers are being added to the group (the book of Acts describes the origin of much future good and evil in the church — in this case the picture of so many new members pouring in might be said to have etched itself on the collective mind of the church as a consummation devoutly to be wished, as perhaps a self-sufficient good, without enough thought being given to the way they were being brought in or to the management and the cultivation, the edification of those new members once they had entered in) —

people are carrying the sick out into the wide streets and putting them on couches and bed rolls so that when Peter comes along his shadow might fall upon them. (5.14-15) Then, lest these facts be dismissed or disapproved of too quickly as the beginning of an idolatrous tendency in the church, a tendency superstitiously to ascribe efficacy to certain holy people, Luke tells us that a multitude from the cities around Jerusalem came together carrying the weak and those afflicted by unclean spirits and that *all* of them were healed, which record surpasses even that of Jesus, who at one point in Galilee at least was stymied, unable to perform many miracles (Mark 6.5). The success of Peter in healing at this time recalls Jesus' promise that his disciples would perform even greater miracles than the ones that he himself had performed because Jesus was going toward the Father (John 14.12).

And at least for awhile the idyll in the church continues. The apostles are arrested and thrown, as Peter and John had been earlier, into the public keep, but from there they are miraculously delivered at night by an angel of the Lord. (5.18-19) He sends them off to the temple to speak "the things concerning this life". (5.20) Their would-be examiners (who are defined as "the high priest and those with him, the existing faction of the Sadducees" — it is worth noting that in Acts Luke seems anxious not to implicate the Pharisees in any actions against the church) foregather on the following morning and of course the attendants whom they send to bring the prisoners back find the guard-house empty. The apostles are found teaching in the temple, they are brought back a second time, not forcibly, and now the examination begins. (5.21-26)

The reply which Peter makes (Luke says that he makes it along with the other apostles) again shows a mixture both of insight and of misunderstanding. For example he says that the apostles are witnesses in collaboration with "the holy spirit which God gave to those who obey him" (5.32), thus suggesting that he has remembered some words of Jesus: "Whenever they bring you in beside the synagogues and the rulers and the authorities, do not be anxious how or what you will speak in your behalf or what you will say, for in that hour the holy spirit will teach you what you must say." (Luke 12.11-13) In other words, just as with the healing of the crippled beggar in Acts 3, Peter ascribes the effectiveness of their witness in general to some power other than what they as human beings possess unaided. Furthermore, on the side of insight, i.e. more in keeping with Jesus's explanation of the salvation process that was set in motion with his passion and which culminated in his resurrection and assumption, Peter also now seems to understand Jesus as ruling in full power at the right hand of God rather than waiting as some sort of Christ-designate to return to the earth and establish his rule there later. Peter still reveals, however, the rather serious misunderstanding that this reign of Jesus from heaven benefits only Israel: "God exalted this one as leader and saviour at his right hand to give repentance to Israel and forgiveness of sins" (Acts 5.31) In this way Peter ignores the wish Jesus had expressed that the salvation-process benefit the whole world. (Matt. 28.19; Acts 1.8)

Once again, whatever criticism may be made long after the fact, one cannot deny that Peter's remarks produce significant results. This time Peter manages to enlist the sympathies of one supremely powerful ally. Gamaliel, "a teacher of law esteemed by all the people," (5.34) reveals by his response to Peter's remarks that he is inclined to see the movement which Peter advocates as being of divine origin. At least he is not ready to commit the resources of the religious establishment to an attempt to suppress it. Gamaliel mentions certain revolutionary movements which once seemed to pose real threats but which in time came to nothing or were scattered. (5.36-7) He then suggests a course of action in relation to the church and offers his rationale for it: "And now I say to you, stand away from these men and leave them alone. Because if this plot or this work be from human beings, it will be dissolved, but if it be from God you cannot dissolve them, lest you also be found to be God-fighters" (5.38-9) The apostles end up being beaten and again commanded not to speak on the basis of Jesus' name. (5.40) Otherwise this counsel of Gamaliel's prevails among the Sanhedrin and it seems that the church has won a significant victory or at least achieved a stalemate and should be ready now for new gains.

v. PETER'S ROLE IN PROBLEMS OF THE MATURING CHURCH.

The fact is, though, that the first great schism is about to develop if it has not been developing already. One of the difficulties which one faces in dealing with the next several chapters of Acts is that Luke may have wanted to give a more harmonious picture of the church at this time than the facts which he possessed would have warranted, or he might at least have been trying to tone down controversies when he could not avoid recounting them. One can wonder, for instance, whether there might not have been tension all along between the Hellenists and the Hebrews in the church, with both groups giving out different versions of the Gospel, and whether this tension may not have been eased temporarily when the Hebrew apostles gave some kind of official function or title to the Hellenists' leaders. At any rate, what Luke now tells us is that a grumbling of the Hellenists arose against the Hebrews because in the daily distribution of food the Hellenists' widows were being overlooked and that the twelve assembled the multitude of the disciples in response to this grumbling. (Acts 6.1)

As always, when one is dealing with a pronouncement of the apostles, one assumes a serious if not a preëminent involvement in it on Peter's part. What the twelve say here is rather shocking if one recalls once more Jesus' injunction to the disciples: "Let the greatest among you become like the youngest and the one who rules like the one who waits on tables. Who is greater, the one who sits or the one who waits on tables? Is it not the one who sits? But I am in your midst as the one who waits on tables." (Luke 22.26-27) In contrast to this directive the twelve say to the multitude in Acts "It is not right that we forsake the word of God to wait on tables" (6.2). They also go on to speak of their need to continue "in prayer and in the service of the word." (6.4) In other words they have set up a distinction between various ranks of work in the church where Jesus intended there to be none. They are docetizing the work of a disciple, splitting off so-called spiritual functions from the supposedly baser ones which are concerned with merely physical needs. They are perhaps pretending that they are too good to perform that work which Jesus described as his prototypical function (and of course Jesus actually went farther in deed than simply to wait on tables: he washed the disciples' feet, and that job was considered fit only for women or for slaves; it is worth recalling here what was pointed out earlier, namely that women seem to have an easier time being born from above than men do; this may be because for whatever reasons, perhaps because society forces such a stereotype upon them, they are already doing what Jesus enacts for his disciples as, paradoxically, a lofty ethical goal to be aimed at — not that society can be excused because it does women a kind of favor in preparing them for the kingdom, but inasmuch as women have been excluded from the extant power-structures, they may already be much closer to a kingdom that is not of this world). In denigrating one branch of Christian service, in suggesting that one branch (that of the word) is more important than another (that of the body), they are flirting with one of the worst sophistical traps that imperils Christians, a trap that the New Testament warns against: "If a brother or a sister be naked or lacks daily food, and one of you says to them 'go in peace, be warmed, be satisfied,' but you do not give them the things necessary for the body, what is the profit? So faith is if it does not have works, of itself it is dead." (James 2.15-17)

As we suggested above, it is possible to wonder whether the dispute at this time involved only the church's neglect of the needs of the widows. Luke says that the Apostles tell the Hellenists to choose "seven attested men, full of spirit and wisdom" who can be put in charge of this program for the widows (which sounds like a sort of first century meals on wheels perhaps without the wheels). (Acts 6.3) It is this solution which suggests a more complicated problem than the one which Luke has depicted. Perhaps these Hellenist men, full of spirit and wisdom, whose number seven is as sacred as was the number twelve of the apostles, had already been at work preaching their own version of the Gospel which did not agree with that of the Apostles, perhaps they finally had to be given some kind of official sanction. The exceeding Greekness of the names of five of the seven men whom the Hellenists choose suggests one basis of what could have been the original tension between them and the Hebraist apostles: the names Stephen and Philip had pretty much been assimilated into Jewish use, but the names Prochoros, Nikanor, Timon, Parmenas, and Nikolaos would have seemed extremely foreign to the xenophobic Galileans. In the end, the religious outlook of the Seven would have constitued an even more significant and also a more permanent basis of tension between these two groups. Of course Luke denies that there is any tension after this apparent settlement of the conflict; he gives one of his standard optimistic refrains about the increase of numbers within the church (6.7), but then not even he can cover over the rancor that is directed against Stephen, the most brilliant of the Seven, the one who "full of grace and power, was doing great signs and wonders in the people." (6.8)

It is a group of Hellenistic Jews who eventually bring suit against Stephen, who had once been one of them (6.9). Probably out of a concern to prove that they are more Jewish than even the Hebrew

Jews are, these Hellenistic Jews suborn certain men into saying that Stephen had spoken out against Moses and God (6.11). When the Sanhedrin tries him, they set up certain witnesses whom Luke calls liars but who actually, as his ensuing speech will reveal, are telling something partially true about Stephen, namely that he is saying things against the holy place and against the law. (6.13) What it is important to remember, however, is that since they had continued to act as observant Jews, making the Temple the center of their preaching mission, the Apostles would have been sympathetic to those who had brought such charges against Stephen. There is a harsher and perhaps more accurate way to describe the difference between the Apostles and the Seven: one could say that the Apostles had settled back, a little complacently, into an acceptance of all sorts of Jewish practices and assumptions, especially in that such an acceptance seemed to bring them legal security, whereas the Seven, who had been Jerusalem disciples of Jesus, had understood and adopted the Master's position (which we have seem him expounding to the woman at the well) that God is not pleased by the system of sacrifices and edifices which human beings want to pour so much money and energy into, that God is interested in other things (mercy, not sacrifice; true spiritual worship as opposed to astrological idolatry which Stephen explicitly links the Temple system with by quoting from Amos in his speech [7.42-3]). Furthermore, the story of the dispute between the Hebrews and the Hellenists in the church is sprinkled with hints of how Stephen and by implication the six other members of the Seven with him have an understanding of Jesus which is grounded in what is still perhaps the divisive notion of the Suffering Servant, whom Stephen for instance envisions at the moment of his death (7.57) and whom Philip expounds to the Ethiopian eunuch (8.27-40).

Less radical, the Twelve had somehow managed to achieve a truce with the religious authorities, as we have seen above, and would not have wanted to see that truce endangered by any fiery professions which might have implicated them, and so while they did not actually instigate the attack on Stephen, they neverthelss did nothing to combat it even though they might very well have been able to do so: as we have seen, they were approved of by "the people" (5.12) who in this case had been stirred up against Stephen (6.12); they could have used their influence with "the people", but instead they simply abandoned their brother in Christ, about which abandonment it is not too strong to say that it constituted a second denial and abandonment of Jesus on the part of Peter and the Apostles.

Luke seems to suggest such an equation when he puts in Stephen's mouth as he dies words which resemble words which Jesus spoke from the cross: "Lord, do not stand this sin against them." (7.60; cf, Luke 23.34, although there are textual problems with this verse) And even Luke who, as we have seen, may have been trying to make the church look as harmonious as possible, can no longer disguise what the Twelve have done, he finally has to come out and summarize their whole monstrous apostasy in one devastating sentence after he has told of the death of Stephen: "In that day there arose a great persecution against the church in Jerusalem, and all were scattered along the regions of Judea and Samaria *except the Apostles* [italics ours]". (8.1) Thus two groups now emerge from Luke's account: on the one hand the true witnessing church which has had to leave Jerusalem and on the other hand the Apostles, who have colluded with the powers then in existence. Of course it is not quite so simple as that, one can not simply dismiss the Twelve as uncommitted neutrals, but if one reads a little between the lines in Acts, the behavior of the Apostles at this time starts looking like what Dante might have called a *gran rifiuto*, a great denial.

The scattering of the Seven (now down to six) does have one unintended beneficial result: they begin preaching the good news in Judea and Samaria just as Jesus had wanted it to be preached and just as the apostles had failed to preach it (Acts 8.4). Luke focuses in particular on Philip as an implementer of this program. The story of Philip preaching in an unnamed Samaritan town soon involves the story of Simon, a local magician whose works lead the inhabitants of the region to say "This is the power of God which is called great". (Acts 8.10) Simon, recognizing an impressive power in the works which Philip is performing ("Many of those who had evil spirits shouting with a loud voice came out, many paralytics and lame were healed" — 8.7), and also seeing his usual clientele of admirers lining up to be baptized by Phillip, submits to be baptized himself.

It is at this point that the apostles in Jerusalem hear that Samaria has received the word of God. The Jerusalem group sends Peter and John down to investigate — the language of Luke does not reveal with what sort of intent the two went down; one tends to assume that their intent was somewhat hostile or at least suspicious. When Peter and John arrive, however, they are favorably enough impressed to pray that the Samaritans might receive the holy spirit. It seems strange of course, given all the power and the insight which the Seven had obviously possessed, that one of their number, Philip, is not able to bring down the holy spirit as he is baptizing in a place, but such is the fact as Luke reports it: "for it [the holy spirit] had not yet fallen on any of them, but they had only been baptized into the name of the Lord Jesus" (Acts 8.16) The apostolic emissaries succeed in remedying this defect: "They then laid their hands upon them and they received the holy spirit" (8.17)

A rather impressive encounter between Peter and Simon the magician follows. Simon has been impressed with this feat of bringing down the holy spirit and he attempts to buy the power to perform it from Peter. This attempt gave him his infamous reputation in the later church as the great example of the abuse that was named for him, i.e. simony, the purchasing of ecclesiastical power with money (he was also known as the father of Gnosticism). In a show of that commanding and awesome presence that he can sometimes summon, Peter not only faces Simon down on this point but actually convinces him to repent (8.20-24). It is probably more significant as an indication of Peter's real inward state at this point, however, that he has managed to make some sort of truce with a member of the Seven, that he has been won over by the evidence Philip's work. It would seem to be a sign that Peter has matured somewhat.

It is hard to know just what sort of arrangement now obtains among the once antagonistic Christian factions. Luke says that "Those who solemnly bore witness to and spoke the word of the Lord returned to Jerusalem, and they preached the good news to many villages of the Samaritans" (8.25) It is not quite clear to whom Luke is referring here, i.e. does he mean Peter and John, in which case a remarkable change of heart on the part of two formerly rather exclusivist apostles had taken place, or does he mean that it was safe for some of the seven to return to Jerusalem now and that on the way back they visited some villages in that region which had come to be their special concern by dint of their being scattered? There would seem to be no definite answer to these questions. Another picture of the church, perhaps referring to this same period right after the excursion of Peter and John, is given slightly farther on: "The church then through all of Judea and Galilee and Samaria had peace, being built up and proceeding in the fear of the Lord and it was filled with the consolation of the holy spirit." (9.31) This sounds like the achievement of another idyllic phase although at the considerable price, one must remember, of the loss of perhaps the most remarkable follower of Jesus up to this time.

vi. PETER'S FINAL PHASE: ADVANCES AND RELAPSES.

After some important intervening material Luke than reports two more healings, or rather one healing and one resuscitation by Peter. (Acts 9.32-43) He may at this stage only be partially born from above, but Peter does retain an impressive therapeutic gift. As the next episode will show, however, he still is in the process of being born from above.

The tenth chapter of Luke, which recounts the continuation of this process, at first does not seem to be about Peter at all. A marvel of masterly narration in every way, this chapter exhibits one of those deceptively simple, seemingly offhand, matter-of-fact expositions with which so many of the greatest Biblical stories begin: "A certain man in Caesarea whose name was Cornelius, a centurion from the cohort called the Italian, pious and God-fearing along with all his house, doing many works of mercy to the nation and constantly praying to God . . ." (Acts 10.1-2) Before one moves on to the verb of which this series of phrases is the subject, one needs to look more closely at the information which the series has conveyed. Cornelius is what at this time, in this region, would have been called a proselyte of the gate: this term referred to someone who had a profound sympathy for or an interest in the religion of the Jews but who could not quite commit himself first of all to being circumcised and then to taking up the full burden of the law. Nevertheless, despite such scruples or such hesitations, he would have been considered a serious monotheist, the fruits of which outlook on his part Luke has made plain: Cornelius fears God, he performs acts of mercy among the people he has been sent to rule over as a military officer, and he he prays constantly to God (later on it will be important to speculate as to what he has been praying about since a strange supernatural visitant will tell him that his prayer has been answered).

And yet he lacks one thing: any companions in his religion. He does have the members of his family, and without doubt they are all sincere seekers, but as a religious group they constitute a rather forlorn little cell in an alien land. Although it has permitted them the marginal status of proselytes at the gate, Israel has not really made any provision for people even of this type, not to mention for those who are even less sympathetic or enlightened. Cornelius's household might be said like Peter to be struggling to be born into some kind of divine family; they might even be said to have gone just about as far along the canal which leads toward such birth as Peter himself has, it might be said that through separate spiritual channels both Cornelius and Peter are struggling to be born into the same divine family of spiritual worshippers which God is willing into existence, a family not based upon bloods or on the keeping of any untainted lineage (as the Jews and to their shame the Apostles, who should have known better, have thought), i.e. not upon membership among the children of Israel, but rather, as the first chapter of the Gospel of John tells us, upon trust put in the name of the Word. What the tenth chapter of Acts is about is how divine pressure is brought to bear, how a divine squeeze precipitates both Cornelius and Peter out into the open air of this new divine group. To change the metaphor: God is not finished with Peter yet, and he uses Cornelius as the forceps to pull Peter out into the atmosphere and light which Peter up until now has kept shunning.

But to return and rescue Cornelius from the mid-sentence suspension in which we left him up above: this man, whose essential attributes have been presented, is on this occasion granted a vision of an angel of the Lord approaching and calling his name (10.3) The angel instructs Cornelius to send for Peter in Joppa where he has been shown to be staying (9.43). Cornelius complies with these instructions. (10.7-8)

The next day, as Cornelius's messengers are arriving at the city of Joppa, Peter goes up on the roof to pray at about the sixth hour (twelve o'clock). He becomes hungry and wants to eat. As some unspecified number of people are preparing a meal for him, what Luke refers to as an "ecstasy" comes upon him — the word "ecstasy" in Greek denotes a trance or vision, a cessation of ordinary consciousness so that something in another realm or at another level of consciousness can come into mental view, but it also can connote something unpleasant or frightening. In this particular ecstasy Peter sees "the heaven having opened and a container, something like a great napkin being let down upon the earth by the four corners, in which were all the quadrupeds and creeping things of the earth and all the birds of heaven" (10.11-12) Then he hears a voice which says

"Arise Peter, sacrifice and eat" (10.13) The Greek word which has here been translated as "sacrifice" could possibly be rendered in English as "slaughter", but a survey of the appearances of it in Greek suggests "sacrifice" as the far likelier meaning. The suggestion of eating these unclean animals so forcefully prohibited by Pentateuchal regulations after dedicating them to the Holy One by sacrificial slaughter shows that Peter is under divine pressure to revamp his notion of what the holy is. Up until now, for Jews, holiness had involved separation and segregation, and had consisted of putting up barriers behind which God's chosen people could be kept worthy and clean. Jesus had enacted another kind of holiness, a holiness involving openness and freedom in one's relations with all people. His life and his attitudes should have remained the touchstone of holiness for his followers, but they neglected his example, they relapsed from or rejected the standard he had set. In Stephen's speech and Peter's dream, Luke has shown God again trying to get through to the human race with this message of a new kind of holiness, the only kind that would be pleasing to Him.

Peter emphatically refuses to obey this divine imperative to sacrifice and eat. His answer is blunt — "No way, Lord, for I have never eaten anything common or unclean" (10.14) — and it shows him resolutely forgetting or at least neglecting to remember what Jesus had taught: "Don't you understand that nothing which goes into a person from the outside can make him common because it does not go into his heart but rather into his belly, and it goes out into the latrine" — "making all foods clean" is the Gospel writer's gloss to this statement of Jesus. (Mark 7.19) In other words, Jesus has dissolved the category of the unclean or common and yet as with so many other later liberating options, Peter has refused to avail himself of this one that Jesus had offered, Peter has preferred to keep on hemming himself inside the fence of the law. The voice in the ecstasy repeats to Peter now this lesson which he had once heard from Jesus: "Don't you make common those things which God has made clean." (10.15)

At this point Luke includes a remarkable and at the same time possibly ominous detail: "This happened three times and immediately the vessel was taken up into heaven." (10.16) In Peter's life the number three is associated with denial. Using the number three as a sort of leit-motif here, like a sort of gonging alarm bell, Luke seems to be saying that Peter is denying Jesus again by refusing to obey the voice in the vision.

And yet Peter is being led into obeying this divine directive almost in spite of himself: "As in himself Peter was perplexed what the vision which he had seen might be, behold the men sent by Cornelius, having learned the house of Simon by inquiry, were standing at the gate." (10.17) Peter is at this point in the midst of "trying to understand about the vision". (10.19) The spirit tells him to rise, go down, and follow the men unquestioningly. Peter is far less loath to follow this directive than he was to follow the dream's directive, and he presents himself to the men. He entertains them as guests that night, the next day they travel to Caesarea. (10.20-24) In terms then of being born from above, one may deduce from the present case that it is not enough for someone simply to hear the voice or to receive a vision (visions can be false after all, one needs to be a little skeptical about them); it would seem rather that some human contact to catalyze or galvanize the birth process is required as well, that the spirit which is the agent of birth from above works best through the medium of sociality. Later when he is retelling the story of this vision and its aftermath to Cornelius, Peter says that he came without objection when he was sent for (10.29) — this is a true statement, but it highlights again how much the human call was needed in addition to the divine, how the divine alone was not enough.

Cornelius is expecting Peter and the messengers when they arrive; he has in fact proleptically gathered a group of "his relatives and indispensable friends" to celebrate the arrival. "As it happened that Peter came in, Cornelius met him, fell upon his feet and worshipped him. Peter raised him up and said, Get up, for I also am a human being." (10.26) The significance of this response on the part of Peter would seem to be that in order really to start to undergo the birth from above one has to acknowledge one's human shortcomings; perhaps it was those shortcomings which Peter had tended to forget when he was allowing people to lay at his feet the proceeds of property sales in successive acts of obeisance or when he was striking people dead with bolts of the divine lightning.

Having surmounted this potential stone of stumbling, Peter then proceeds to confront another; he finds that there are many who had come together to be with Cornelius. He says to them "You understand how unthinkable it is for a Jewish man to associate with or go toward a member of another race." (10.28) One may note here in connection with what is apparently the greater ease which women have in being born from above that it is the Jewish *man* who cannot think of associating with a member of another race or nation. The role of the Jewish woman is restricted to a very specific subset of the law; she has to be concerned with dietary regulations and matters of ritual purity. It is the Jewish man who, among his many other wide-ranging legal responsibilities, in the role of some sort of excluder, has to deal with the foreigner. In other words, it is the job of the Jewish male (and of the males of other cultures too) to build up those protective palings which prevent the divine family, which admits of no nationalistic divisions, from coming into existence. This fact of his conditioning may be one reason why the male finds it more difficult to be born from above than does the female. Therefore Peter's next pronouncement really does bespeak some kind of falling of the scales away from his eyes even if Peter is not quite correctly quoting from the vision he has had. What the vision had said and what Peter had refused to accede to at the time was "Don't you make common those things which God has made clean" (10.15) Peter changes this command in recounting it to the group around Cornelius: "God showed me not to call any person common or unclean." (10.28) This shift is extremely important: as we will see when we discuss Galatians (2.6-10), Peter later relapses into his old-style exclusivist outlook over the issue of food. In directing Peter to focus first on overcoming his conditioned aversion to certain kinds of food, the dream was showing a certain pedagogic soundness (like Paul's first feeding his recent converts with milk) and psychological shrewdness. If and when Peter had changed his attitude toward certain non-kosher kinds of food, there would then have been time for him to proceed to a new and more enlightened attitude toward people. By leapfrogging over food to the more advanced problem of people, he resembles a piano student who decides to play the Appassionata Sonata without first having mastered the elementary business of scales.

But the consequences of such rashness on his part lie somewhere off in the future. In the meantime, as far as this scene in chapter 10 of Acts is concerned, revelations and self-revelations also emerge from Cornelius's side. He says that the celestial visitor whom he received was a man in flashing apparel. (10.30) He also says that this man had told him that his prayer had been heard. It is at this point that it becomes important to ask the question: what is the prayer to which the coming of Peter would have constituted an answer? Assuming that Cornelius could not have known enough to pray for someone or something so specific as Peter, one is led to posit a sort of general longing for fulfillment along the lines suggested above, some vague awareness perhaps of his need for a community in which his religious life might flourish as it had not flourished in isolation — of Cornelius one could almost say that like Adam in Keats's formulation of him, he "awoke and found his dream truth."

Cornelius now says that he and all his visitors have come together to hear the things which God has commanded to Peter. (10.33) Peter obliges with a major theological speech, the topic sentence of which is: "I perceive truly that God is not prone to playing favorites but that in every nation the one who fears him and performs righteous works is acceptable to him." (10.34-5) This appears to be not quite the vision of the divine family that the gospel of John presents — i.e. works righteousness stands in place of putting one's trust in the name of the logos — but it still represents a remarkable breakthrough for someone who not too long before this time had conceived of salvation solely in terms of Israel, and in fact by the end of this speech, perhaps having warmed to his subject, Peter will describe the matter in a manner much closer to that of the Gospel of John: "To this one [i.e. Jesus] all the prophets bear witness that everyone who trusts in him will through his name receive forgiveness of sins." (10.43) He also talks of God as having announced the good news of peace through Jesus Christ (10.36) — in the context of the speech Peter is giving this peace must be thought of in terms of peace between God and human beings first of all, but then peace between human beings of all types, and in particular between the Jew and the Gentile.

However far Peter has broken through to what for him is a major new insight, this breakthrough is now certified by a descent of the holy spirit upon the people at Cornelius's house (a descent of the spirit which, contrary to the usual order, precedes baptism!). Those from the circumcision who had come with Peter to Cornelius's house are amazed that the gift of the holy spirit has been poured out upon the Gentiles. (10.45) Peter seems almost relieved to receive such a confirmatory sign which he can pit against what he assumes to be their skepticism: "No one can deny water, can he, so that these may not be baptized who have received the holy spirit just as we have." (10.47) At any rate no one does deny that water and so the people at Cornelius's house are baptized in the name of Jesus Christ.

Peter soon has to defend this course of action back in Jerusalem against other Christian brothers who are from the circumcision. Luke says that they are at odds with Peter and that they say "You went in toward men who are uncircumcised and ate with them." (11.3) It is in response to this charge that Peter re-tells the story of his vision and of his summons to visit Caesarea, building up toward a climax in the descent of the holy spirit upon those who had gathered at Cornelius's house: "As I began to speak the holy spirit fell upon them just as also upon us in the beginning. But I remembered the Lord saying as he had said, John baptized with water, but you will be baptized with holy spirit. Therefore if God gave them the gift equal to what he gave us who believe upon the lord Jesus Christ, who was I to be able to hinder God?" (11.15-17)

At first reading it would appear that once again Peter has conveniently forgotten what he was really charged with. Those who were at odds with him had not said anything for or against his baptizing the people at Cornelius's house, their concern rather had been with Peter's eating with uncircumcised men. One would expect Peter to defend himself against *this* kind of charge, and in fact by depicting the baptism by the holy spirit of the people he has met in Cornelius's house he actually does defend himself, but it takes an understanding of the procedures by which a Gentile convert was taken into the Jewish religion to recognize how he has done so. Normally a candidate for Judaism would have had to be circumcised before he could be baptised. By describing the baptism by the holy spirit which the people at Cornelius's house had undergone, Peter seems to suggest that in this case the normal procedure has been circumvented and that his antagonists will have to simply accept an accomplished fact. The holy spirit has seen fit to skip circumcision and proceed directly to baptism, therefore who are mere human beings to insist on their normal progression of acceptable steps? And those who have accused Peter really do seem satisfied according to Luke's account: "When they had heard these things they were silent and began to glorify God, saying therefore also to the Gentiles God gave the repentance unto life." (11.18)

But is this sudden happy ending to such a sharp confrontation a little too good to be true, and might Luke not be attempting here, as he has attempted before, to make the church look like a more harmonious body of people than it in fact was? Or even if he was not impelled by such cosmetic motives on this occasion, could he not possibly have had more material about this confrontation which he has suppressed or shifted somewhere else? The authors of this study believe that Luke actually did have other material about this examination of Peter and that this material appears in chapter 15 as part of the so-called Council of Jerusalem. In chapter 15 the controversy which arises is said to involve circumcision and yet the decree that is accepted counsels Gentiles against the eating of ritually impure food. This discrepancy alone might be reason enough for removing the matter having to do with food from chapter 15, but then there is the further reason that when Paul in Galatians 2 talks about going up to Jerusalem on the occasion which Acts 15 also depicts, he does not mention any full-scale gathering of apostles and elders, as in Acts 15.6, to see about what he had said. Rather, according to Paul, whatever he discussed in Jerusalem he discussed only with James, Peter, and John, the so-called pillars of the church. By removing most or all the material of the council from chapter 15 to chapter 11 of Acts, one harmonizes Luke's account and Paul's account of the Apostle's second trip to Jerusalem; one also gains what seems like plausible and valuable added information about the confrontation between Peter and those apostles and Christian brothers of Jewish persuasion who were examining him about the episode at Cornelius's house.

There is some reason for thinking that Peter's speech in Acts 15.7-11 is not entirely out of place where it now stands. The subject of this speech is circumcision, and we learn from Galatians 2.3 that the question of circumcision was in some way at issue when Paul made his second Jerusalem trip. Acts 15.7-11 then may very well reflect an accurate tradition about what Peter said on the occasion of this trip. Luke's only mistake would have consisted of having Peter utter these words before a council when they had actually been uttered in the private conference which the three pillars held with Paul. (Gal. 2.9) On the other hand, though, Acts 15.7-11 would supplement what Peter says in Acts 11.15-17 since on that occasion, as we have shown above, Peter's defense of himself before his accusers involved the fact of baptism by the holy spirit and the way in which it had superseded the old stages by which a proselyte was brought into the Jewish fold. Peter's words in Acts 15 could have been applied to just such a defense: "Men, brothers, you understand that from early times among you, God chose for the Gentiles through my mouth to hear the word of the gospel and to start believing. And the God who knows hearts bore witness to them, giving the holy spirit just as to us, and he did not in any way discriminate between us and them, cleansing their hearts by faith. Now then, why are you putting God to the test, putting upon the neck of the disciples a yoke which neither our fathers nor we were able to bear?

But by the grace of the lord Jesus we trust that we will be saved in the same way as those." (Acts 15.7-11) The yoke referred to would be the law the full weight of which every circumcised person is obliged to bear, as Paul says (Galatians 5.3). To make people carry that yoke one would have to circumcise them first, so that Peter in this speech could be using different terms to object to the idea that Gentile converts would have to be circumcised before he could eat with them. Along this line the speech would be well suited to his defense of what he did at Cornelius's house.

One would have fewer doubts about moving the speech James makes in Acts 15 back to the examination of Peter in chapter 11. James's speech in fact almost seems designed to carry directly on from Acts 11.17. For instance its opening words are "Simon has told how God first cared to receive from the gentiles a people to his name" (15.14) and these would far more aptly refer to Peter's long story about the conversion of those who were at Cornelius's house than they do to what Peter says in Acts 15.7-11. The same thing could be said of James's argument that follows if one assumes that the people back at the beginning of chapter 11 who had objected to Peter's eating with uncircumcised men had not been completely placated by his speech about baptism by the holy spirit and wanted to deal with what they considered to be a further problem, namely the defiling of a Christian convert (who was in their minds becoming a Jew also) by the introduction of unclean food into his or her mouth. The citation from Amos (15.16-18) shows James's sympathy toward an ingathering of the gentiles, and he stresses the fact that he does not want to add extra difficulties to those of the gentiles who have turned to God (15.19), but on the other hand he does not feel free simply to abrogate longstanding dietary laws and so he wants to instruct gentile converts "to abstain from the defilements of idols and from sexual immorality and from what is strangled and from blood." (15.20)

James goes on to justify his insistence on this much orthodox Jewish piety (which is based on various Old Testament texts, primarily Genesis 9.4) from gentile converts to Christianity: "For Moses from the generations of old has had those proclaiming him from city to city in the synagogues on every sabbath and is read." (15.21) Twentieth century scholarship has revealed that there were great numbers of Jewish missionaries who were active at this time and were in fact the agents who brought proselytes like Cornelius to gate or sometimes fully into the Jewish fold; James probably has these missionaries in mind here, i.e. he feels that Jewish practices would have had a fairly wide publicity already and that gentiles would almost expect to adopt some of them when they came into an apparently Jewish religious movement like Christianity. But then by slipping in the prohibition against sexual immorality, James has limited the freedom of newly converted Christians in more than just the area of food. There is much dispute about the proper text of James's speech here, i.e. does the term "sexual immorality" even belong in the list of prohibitions? Assuming, though, that this term does belong in the text,[3] we are then faced with an apparent attempt by James, at the last moment, to take away with one hand what his other hand has granted: i.e. after all his fine words about bringing Gentiles into the Christian church, what he seems to really want is to hold them accountable for a larger and larger segment of the Jewish legal requirements. The term *porneia*, which we have translated as "sexual immorality" may have referred to certain kinds of forbidden marriages or to mixed marriages with pagans or even metaphorically to participation in pagan worship (which in Old Testament terms would have been thought of as spiritual adultery). Whatever it meant, its inclusion in this decree seems to reveal a certain nervousness, a certain need on James's part to supervise incoming Christians, a discomfort with what Paul calls the freedom of the Christian person.

We will be dealing more with this nervousness of James in connection with Paul's career and with his birth from above. In the meantime, we have now discussed why we think that the decree which Luke shows being promulgated in Acts 15 is more likely to have arisen in the wake of Peter's experience in Caesarea at the house of Cornelius (Acts 11), and if our opinion is correct, and if Peter acceded to this decree, then after his big breakthrough at Cornelius's house, he has relapsed into a state of merely partial birth from above. One only has to consider Paul's enlightened views on the subject of food to realize how much resistance Peter would here be showing to the expressed wishes of Jesus (Mark 7.14-23), with which Peter certainly was familiar. Furthermore, in the paragraph following Peter's examination in Acts 11 Luke makes it clear that from this time forth the Gentile question will be impossible for the Christian church to avoid. He observes that disciples or descendants of the Seven are going through as far as to Phoenicia and Cyprus and Antioch and that some of them are preaching only to Jews but that of their number, certain Cypriot and Cyrenean men are preaching to

Greeks in Antioch and having a great success (11.19-21)[4] Therefore at this point the question of how Gentile converts need to be treated becomes of major importance to the church.

Despite (or is it because of?) this spread of the faith, the Jerusalem church seems by now to be set in a policy of quasi-inquisitorial vigilance concerning outbreaks of successful preaching wherever they occur: for instance on this ocassion just mentioned they send Barnabas down to Antioch to investigate. Because he is "a good man and full of the holy spirit and of belief" he rejoices at and approves of what he sees (11.22-4), but what will happen if those in Jerusalem send a less good man somewhere else? In other words might not the church's presuming to rule on what is orthodox and what is not, what is kosher and what is not, its concern to confine the spreading church to certain strictly specified practices and attitudes be dangerously contrary to a more tolerant attitude which Jesus himself seemed to espouse: "John answered and said, Master, we saw someone in your name casting out demons and we prevented him because he isn't following along with us. But Jesus said to him, Don't prevent him, for the one who isn't against us is for us." (Luke 9.49) If Peter goes along with decrees like those which James and the Jerusalem church put out concerning food, then he is still not in full accord with the mind and intention of Jesus.

If one excludes chapter 15, then there is only one more story about Peter in Acts, namely, in chapter 12 his miraculous deliverance from the prison into which he has been thrown by Herod Agrippa I. The beginning of chapter 12 marks the breakdown of what, in reference to Acts 5, might be called the Gamaliel peace between Christians and Jews. The Jews seem now to want to see the Christians, which would mean the apostolic branch in Jerusalem, persecuted: Luke records that, having already killed James the son of Zebedee, Herod goes on to arrest Peter because he sees that such an action is pleasing to the Jews. (12.3) The story of Peter's escape from prison constitutes a marvelous adventure, contains several noteworthy psychological touches, but adds little to any consideration of Peter's being born from above.

The only other important story concerning Peter appears in Paul's letter to the Galatians. This letter will have to be examined more carefully later when we come to deal with Paul's birth from above. Right now, though, in relation to Peter, it contains one last equivocal glimpse of that enthusiastic but often misguided follower of Jesus. Paul relates to the Galatians that Peter has come down to

Antioch and that he, Paul, has opposed Peter to his face because he, Peter, stood condemned (2.11).

Paul says that before some had come from James, Peter had eaten together with the Gentiles but that when these people did come from James, Peter then drew back and separated himself, fearing those from the circumcision (2.12). Again, we will be trying to deduce the full import of these messengers sent from James and all the circumstances of their mission in our next section, when we deal with Paul. It will be enough to say here that since Peter suddenly withdraws from table-fellowship with the Gentiles, their mission must have had to do with some dietary edit of the sort which we think came out after Peter had eaten with the Gentiles in the house of Cornelius (Acts 10-11). The arrival of these messengers now in Antioch affects not only Peter. According to Paul the other Jews joined in acting insincerely with Peter so that even Barnabas was carried off by their pretence. (2.13) Paul gives a vivid interpretation of their behavior: he says that "they are not straight-footing it toward the truth of the gospel" and that when he realized this fact about them, before the whole group he confronted Peter with the words: "If you who are a Jew live like a Gentile and not like a Jew, how can you compel the Gentiles to live according to Jewish regulations?" (2.14)

In other words, what is good enough for Peter ought to be good enough for the Gentiles too, they should not now, after Peter has implicitly approved of their way of life by participating in it, be forced to step backward out of what Paul refers to in this letter as freedom into some kind of retrograde Jewish dietary regimen. For Paul, this conflict seems to be connected with all the fundamental issues of the gospel as he preaches it (he sometimes calls it *his* gospel) or at least discussion of this conflict then prompts him to discuss the whole matter of justification by the faithfullness of Jesus Christ, but as far as Peter, who is still our principal subject, is concerned, this episode represents one last example of his tendency to deny or to desert a person or a cause under pressure. He is here called rather abrasively to account for it by Paul, just as he was called more hauntingly, more tenderly to account for it when Jesus gave him that one penetrating look outside the praetorium, but what it is probably most important to note here is that the person who is born from above, as Peter undoubtedly was, is not suddenly forged into some infallible instrument of the lord but rather remains heir to many of the same personality faults that he or she was heir to before the entry into the new life.

Birth from above, it must be asserted then and as the career of Peter reveals, is not some kind of personal panacea. It may focus certain previously diffuse energies, it may orient a person toward some more valuable goal which he or she was not aware of before, but in many way it will still be the same basic person with the same refractory virtues and failings to whom these benefits accrue. This aspect of being born from above is as evident in the career of Paul as it is in that of Peter, and since Paul has already started intertwining with Peter in our account of the early church, we should perhaps return to the paradoxical beginning of Paul's service to the Christian church and try once more to understand birth from above by studying the whole process of it in the life of one more New Testament figure.

CHAPTER 4.

PAUL AND THE STAGES OF THE NEW LIFE

I. THE ACCOUNT IN ACTS

For those who, in a book on being born from above, would have expected to read about sudden cataclysmic interruptions, existential watersheds with persons' lives dramatically and decisively being divided into before-and after-segments, a chapter on the apostle Paul might be thought to promise at last an example of the real thing. After all, isn't "having a Damascus road experience" what most people mean when they talk about being born from above?

Unfortunately for those who would like such a clear-cut picture of the birth from above, several facts must be remembered. First of all Paul himself never mentions any cataclysmic conversion in his own letters. He does divide his life into before-and after-periods, and we shall be attempting later to understand such divisions as he himself cares to make, but it is important to note that he never talks about any experience of sudden blinding or sudden revelation on the road to Damascus. It is Luke alone in the book of Acts who tells of such an episode in Paul's life. Furthermore, the Damascus road experience is recounted three times in Acts, once in a third-person narrative and twice in speeches by Paul, and the details differ in each telling. Even if we posit this experience of Paul's as the model for a true birth from above, careful analysis of the three versions in Acts will eventually lead us to realize that our model is more complicated than we had at first assumed it to be.

The Damascus road experience as narrated in the third person by Luke grows out of the trial and eventual stoning of Stephen. In that episode, Stephen is defending himself before the Jewish Sandedrin with his own tremendous interpretation of Jewish history and of the true nature of God (Acts 7), an interpretation that is not calculated to find favor with the Jewish authorities. Emotions rise against

Stephen, the scene approaches its terrible climax, at which point Luke almost brings it to a halt by introducing one strange detail: "And the witnesses were laying down their cloaks by the feet of a young man named Saul[1]." (7.58) Luke proceeds to describe Stephen's death by stoning, and then he adds another arresting detail: "And Saul was approving of his murder." (8.1)

One is tantalized by such details, they seem to offer (probably just beyond reach) some clue as to the state of mind which Paul was in on the brink of his conversion. If nothing else, one would like to know who these "witnesses" referred to in verse 7.58 are, assuming that a person's associates may provide some clue to his or her outlook. The problem is that as with so many of the other critical and historical problems which Acts raises, the identity of these witnesses is not easy to determine. Ernst Haenchen argues that the witnesses "recall the offical procedures laid down for stoning in the Mishnah,"[2] that is he seems to think that the witnessess in 7.58 constitute a new group picked up from among those who were present at the trial of Stephen, a group whose job it is to set in motion the prescribed stages of an execution. Haenchen argues for such official standing on the part of these witnesses even though he admits that the Sanhedrin cannot carry out capital punishment officially in this period and that the story of Stephen's execution suggests an instance of lynch law.[3] Haenchen's identification raises doubts in that he has to import it from outside the text, using materials that may or may not be germane to Luke as his source.

If one simply stays within the text of Acts, various groups are shown to be hostile to Stephen, and the term "witnesses" is even applied to one of these. It seems more likely that in 7.58 Luke would be referring back to one of these groups, although then one is faced with the fact that the members and the boundaries of the group are not always easy to determine. For instance, Luke states that "some from the synagogue called of the Libertines and Cyrenians and Alexandrians and of those from Cilicia and Asia rose up to argue with Stephen and could not withstand the wisdom and spirit which he spoke with." (6.9-10) Endless (it seems) arguments have been conducted over the number of synagogues being referred to here (the numbers five, two, and one all have their proponents on the basis of history and grammar). Nor has the text itself gone unchallenged. The word "Libertines" probably refers to a Jewish group taken as slaves by Pompey in 63 B.C and shortly thereafter released. The synagogue or one of the synagogues referred to in this passage from Acts would consist of descendants of those from this group of freed slaves who had migrated back to Jerusalem. Some scholars, however have thought that "Libertines" should be replaced with some other word meaning "Libyans". Among other supposed advantages, this emendation would give the passage a nice sweep around about half of the Mediterranean basin, starting in northwestern Africa and ending up in Asia Minor. Whatever one's proposed solution to the problems of the passage, here at least is one group (or several groups) that is (are) mentioned as being hostile to Stephen.

Luke then recounts how this group or groups suborns another group into testifying that they had heard Stephen speaking blasphemous words against Moses and God (6.11) One of these two (or more) groups mentioned thus far (the antecedent of the "they"-subject implied in the Greek verb is impossible to determine) then stirs up the elders and the scribes; they stand up and seize Stephen and bring him to the Sanhedrin. (6.12) There, another group hostile to Stephen (or possibly the same group that was suborned above) is put into action, namely false *witnesses* who say that Stephen does not stop saying things against the holy place and against the law, and that they have heard him saying that Jesus the Nazarene will tear down the temple and alter the customs handed down by Moses. (6.13-14)

We assume that it was members of one of these hostile groups who were laying their clothes at the feet of a young man named Saul before they stoned Stephen, but even here the critical problems continue to multiply. One wonders, for instance, what one should conclude from the fact that Paul, who later was to describe himself as a "Hebrew of the Hebrews," (Phil. 3.5) is here shown to be consorting with the Greek Jews. There had been tension between the "Greek Jews" and the "Hebrew Jews" dating from the time which the Books of the Maccabees depict. Paul himself, if we can assume that at some point he came up to the capital from Tarsus (in southern Asia Minor northeast of Cyprus) and made himself over into what he says he was, an impeccable Hebraist as opposed to Hellenist Jew, would nevertheless have continued to have ties to the Hellenist camp simply by dint of the facts of his life. He was, after all, a Roman citizen, he possessed complete mastery of the Greek language (in contrast to some of the other New Testament writers), he may even have posessed knowledge of "pagan" Greek writers (Luke has him draw an argument from one such "pagan" in his speech in Athens

[Acts 17.28] and Paul himself quotes another such writer in his first letter to Corinth [15.33]). Furthermore, having come from Tarsus, he might very well have felt at home or at least in some way drawn to a group like the one mentioned above (6.9) which included people from his native province of Cilicia — such attraction might have depended on how secure Paul had felt in his "Hebrew of the Hebrews" identity — some people, trying to escape their provincial pasts, would have wanted to stay as far away as possible from the down home crowd for fear of taint or contagion.

The problem of the "witnesses" in 7.58 and Paul's association with them becomes further complicated when one asks whether the Greek Jews who rose up against Stephen might in addition have been Christians, who thus attacked Stephen because they did not want him to give Christianity so radical a name that it would be thrown out of the Jewish fold, i.e. Greek Jewish Christians who might have been hoping for an accomodation with the similarly conservative Apostles, hoping to make Christianity an acceptable sub-set of the Jewish religion. Luke does not say that those from the synagogues that rose up against Stephen are Christians, but he has just been talking about one group of Greek Jews (i.e. the Seven) who *were* Christians, and Paul is shortly to set off for Damascus, the synagogues of which are said to be harboring Christians. Many synagogues at this point do seem to be spawning Christians and hence the need to ask whether the group Paul was associating with could possibly have been a Christian group.

The traditional, the almost unanimous interpretation has of course been that Paul was a hyper-committed Jew at this point, intent on extirpating every Christian weed which he could find. Although we recognize the likelihood of such a universally subscribed-to interpretation's being the correct one, we have also felt compelled to point to the little fault-lines in it, the kinds of fault lines which seem to threaten almost any conclusion which one ventures to reach on the basis of "facts" in Acts, We are also somewhat prompted by a statement which, although it comes from one of Paul's letters and is therefore risky to use as a tool in interpreting Acts, continues to tease and intrigue us, namely the statement that the risen Jesus appeared to Paul as to an abortion (1 Cor. 15.8). Could Paul by this statement possibly have meant that he had been some sort of stillborn Christian (i.e. one who persecuted his Christian brothers and sisters), one who had not immediately been born out into a viable form of the faith, that he had needed some sort of additional birth from above to really enter into life as one of Jesus' true followers? The material from Acts that we have just summarized, material which is apparently so calm and clear on the surface but which underneath seems charged with so many problems, seems calculated to keep such questions stirred up without really providing any clear-cut answers.

Furthermore, there could even be a certain ambiguity in the actual words which Paul hears on the Damascus road. "As he was going," Luke says, "it happened as he drew near to Damascus that suddenly a light from heaven flashed round about him and he fell to the earth and heard a voice saying to him 'Saul, Saul, why are you persecuting me?' He said, 'Who are you, Lord?' He said 'I am Jesus whom you are persecuting. But get up and go into the city and you shall be told what you need to do.'" (9.3-6)

The question asked by the voice could (and has been generally taken to) mean simply that as a Jewish zealot Saul was pursuing Christians of all kinds, "breathing threats and violence," (9.1) trying to stamp them out as enemies to the one true religion. In this case, Jesus would be intervening drastically in the case of one who had never known him or in the case of one who, if he had heard of Jesus, had never wanted to know him. But one could read Jesus' question in another way, a way which stresses certain key words, namely "Saul, Saul, why [of all people] are *you* [of all things] *persecuting* me?" If the question were asked in this way, it might imply that Paul had thought he was doing something else for (maybe serving?) Jesus and needed rudely to be awakened from such a deluded course of action. According to this interpretation Saul could be seen as some sort of Jewish Christian who had thought that he was serving the Lord Jesus by stamping out the Hellenistic universalist, anti-Temple heresy which men like Stephen represented and of which, in Paul's opinion, the Lord Jesus could never have approved.

One does seem safe in stating one fact about Paul (as depicted by Luke) before his encounter with Jesus on the road to Damascus, namely that whether or not he had developed some sort of allegiance to a form of Jewish Christianity, he was leading a totally disciplined life. Paul himself makes this point when he tells the story of his conversion before Agrippa: "All the Jews know the way of life I followed from youth, from the beginning in my nation and in Jerusalem, since they knew me beforehand from the beginning, if they care to testify, that according to the strictest sect of our piety I lived a Pharisee. And now I stand judged, having come by the hand of God into the hope of the promise unto our fathers, unto which our twelve tribes hope to attain by earnestness serving night and day, concerning which hope charges are brought against me at the Jews' hands, o king." (26.4-7) It is important to notice here that the life Paul was leading before his Damascus road experience was in keeping with the strictest sect of Jewish piety. In his case at least, birth from above is not out of some state of wallowing in lascivious self-indulgence or intemperate habit into some new-found rigorous self-control: Paul had as much self-control as it is possible for a human being to have *before* he was born from above.

In fact he would seem to have had so much discipline and repressive power at his disposal that he needed areas other than his own psyche in which to apply them. Where he saw religious heresy arising, he felt compelled to act: "Against the name of Jesus Christ[4] I considered myself obliged to commit many hostile actions, which I performed in Jerusalem, and I locked up in prison many of the saints, having received authority from the high priest and cast my vote against them when they were being killed. And many times through all the synagogues I punished them and forced them exceedingly to blaspheme and I was enraged at them and kept pursuing them as far as the cities outside." (26.9-11) Of course the question arises as to what sort of inner motivation could have prompted such inquisitorial zeal: could Paul, for instance, have been projecting some feared aspect of his own wavering psyche out onto reality so as to blot it out, so as to still the war of factions inside his own mind? Stephen, for instance, had attacked the tradition which Paul had striven all his life to uphold. Paul later promotes a version of Christianity that is a great deal like Stephen's. Might Paul, when he approved of Stephen's death, already have been having some doubts about that tradition, doubts which he was terrified to admit, doubts which (as the image of his own buried but inadmissable fear) it so terrified him to hear the Hellenists boldly proclaiming that he wanted to see them obliterated?

A positive answer to this question may be hinted at in the addendum to the remarks made by the voice on the road to Damascus which Paul reports in the version which he gives of those remarks before Agrippa. Before Agrippa he says that in addition to asking the question "Why are you persecuting me?" the voice made the observation that "it is hard for you to kick against the goads" (26.14). This expression was proverbial and appears in Greek and Latin literature. It refers to the self-defeating action of a plow-ox which, if it kicks against its harness, will only injure itself repeatedly. The proverb is usually, in a human sphere, applied to people who are bucking the inevitable. As applied to Saul, this proverb could in part have meant that he was having a difficult time resisting the spread of the church, which had been willed by God, it could have meant that he was becoming one of those futile God-fighters whom Paul's teacher Gamaliel had urged the Jewish leaders not to be. (Acts 5.34-40). Saul had thought of himself as always fighting *for* God, not against God, especially when he persecuted the Hellenistic Jewish Christians, and so in this sense the words of the voice would have constituted a real shock to his self-assurance, his cherished notions of himself. But the voice might also have been saying that it was hard for Paul to kick against what the mind behind the voice recognized as Paul's inevitable destiny, namely to become the very kind of Hellenistic Christian which at that point Paul was trying to annihilate. The voice that is may have been reflecting and confirming the fact that Paul was fighting against something in himself in fighting against a certain group of Christians.

So much for what we apparently can learn from Acts about Paul's state of mind and being before he met the light and heard the voice on the road to Damascus. As we have seen before, most fully in the case of Peter, it helps to understand the nature of a person's birth from above if one knows something about the person's pre-birth state. If we now try to ask what Acts may tell us about the birth itself, about the new condition out into which Paul was born, we find that at first Acts says very little. The aftermath of the original third-person account in chapter nine shows a blinded Saul being led by the hand to Damascus. (9.8) The character of Ananias is introduced; Ananias is to be the instrument, albeit reluctant, of the restoration of Paul's sight and therefore, we might say, of the completion of the birth process. The point would, as in the case of Peter and Cornelius, be that birth from above requires some element of sociality for its completion, that at least as depicted in the New Testament, it is not a solipsistic process.

This is an important point, but it still does not tell us too much of what Paul was undergoing on the inside. It does seem significant that in describing Paul to Ananias as its "vessel of choice" the voice of Jesus says that it will show Paul "those things which he must suffer on behalf of my name." (9.15-16) These words recall the concept that we have examined at length already, namely that it was necessary for the Son of Man to suffer. Evidently it is necessary for the kind of disciple of the Son of Man that Paul is destined to be to suffer similarly, a fact which Paul discusses (and which we will examine) in his letters. These words of the voice of Jesus may constitute the beginning of a picture of the life which Paul is being born into from above.

A much fuller picture seems to emerge from the second of Paul's two re-tellings of the Damascus road encounter, from the version of it which he presents to King Agrippa, or perhaps, to be more accurate, we should say that a version of the birth from above which Paul has been designated to help others undergo emerges from that speech. It may be somewhat risky to do so, but we assume that in order to help others to undergo this birth from above, Paul must have undergone it himself; we assume that we can apply the description of this birth from above to him. In his speech to King Agrippa Paul is discussing in a fuller form than any which a reader of Acts has been shown elsewhere, what sort of guidance he received from the voice after having been struck by the light. The voice had said: "Arise and stand on your feet. Because I appeared to you for this reason, to choose you as assistant and as witness of the things you saw of me and concerning which I will appear to you, selecting you from the nation and from the people unto which I will send you to open their eyes, to turn them from darkness unto light and from the power of the Satan unto God, so that they will receive forgiveness of sins and a share among those who have been made holy by an attitude of trust in me" (26. 16-18)

The terms of this process which Paul is told to make available to others and which we assume he underwent himself bear a remarkable resemblance to the terms of the birth from above which we discovered in the first and third chapters of the Gospel of John. Darkness and light are again opposed and by parallelism are shown to stand for the power of Satan and the power of God. The power of Satan (the Accuser, the cosmic prosecuting attorney) in the Acts passage would be his policy of judgment as it is carried out by (to use the phrase from the first epistle of John as we interpreted it) "the one who is doing sin," i.e. the one who, out of reflex or habit or conscious decision, has adopted judgement as his or her set policy. It is this realm of darkness in which and by which is communicated the conviction of the evil of one's own deeds which prevents one from coming to the light ("this is the judgment" — John 3.19). This is the realm in which the "shabby" works of the law which make one hate the light (John 3.20) are performed in an attempt to earn the status of "not guilty" against the cases conducted by Satan.

In the realm of light, by contrast, forgiveness of sins is conferred, as well as status in the divine family, a status which is here described as a share among those who have been made holy by an attitude of trust in Jesus. In the key born-from-above passage in the first chapter of the Gospel of John (1.12-13), we saw how trust in the name of the word results in the restoration of the authority grant which came with humans' having been made as the image of God. In Paul's speech before Agrippa, a group is envisioned as being restored or raised, on the basis of their trust in Jesus, to another sort of divine status, in this case holiness. For this restoration or for this elevation to take place, people must open their eyes and perceive what the disposition of God makes possible for them. Following this perception, they must accept the fact that they are accepted by God. We have already discussed this sort of requirement for salvation in connection with the third chapter of the Gospel of John.

Thus the Paul of Acts (without any attention being given to the vexed critical question as to whether he may partly or mostly be an invention of Luke) describes the process of birth from above. In his own letters Paul uses different terminology, and it is to these that we will now turn.

ii. PAUL'S LETTERS: DYING TO ONE'S SINS AND BEING BORN FROM ABOVE INTO THE NEW LIFE.

In chapter six of his letter to the Romans, Paul has anticipated an objection to his depiction of a God whose response to the disobedience, the ethical failure of his creatures, has been to invite them into his kingdom anyway, his depiction of a universe in which sin seems to have had such desirable consequences: "What then shall we say? Ought we to remain in sin so that grace may increase? May that thought never arise! We who have died to sin, how shall we yet live to it? Or did you not know that as many of us as have been baptized into Christ Jesus have been baptized into his death? We have been buried with him through baptism then so that just as Christ was raised from the dead through the father's glory, so might we also begin to walk in newness of life." (Romans 6.1-4) Newness of life was what the old legal system had aimed at, a regenerated humanity, and

Paul is saying that the end result of the new system that Jesus has proclaimed and embodied will be that same newness of life, that same regeneration. But in the meantime, "our old person" has to die "so that the body of sin may be abolished, so that we no longer serve sin as slaves." (6.6) The idea here is that we have been in some sort of legal bind, a bind so desperate in fact that the only way for a person to get out of it would be to die, "for the one who dies has been justified from sin" (6.7). By incorporating with Jesus, we avail ourselves not only of this kind of death needed to "justify us from sin," but we receive also the benefit of his resurrection: "The death which he died he died to sin once and for all; the life which he lives he lives to God. So you also reckon yourselves on the one hand dead to sin, but on the other hand alive to God in Christ Jesus." (6.10-11)

That dying to sin equals dying to the law becomes clear farther along in this discussion: "Now we have been released from the law, dying to that by which we were suppressed, so that we might serve by newness of spirit and not by oldness of letter." (7.6) Therefore dying to one's sins means giving up the hope of trying to earn salvation by obedience to the law, within the system where Satan stands as prosecutor before the divine tribunal hoping to win verdicts of guilty against each sinful human being. Paul understands the central tenet of Jesus' message, namely that God is offering free admission to his kingdom, irrespective of one's success in obeying all the multitudes of legal requirements. Satan has been thrown out of heaven (Luke 10.18), there is no further use for a prosecuting attorney there. For Paul, being born from above involves accepting God's gracious attitude, involves surrendering any claim to merit on the basis of one's own efforts. It is important to realize that accepting God's invitation is not an end in itself in Paul but rather the beginning of a whole extended process. This process, as Paul sees it, consists first of "dying to" one's sins and then of being raised to life in or with Christ.

Paul says more about the "dying" part of his process, about the need to "die", in pulling back from the equation he himself apparently has made between law and sin. This equation seems to have frightened him. "What then shall we say? Is the law sin? May that thought never arise." (7.7) The law is not sin, he then goes on to explain, but in some mysterious and unfortunate way that has to do with the makeup of human creatures it seems to prompt sin: "I would not have known sin except through the law. I would not have known covetousness unless the law has said thou shalt not covet. But sin, seizing an opportunity through the commandment, worked up every kind of covetousness in me. For sin is dead apart from the law." (7.7-8) We all know what the Apostle is talking about here: the indifference that we show toward something until we are told that we cannot have it or cannot or should not do it ("Please don't throw me in that briar patch"). In the light of this analysis one could almost lament God's having posted a "do not touch" sign on the tree of the knowledge of good and evil: without the prohibition Adam and Eve would probably never have been interested in its fruit, or so we can imagine. What Paul is talking about here is the problem that arises when, after an indeterminate period of exemption early in life (i.e. babyhood), the will of the individual, who naturally assumes that his or her desires are central to the scheme of things, meets its first check: "I at one time lived apart from the law, but when the commandment [i.e. the first notion of a "do not" or the first limit] came, sin sprang up to life, but I died, and the commandment which was unto life, this was found for me to be unto death." (7.9-10) Prohibitive commandment prompts rebellion. The commandment seems to focus the otherwise diffuse energies of sin, or, once planted as a beneficial cell in the human community, the commandment provides the matter by which the virus of sin may flourish in the social body. Paul recognizes that "the law is holy and the commandment holy and righteous and good" (7.12), he is not talking here about an unjust legal system, but rather about one which he subscribes to. But the commandment seems to engender in the human personality a desire to disobey it (it would never have occurred to me to speed up at that corner if the light hadn't started turning red), sin results from the combination of two elements which in themselves are good, i.e. people and commandments.

At this point Paul pulls back again and tries to be more precise. Instead of calling the law holy and just and good, he calls it spiritual, which characteristic makes it antithetical to the human creature who is composed of flesh, having been sold under sin, that is belonging to the system of slavery which sin comprise. (7.14) By virtue of this condition the human creature ends up being radically at war with himself or herself: "I do not know what I am doing. For I do not do what I want, but what I hate, this is what I do." (7.15) The basis of this war within the self is as follows: "For I delight in the law of God according to the inner person, but I see another law in my members warring against the law of my mind and leading me prisoner by the law of sin which is in my members." (7.22-23)

The law of his mind equals ethical reason, which is able to

recognize that there are rival centers of human consciousness which have claims on reality equal to the claims which his center makes. His members he refers to also as his flesh, where nothing good dwells. (7.18) But in this letter flesh does not stand merely for some sort of locus of appetency, some center of sensual drives, but rather for the entire egocentric delusion, the delusion that reality revolves around him or her, from which each human creature suffers and which at some original point (the end of innocence, the beginning of ethical tension) in our lives makes us perceive it as an outrage to, a betrayal of our sovereignty to be confronted with a commandment from somewhere or something outside ourselves. As a result, reason (law) and flesh (egocentricity) fight within the self and produce stalemate or, even worse, bankruptcy: "I am a wretched human being. Who will deliver me from the body of this death?" (7.24) Hopelessly, the last phrase of this question probably refers to the body in which one receives death as the wages of one's sin (6.23, although the real root of this idea is in 5.12 where Paul asserts that death enters the world through sin). Sin is failure and/or refusal to observe the commandments of God. The law exacerbates sin: it seems to stir up the impulse to sin, as we observed above, it also provides the means by which to judge sin: "Sin was in the world before law [obviously, since Adam the sinner pre-dated Moses], but sin is not reckoned where there is not law." (5.13) Death, sin, and the law are all intervolved in Paul's thinking, like the coils of the serpent in the Laocoon sculptural group. To die to any one of them would be to die to all of them.

Paul recognizes that the way out of the impasse has been supplied: "But thanks be to God through Jesus Christ our lord" (7.26) In him we can die to the sin/law nexus and be re-born or born from above by realizing that now there is no condemnation for those who are in Christ Jesus and that the law of the spirit of life has by Christ Jesus set us free from the law of sin and death. (8.1) Paul elsewhere describes this emancipation as "what has been given to us by God" (1 Cor. 2.12). Not that such a gift is easy for human beings to comprehend. In fact Paul says that we need to receive the spirit of God in order to know what has been given to us by God: since it is birth into a new redeemed life that has been given to us by God, our needing the spirit to comprehend and thereby enter into possession of the gift is the "from above" part of this spiritual birth. (1 Cor. 2.12) The physical person is not so constituted as to be able to receive such wisdom of God, "for it is foolishness to him" (1 Cor. 2.14). The physical person, the person of this world, is geared in terms of achieving his or her own status by dint of his or her own efforts, of judging other persons in terms of what they have likewise accomplished. Such self-reliance is the way of the so-called civilized world — to call it self-reliance is to see it in its best light, it can all too easily shade over into self-interest, though, or even worse, self-centeredness. At best within this human frame people are aiming at some sort of version of the good life (which some would define as status in God's kingdom); at worst, "condemned to hope's delusive mine," they strive for temporary stopgaps or solaces, gratifications such as money or power; in between there are the various degrees of "success," not all of them negligible of course, by which people try to achieve some sense of their own worth, some sense of happiness. As we saw in our introduction, though, failure within this system can lead to a sense of alienation and resentment, further isolating human beings into suspicious cells looking warily out at other people in the world.

To human beings caught within this system of striving, it would make no sense to say that they can have what they are really striving for (whether they know it or not), ultimate acceptance and affirmation of themselves, as a free gift (hence Paul's statement that they see the proclamation of the gift as "foolishness"). In fact, although this gift is free to us, it is not free to God, who pays the complete cost of it in the form of the death of that fairest and best human being who is in some very real form one with God. The forgiveness of God might be called our ticket of admission to the Kingdom which we have hitherto been kept out of by our failure to conform to the will of God, which is that we love one another. The death of Jesus is necessary in order to make the forgiveness of God something other than a counterfeit ticket, a piece of printed paper with nothing to back it up. It is easy and in some ways tivial to forgive someone when you yourself have not been the one to suffer from that person's sin (for example, a man cannot really forgive another man for that other man's devaluation of women, only one of the women whom he has devalued can); if, however, that person's hostility has been expressed toward you and expressed to the uttermost, so as to make you die, and you can still forgive that person, then that person truly is forgiven. In other words God in Christ had to feel the full brunt of the worked-up human resentment against him, the anger human beings feel at the God whom they conceive of (wrongly) as their judge, the one who in the last analysis (they think) keeps them out of the good life, the green field, the everlasting tents which are their aim and due — God had to experience the full brunt of this resentment so as to be able to forgive human beings. Of course there is the great question of whether or not a person would feel forgiven even if, at the moment of death, the person whom he or she was torturing extended full forgiveness: the torturer's guilt or rage in such a case would probably be so overwhelming that there could be no recovery from it. But in the economy of salvation the resurrection of Jesus overcomes this guilt: the victim has been restored to life (although as a human being without foreknowledge he had not known that such a result would occur), giving his torturers a reprieve that is almost beyond the power of the human mind to conceive of even as a possibility.

Another New Testament writer, in a passage which illuminates what we have just been examining in Paul, describes the resurrection of Jesus as the means by which God "according to his great mercy has begotten us again into a living hope." (1 Peter 1.3) This passage implies that hope had previously been dead because of a breakdown within the system of self-striving; beyond and worse than the alienation and resentment which that system had produced was the anxiety about, the despair over the prospect of death toward which each human life had inexorably been bent within the law/sin nexus, soul states which Kierkegaard and his successors have articulated with such vehemence as had the psalmists long before them. By offering hope in life and life as hope, the resurrection creates the condition by which and in which the divine family can or could come into existence: forgiven, freed from the death threat, human beings could stop looking warily upon each other as competitors for a limited supply of gratifications which they think of as there to be snatched at or extracted from the limited matter of earth and (as we at our late threatened date would state the human problem and challenge) start to think of each other instead as equally threatened, equally vulnerable siblings on a planet in peril.

iii. MATURITY WITHIN THE NEW LIFE

Stupendous though this message of what God has given us may be, this message of how reality itself has been transformed by the resurrection of Jesus, Paul refers to it as mere milk for babies (1 Cor.), by which he means that it is the sustenance of the infancy of what he hopes will be a process leading to Christian maturity or adulthood. Birth from above is forward-looking for Paul, not just in terms of an eternal salvation but in terms of the tasks in the kingdom for which such birth qualifies a person if the person moves on to become mature. A new capability is envisioned.

Paul gives several visions or versions of what the mature stage of Christian life might be. One of these appears in Romans after he has shown how a person emerges from the impasse which the system of law inevitably leads to. The way out of the impasse is provided by the fact that "there is no condemnation for those who are in Christ Jesus" (Rom 8.1) and by the fact that "the law of the spirit has by Christ Jesus freed you from the law of sin and death" (Rom. 8.2). At this point Paul can finally answer the objection which he has thought of back in chapter 6, namely that in propounding this system of grace he must also be propounding a system of unlimited license to sin: since it was sin that gave occasion for grace in the first place, he has imagined an objector saying, why not sin all the more so as to bring forth more grace? He answers this question by showing that the law of the spirit of life has released us from the law of sin and death, but for a purpose: "The thing which the law could not do in that it was weak through the flesh, God by sending his own son in the likeness of sinful flesh and on account of sin, condemned sin by [or in] the flesh in order that the righteous deed of the law might be fulfilled by us who are walking not according to the flesh but according to the spirit." (8.3-4) The Christological scope of the first part of this statement is so tremendous as to daunt exegesis, almost to defy it. One could write (and the authors of this study did in fact in our discussions seem to talk) tomes about what it means for God to have sent his own son in the likeness of sinful flesh, i.e. does such a statement mean that Jesus only appeared to be a human being with a natural bias toward egocentrism like the rest of us, that there was something feigned about his human existence? We think that the answer to questions such as these is no, that Jesus really was a human being. The problem remains, however, that having stated such a belief, we are still left with the difficulties of Paul's language in this passage.

For instance, what does Paul mean when he says that, by sending Jesus, God condemned sin in the flesh or by the flesh? First he seems to mean that God acting through Jesus did not cooperate with sin, did not present his members as the servants of sin to use a Pauline phrase, although here one is confronted with perhaps the most difficult question of all concerning Christology: in order to say that God, or Jesus acting for God did not cooperate with sin, is one committed to a position that Jesus never committed a single sin in his entire earthly life, does one sin knock a person over into the column of cooperating with sin, and if so, then what is a sin? These matters would require a separate book for adequate discussion.

In saying that by sending Jesus, God condemned sin in the flesh, Paul also seems to mean that God exposed sin for what it really was, especially when sin in the form of judgmental attitudes, which always further the work of Satan, seemed to be plated with the gold of utmost pious virtue or went wrapped in the vestments of religious authority. Sin's self-exposure culminated in the torture and killing of Jesus. In torturing Jesus, sin was in fact revealing its most heinous and perverse depths, as hostility toward the one who embodied God's gracious disposition toward all human beings. Once sin fully manifests itself in this way, God then reveals his own paradoxical way of condemning it, which is not like the human way: the human way of condemning sin is to attack and punish the sinner, the divine way is to suffer under the sin; through the anointed one, the messiah, God forgives sin and by the resurrection of this anointed one God converts the greatest sin into the greatest benefit for all human beings.

Paul says that such condemnation by God of sin with its two aspects (refusal to cooperate with sin, and exposure and transmutation of it) takes place in or by the flesh — one cannot be certain just exactly how to translate the Greek preposition *en* here. The phrase could mean that sin was condemned in its own territory, i.e. the flesh or human egocentric perspective which sin is so adept at using for its own purposes, or it could mean that sin was condemned in or by the flesh of Jesus: if this latter interpretation were correct, Paul would here be proposing some notion of the suffering servant as presented by Isaiah, i.e. the one who endures and carries away collective human hostility toward God, the sheep who is mute before the shearers.

At any rate, sin, which is part of the system which results in the condemnation and eternal destruction of human beings, is itself condemned. This is the fact that constitutes the milk we are fed as babies in the new life and which we need to keep receiving periodically by re-infusion even when we have passed on into more mature stages. But Paul is at this point interested in more than merely re-stating this fact; he here wants to show that God condemns sin for a specific purpose, namely "so that the righteous deed of the law might be fulfilled by us who are walking not according to the flesh but according to the spirit." The law itself as an effectual system may be bankrupt, but the fulfillment of the law seems still to be a desideratum in the mind of God. Not only that — God has found a way to realize that desideratum, but here it must be stressed that he does so by the spirit and in a group. We have already noticed how for Paul it is the spirit which enables us to take in the milk of our having been accepted by God. Likewise the fulfillment of the righteous deed of the law is by the spirit, but it is a plurality that he envisions walking and working by this spirit; the righteous deed of the law is being fulfilled among *us* (plural). The righteous deed of the law can only be fulfilled by the body of Christ, the church, which has the spirit as the standard which it walks by. Since, as Paul will say later on in a further discussion of the new society which he envisions, love constitutes the fulfillment of the righteous deed of the law (13.10), the condemnation of sin has taken place in or by the flesh so as to free us for love, the expression of which is hampered within the fleshly or legal system, for reasons which we have already noted several times: first of all, in a system where each person has to achieve success or status by his or her own efforts, other people tend to be looked upon as threats or as dismissable nonentities or as actual blots on (perhaps even in need of extinction from) the earth's surface rather than as brothers or sisters in need of our fellowship and help; one cannot love God within such a system because God is conceived of as the condemning, rejecting judge whose commandments one has failed to obey; failure to obey these commandments leads to further alienation, one shuns one's neighbor out of a sense of one's complete unworthiness and failure, out of a feeling that one is what Dostoyevsky calls the unnecessary worm. This whole downward spiral is what lies behind Paul's statement that "the mind-set of the flesh is hostility towards God, for it is not subject to the law of God [here = love], nor can it be" (8.7), that is those who walk according to the flesh are at war with the God whom they conceive of as the judge whereas his will is for them to see him as the parent and to see all other persons as brothers and sisters.

What Paul is telling the Romans is that they are free from this fleshly mind-set, free to have a different outlook and to act in accordance with it: "You are not in the flesh but in the spirit, if the spirit of God dwells among you" (8.9) — again it needs to be stressed that the "you" here is plural and therefore stands for a group; the spirit is not to be found fragmented, parceled out among a number of separate you's but rather circulating within a group. Again he describes for his readers the two-stage transformation by which they can pass out of the old life under the legal system into the new life in Christ: "If the spirit of the one who raised Jesus from the dead will also make your mortal bodies alive through the spirit which dwells among you." (8.11) The mortal bodies are the bodies which have died to sin in the sense discussed above, i.e. which have died to the old legal system. Out of this death one is raised to new life as a child of God: "As many as are led by the spirit of God, these are sons of God." (8.14)[5] Paul takes great pains to stress the difference between the new life and the old life that is being left. "For you did not receive the spirit of slavery unto fear again," which spirit governs the fleshly system of self-preoccupied striving and of seeing God as hanging judge under the law, "but you received the spirit of adoption by which we cry, Abba, the father." (8.16)

Here Paul is again describing the first, the baby-stage, which is what we have been given. There is nothing which can deprive us of this gift, as Paul is always at pains to stress: "The spirit itself testifies along with our spirit that we are children of God." (8.16)[6] But the fact of being children leads on to other benefits: "And if we are children, then we are heirs. Heirs of God, fellow heirs of Christ since we suffer with him in order that we may be glorified with him." (8.17)

Here Paul has imperceptibly slipped into talking about the second stage (maturity) in which demands are made upon us, even demands that we suffer. This section of Romans shows that he cannot really separate the two stages in his mind. He expects that those who are taken in as adopted babies will eventually become the mature adults who suffer along with Christ. He also probably wants to stress the fact that adversity is a confirmation rather than a cancellation of one's status in the divine family, an idea which he proceeds to develop at some length, not always with what appears to be coherent logic although he does come back in the end to the idea that to really be among the chosen of God, one has to share in the form of the image of his son, which form involves adversity.

Paul himself does not seem to ascribe much importance to any sufferings themselves, he seems to brush them away almost as minor irritants en route to something far greater: "For I suppose that the sufferings of the present time are not to be compared with the coming glory to be revealed unto us." (8.18) This glory will include the restoration of the creation which had been involved in the fate of Adam ("through one man sin came into the world and through sin death" — 5.12), which had been sentenced along with him ("on account of you the earth is cursed" — Gen. 3.17). Thus creation is as eager for the next phase of the cosmic drama as the human race is or ought to be. Paul actually uses a term that refers to drama, to the theater here, for when he says that "the eager longing of the creation expectantly awaits the revelation of the sons of God," (8.19) the word which we have here translated as "eager longing" means an eager stretching of the neck of the kind seen among theater-goers who are impatient for the curtain to go up and for the show to get started. The picture seems to be of the creation as a vast theater-audience waiting for the curtain to go up on the show which the revelation of the children of God will constitute. "For the creation has been subjected to meaningless futility, not willingly but on account of the one subjecting it [= Adam], in hope, because the creation itself will be freed from the slavery of corruption into the freedom of the glory of the children of God [or in hope that the creation itself will be freed from the slavery of corruption etc.]." (8.20-21)

One might have expected Paul at this point to go on extolling the kind of glory which must truly be great if even the creation is so eagerly extended waiting for it, but the state which creation is in seems to recall to Paul the state that the readers of his letter are in, or it may be that he had intended to deal with the state of his readers anyway and that he is actually returning to it and to them from some sort of diversion. Whatever the case may have been, the subject which Paul now proceeds to take up is that of "groans". "For we know that until now the whole creation has been groaning and suffering birth pangs together. Not only that, but we too, who have the downpayment of the spirit, we also among ourselves are groaning, eagerly awaiting adoption, the redemption of our body [probably = the church, i.e. the body of Christ although it could possibly, in terms of Hebrew and Greek usage = our bodies, i.e. our bodies dead to sin]." (8.22-23) He seems to be warning his readers that despite what he has been saying about the gift they have received, i.e. the gift of status as children of God, despite their in a sense already being where they want to be, they are in another sense not "there" yet owing to the fact that they and Paul had been saved not in realization but in hope, and hope by its nature is about something which one does not yet have. (8.24-5)

The argument as it develops (or however it develops) seems to be designed to counteract fears or suspicions that if one is not in a state of constant euphoria, one is somehow not a child of God or perhaps to counteract fears that groanings are a sign of deplorable weakness. As a matter of fact, Paul now goes on to argue, the heavenly powers can make use of our groanings, that is we don't know how we ought to pray anyway, but the spirit is able to make use of the inarticulate groans which we make in order to intercede for us (8.26). A kind of alchemy of prayer is being posited by Paul, or some sort of heavenly transformation by which the spirit picks up our scratchy signals and in some way manages to filter and/or to amplify them so that God can understand them: "the one who searches hearts [= God] knows what the spirit's way of thinking is, because with reference to God the spirit intercedes on behalf of the saints." (8.27) There is a deep consonance between the spirit and God which works to the advantage of the saints, and furthermore "we know that he [meaning God, who is explicitly identified as the subject of this verse in some manuscripts[7]] cooperates for good in all things with those who love God, with those who are called according to plan." (8.28)

With this mention of a plan according to which those who love God were called, with this use of language that recalls the Old Testament language of God's foreknowledge of Israel, Paul is broaching the idea of God's redemptive purpose for the world, which purpose in Paul's mind, as we shall see, requires a lineage of suffering servants, or at least this is what Paul seem to mean in the next few verses, especially if one sees these verses (in keeping with Hebrew chiastic structure which would have been second nature to him) as rounding back to a theme which he had already announced, namely that we are God's heirs, Christ's fellow heirs, since we suffer along with him in order to be glorified with him. (8.17) Here he repeats that theme more figuratively: "Because the ones whom he[= God] knew beforehand, he also set apart beforehand as form-sharers of the likeness of his son, so that he would be the first born among many brothers. The ones whom he set apart beforehand, these he also called. And the ones whom he called, these he also justified. But the ones whom he justified, these he also glorified." (8.29-30) Among the many ideas which Paul here presents, we may isolate one as important to our theme. It would seem that in Paul's opinion, the Son of Man (although Paul does not use this exact term) is still meant to be some kind of group, a group of brothers (or siblings as we would prefer to say, using non-sexist language) of whom Jesus will have been the first born. The successors, that is the later siblings are meant to share in the form of the likeness of God's son, which form we take to be that of the uncomely one in Isaiah 53, the suffering servant. That such apparent outcast status, far from calling in question one's status as an adopted child of God, is actually a high privilege and also the guarantee of one's eventual glorification, is the stumblingblock which we have repeatedly come upon in our discussion of birth from above. This idea is central to Paul's conception of that birth, and we will now turn to a passage in his second letter to the Corinthian church which contains perhaps his most complete discussion of it.

iv. TRUE GLORY AND THE REFUSAL TO FLASH CREDENTIALS.

To put one's trust in "Son of Man/Suffering Servant" as the proper name for the revealing activity of God in the world, is to renouce all worldly success or worldly status as a goal for the enterprise of the body of Christ, as Paul shows when he comes under attack in Corinth. He has evidently come under attack for not living up to some notion which the Corinthian congregation has of what a minister of the gospel ought to be. The Corinthian church has been drawn to certain rival preachers of the word, rival preachers who come equipped with proper endorsements and introductions, seals of approval from the ecclesiastical big-wigs back in Jerusalem. Instead of competing with these rival preachers on their own level, instead of producing credentials of his own, Paul insists on what, in the eyes of most people, would stand as signs of failure — he insists paradoxically upon these as the signs of his deeper success, as signs of his fitness to be their true spiritual leader.

He does so first by using a metaphor which refers to the pageants with which Roman conquerors were in the habit of celebrating their military successes: "But thanks be to God who is at all times leading us in triumph along with Christ and who is revealing the odor of the knowledge of him by means of us in every place." (2 Cor. 2.14) The ones who were led in triumph in these Roman processionals were the prisoners of war, the captured soldiers, the emperors' opponents; they were paraded in humiliation through the streets of Rome. In Paul's version of this scene it is God who stands as the emperor, and Paul and Christ who stand as the prisoners of war being led around in every place by God. Paul is referring here to Jesus in the role of Suffering Servant, a role which Paul identifies with completely. As for the odor in Paul's metaphor, some scholars have connected it with the fragrance of the various sacrificial offerings which were a feature of these triumphal pageants. Others have connected it with a cosmetic odor which was necessary on these occasions to counteract the stench of the prisoners who, after all, would hardly have been offered baths and spices as one of the privileges of their defeated status. The prisoners smelled so bad in fact that the processionals also had to include censer-swingers, who would waft incense out along the way in an attempt to counteract the prisoners' smell. Some modern scholars have therefore interpreted the odor in Paul's metaphor as a reference to this incense being sent out from censers: Christ and Paul are being led as prisoners, but the upshot of the message that comes forth from this fact is sweet. The gospel in fact is considered to be the source of the odor by many scholars even when they do not see the censer-swingers as producing it. They pick up the words "good odor of Christ" from the next verse in this passage and assume that Paul in both these verses must be referring to some pleasant fragrance of the gospel message. We, however, believe that the metaphor is somewhat more audacious than that. We interpret Paul to mean that the odor comes from Jesus and from Paul themselves as sweating prisoners, as suffering servants being led captive by God. In 1 Corinthians Paul had referred to the offensive nature of the message of the cross. Here he is referring more directly, more personally to the offensive nature first of Jesus as the Suffering Servant who had to undergo crucifixion and in whom there was no comeliness to use Isaiah's term of description, then by extension to the offensive nature of all those who have decided to follow Jesus in this uncomely career.

Under attack in Corinth as not successful enough, as not authoritative enough in appearance, Paul prefers to flaunt his non-success or to hold it right under the Corinthians' noses if one wants to sustain the olefactory metaphor. He and Christ are God's malodorous prisoners being led captive at all times in every place through the world, but then Paul goes on to insist that this odor that they emit is the odor of the knowledge of God, the odor that reveals to the world what God's essential nature is: in this metaphor God is the emperor leading Christ and Paul as prisoners in his triumphal procession, but at the same time it is the prisoners who are revealing what God is really like. This may be the point at which the offense arises in most human, or most religious nostrils: people resist a portrayal of God as sweating among the failures and the outcasts, of God as some kind of refuse, of God as taking abuse, but it is this portrayal on which Paul insists not only here, but also by implication in a passage in 1 Corinthians where he says "And we labor, working with our own hands. When we are insulted we bless; when we are persecuted, we patiently put up with it; when we are slandered, we speak words of encouragement. We have become until now like rubbish, like the scum scoured off from all things." (1 Cor. 4.12-13) Identifying in this passage with the Suffering Servant's mission, Paul sees it as his task to be the scum, to carry off all the bad odors and bad vibrations of the human race until the race stands purified, and similarly, in the passage which we have been examining from 2 Corinthians, Paul says that by performing such a task, he and Jesus are revealing the essential nature of God, which is as victim.

This revelation of God, Paul then goes on to assert, divides the human race into two groups: "Because we are the good odor of Christ to God among those who are being saved and among those who are perishing, to the one group a smell out of death unto death, to the other a smell out of life unto life." (2 Cor. 2.15-16) Here Paul states directly that he is the odor, he is not transferring the odor to something else, such as the gospel message. To some, Paul says, this odor of the suffering servant, of the loser, of the outcast, reeks of nothing but death, rejection, and failure. This was, for instance, the way the path to Calvary registered at first on the nostrils of Peter, i.e. as the total failure of the mission which he thought he had embarked upon with Jesus. Others, however — and here we might identify those others as the ones who have been born from above or who are capable of being born from above — are able to recognize this odor as arising out of the new life which the true servants, the true children of God may enter, the odor arises out of this new life and it leads on into further dimensions of that new life.

Paul goes on in this passage to point out the real dangers that exist in any attempt on the part of gospel preachers to try to compete in a worldly way with the enticements of the world. "For we," he says "are not like the many who huckster God's word, but as from a sincere motive, as from God in God's presence we speak in Christ."

(2.17) Being "in Christ" frees Paul on this occasion from the need to present any dossier or credentials to the church at Corinth which he himself has founded, to compete in a worldly way ("huckster") with more "successful"-seeming preachers: "Are we starting again to recommend ourselves? Or we don't need like some any letters of recommendation to you or from you, do we? You are our letter written in our hearts, known and read by all people, revealing that you are Christ's letter taken care of by us, written not with ink but with the spirit of the living God, not on stone tablets but on fleshy heart-tablets" (3.1-3) As with many of Paul's metaphors, this one seems to become a little bit tangled in the details. What one wants this passage to say is that the Corinthian congregation itself constitutes Paul's letter of recommendation, that this letter is written on *their* hearts, and that he therefore needs no other document, and in fact there is some evidence for a text of this metaphor that begins "You are our letter written in your hearts", but even if one submits to the more difficult reading, namely "you are our letter written in our hearts", a strong general assertion still arises out of this passage: in fact, if Paul means for the letter to have been written in his heart, he could be saying that "in Christ" he has such inner assurance of his own qualifications that the idea of a letter of recommendation is one which he can scorn, he knows in his own heart what his own worth as a gospel preacher is. In relation to such an idea, one thinks of Jesus' question in the Sermon on the Mount: "Is not life more than food and body more than what you put on it?" (Matt. 6.25) In accord with such a question, which concerns the difference between what Aristotle calls accidents and substance, Paul is saying "Is not the office of an apostle more than any credentials which he or she can produce?"

Paul therefore has an answer for the Corinthians insofar as they have asked him to produce a dossier, insofar as they have asked him to compete with rival preachers who have come in and seduced his congregation to another message. Not that he has been through some kind of therapy or arrived at some enviable belief in himself, some marvel of Emersonian self-reliance or Thoreauvian scorn for the business-suit: "But we through Christ have this assurance toward God. Not that we ourselves are sufficient to take credit for anything as coming from ourselves, but our sufficiency is from God, who has empowered us as servants of a new covenant, not of letter but of spirit. For the letter kills, but the spirit makes alive." (3.4-6) The new covenant which he is talking about here is one that God has unilaterally put into effect whether or not people subscribe to it (just as in the original convenant with Abraham in Genesis 15, it was God who took all the obligations upon himself), this covenant comprises the desire on God's part to adopt every human creature as a true child; this is a kind of acceptance which one never needs to doubt, this is an acceptance of oneself as being of infinite value to God, this acceptance involves being "loved for oneself alone" as William Butler Yeats put it, and not for one's golden hair or any other desirable attributes or accomplishments or commodities that one may happen to come festooned with. The psychiatrist Alice Miller has written of a syndrome which she calls "narcissistic wounding." In this syndrome, in this predicament, children perceive that they are valued only for whatever glory they can reflect upon their parents, not for themselves as persons. This perception which may harden into conviction leads to lifelong frenzies of striving for success, for self-validation in the eyes of that forever demanding even if, after awhile, only imagined or internalized parent, that parent who withholds his or her love unless or until the child delivers something, physical beauty perhaps, even though that is the most transitory of all commodities (since "rosy lips and cheeks/Within [Time's] bending sickle's compass come"), or some kind of success or accolade, some kind of worldly achievement, although these too are foundations of straw upon which to build up a sense of the self, as Time Magazine showed several years back in an article about what it called the imposter syndrome: sufferers from this syndrome, even people who have achieved a great success in the world of business, are prey to serious self-doubts, to fears of being found out as phonies, as the dependent creatures they are; they experience feelings of emptiness and meaninglessness, the torment of satisfied striving.

The covenant Paul is talking about is one in which people can have trust since under its terms they are valued at the level of their real substance, not at the flashy level of accidentals. It is as with Lycidas in Milton's poem, Lycidas who has died before he has had a chance to "prove himself" or "make a name for himself". The divine voice in Milton's poem proclaims that God knows what Lycidas's true worth is anyway, even without the assistance of a bag-full of earthly trophies:

> "Fame* is no plant that grows on mortal soil
> Nor in the glistering foil

*[Here meaning the true valuation of a person's worth.]

Set off to the world, nor in broad rumor lies,
But lives and spreads aloft by those pure eyes
And perfect witness of all-judging Jove;
As he pronounces lastly on each deed,
Of so much fame in heaven expect thy meed.

One's ultimate worth depends upon God's evaluation, and God who values each living creature can make good the mangled evidence of a life cut short. The doctrine which Milton proposes here is almost like the one of Paul's discussed above in which the Holy Spirit makes good the deficiencies of even an inarticulate human prayer: God makes good the deficient record of human lives and loves us just the way we are.

In the meantime there remains the problem of the old legal covenant of the letter written in stone which still tends to hold sway over the human race. As in Romans, Paul here equates the law with death, first of all because literally, the penalty for failure to observe the apodictic law of the Ten Commandments was death. Not that the legal covenant lacked divine splendor — on the contrary, just as in Romans (7.12) when he acknowledged that "the law is holy and the commandment is holy and just and good," Paul here in 2 Corinthians acknowledges that the legal covenant, even though death-directed in the verdicts it pronounces on those who fail to fulfill its demands, did at one time radiate or reflect the divine glory. But he makes such an acknowledgement for the purpose of showing that the new covenant which he proclaims radiates a glory which far surpasses that of the old: "But if the service of death engraved in stone tablets came into being in glory, so that the children of Israel could not gaze into Moses' face on account of the perishing glory of his face, how will the service of the spirit not be more in glory? For if there was glory by the service of condemnation, how much more will the service of justification abound in glory? For also that which has been glorified has in this respect not been glorified on account of the surpassing glory. For if the perishing thing is through glory, how much more is the thing which remains in glory" (2 Cor. 3.7-11)

In this difficult passage Paul is alluding to an episode in Exodus. This episode in fact becomes the basis for a sustained comparison of the two covenants, old and new, a comparison which is aimed at answering the original question of whether or not, as preacher of the gospel, Paul needs to produce credentials. In Exodus 34 Moses is receiving the Ten Commandments or, as they are there called, "the ten words" from Yahweh. "And Yahweh said to Moses, Write for yourself these words because according to these words I have cut with you and with Israel a covenant. And he was there with Yahweh forty days and forty nights, he did not eat bread or drink water, and he cut on tablets the words of the covenant, ten words. And as Moses went down from Mt. Sinai, and the two tablets of the stipulations were in the hand of Moses as he went down from the mountain, he did not know that his face was beaming light when he was talking with him. And Aaron and all the sons of Israel saw Moses and behold his face was beaming light and they were afraid to approach him. And Moses called to them, and they returned to him, Aaron and all the leaders in the assembly, and Moses spoke to them. And after that all the sons of Israel approached and he commanded to them all that Yahweh had told him on Mount Sinai." (Exod. 34.27-32) Paul is alluding to this story when he says that "the children of Israel could not gaze into Moses' face on account of the perishing glory of his face", i.e. they fled at first in fear and had to be reassured by Moses into coming back to listen to him. That much is clear from the Old Testament story. What is not clear, at least from what we have retold of the story so far, is why such glory should be called perishing by Paul. First of all, it should be pointed out that not all translations put the matter of the glory's perishing quite so baldly or boldly as we do. Many scholars have tried to construe the idea of the glory's perishing as a sort of afterthought or aside, making this part of Paul's sentence read something like "the children of Israel couldn't gaze into Moses' face on account of the glory (albeit perishing) of his face." If the sentence is rendered in such a way, then stress is put on the glory, which glowed too brightly for the children of Israel to endure, even though it was perishing, being about to fade, since it had to go out eventually. On the contrary, we think that Paul meant to put the stress upon the glory's fading nature and that he was asserting that the function of the veil that Moses eventually puts on was to hide the fact that the glory *had* faded; furthermore, we think that he derived this stress from the Exodus story itself as it continues telling how Moses was entrusted with the ten words.

The last section of chapter 34 describes some rather mysterious goings and comings on the part of Moses: "When Moses had finished speaking with them, he put a veil on his face. And when Moses went before Yahweh to speak with him, he took away the veil until he went out, and he went out and told the sons of Israel what he had been commanded. And the sons of Israel saw Moses' face, that Moses' face was beaming light, and Moses returned the veil to his face until he went in to speak with him [i.e. Yahweh]." (Exod. 34.33-35) One learns earlier in this passage that unbeknownst to himself Moses' face was beaming light when he was talking to Yahweh. It was also beaming light when he went down to rejoin Aaron and his fellow Israelits. This face at first frightened them away, but he was able to coax them back and talk with them, all of this without a veil, i.e. the passage does not suggest that the actual beaming brightness was too much for them to look at, they did look at it while Moses was speaking to them. Moses' face evidenlty starts to lose its refulgence sometime after he stops speaking and he puts the veil on in order to hide this fact, he puts the veil on so that he can hide the perishing glory until he can go back to Yaheweh and get infused with another dosage of it. He takes off the veil, Yahweh lights his face again, the children of Israel see this glow when Moses comes back down and talks to them, then Moses puts the veil back on until he goes in to speak to Yahweh again.

It is this facet of the Exodus story which Paul has in mind when he calls the glory of Moses' face a perishing glory. He first mentions this perishing glory associated with the giving of the old covenant of the letter so as to contrast it with the far greater glory associated with the giving of the new covenant of the spirit. The language he uses to make this comparison is so compressed as almost to bewilder exegesis, especially when he says "That which has been glorified has in this respect not been glorified on account of the surpassing glory." (3.10) The surpassing glory is that of the new covenant; when compared to it, the glory of Moses' face, which had seemed incomparable, suddenly looks quite lusterless. A paraphrase meant to bring out the meaning of this verse more clearly might read: "That which once seemed so glorious is in this respect, i.e. because of the surpassing glory, not really so glorious at all." In the next verse Paul again contrasts the two glories: "If the perishing thing was through glory, how much more is the thing which remains in glory." (3.11) The perishing thing is the glory that was on Moses' face, the thing which remains is the glory on the face of those who proclaim the new covenant, a glory which Paul has yet to describe.

In the next paragraph he leads up to such a description, partly by continuing to allude to the story of Moses and his veil. He begins by saying "Having this kind of hope then, we act with much openness".

(2 Cor. 3.12) He is here resuming the topic of his assurance, his freedom from the feeling that he would need to produce credentials in Corinth, and in so doing he compares his openness to the circumspection of Moses: ". . . we act with much openness and not as Moses was placing the veil upon his face so that the children of Israel could not look into the end [= Greek *telos*] of the thing that was perishing" (3.12-13) The Greek word *telos*, like the English word "end" which translates it, can mean either the termination of something or the goal toward which it is moving. We think that by using *telos* here, Paul is referring specifically to the going out, the extinction of the glory on Moses' face, he is saying that Moses put the veil on his face so that the children of Israel could not see that he had lost the splendor which his face would beam when he was talking with God. "But their minds were hardened," Paul says, "for unto this present day the same veil remains upon the reading of the old covenant, it not being discovered that by Christ it is being abolished." (3.14) The minds of the children of Israel were hardened into an expectation of glory from an old source, a source from which the glory had in fact faded. This statement is breathtakingly bold in its devaluation of the law: the law, Paul says, is a fading ember which keeps up behind a veil the pretence of its own abiding splendor. The hardening of the Israelites' hearts which he alludes to might involve the effect of having been deceived or maybe self-deceived too long. Yeats says that "Too long a sacrifice can make a stone of the heart." The sacrifice in this case would be that of basic honesty, the Israelites having sacrificed an honest admission of the facts to the pretence of maintaining an outworn cultus and creed from which the life has departed.

Paul actually seems to go even farther in speaking of self-deception on the Israelites' part. First, in the verse we have been looking at, he says that the veil remains upon the reading of the old covenant. An Israelite would have had to put this veil over the old covenant, although one could perhaps say that this is a picture of the priestly class, the custodians of the law, trying to hoodwink the people and also themselves (as in Bergman's harrowing movie *Winter Light*) into thinking that there was still some life in the old religious practice. But Paul then proceeds to shift the locus of the veil: "But until today, whenever Moses is read, a veil is laid upon their hearts." (3.15) Of course with this verse too the question could be "Who has laid this veil on their hearts?" but since the veil has now been located throughout all the people, one assumes that they are somehow complicit in the obfuscation which the veil causes, in the fraud being carried out. The people must have colluded in their own hoodwinking. At this point too, if one tries to stay with Paul's metaphor, it seems as if there would have to be a relocation of the fading of the fire of glory too since, in terms of the original Exodus story, that fading takes place behind the veil: the glow on the glory has now gone out of the hearts of the children of Israel, the heart being, in Hebrew terms, the center of ethical and religious consciousness.

It may be that we do not have to struggle to hold together Paul's metaphor for him, it may be that even if inconsistencies do creep in, if the metaphor seems to be starting to crumble, a bold idea arises from these verses nonetheless. One needs to remember too that the idea which governs this whole discussion, the subject to which Paul always returns and for which in this section he is building up an impressive weight of metaphorical glory, is the subject of his having to present credentials as a preacher. In the light of this subject, Paul reminds his readers of the one infallible way to regain the glory when it has ceased to shine: "Whenever he returns to the Lord, the veil is removed." (3.16) This verse is probably Paul's quotation from memory of a part of the Septuagint version of Exodus 34.34 (which above we translated literally from the Hebrew as "And when Moses went before Yahweh to speak with him, he took away the veil . . ."). There are problems with regarding this verse as a quotation from Exodus and thus with regarding Moses as the antecedent of "he". First of all in the Septuagint (which is faithful to the Hebrew) Moses is explicitly stated as the subject of the verb, and the verb (also faithful to the Hebrew in this) is "to go in," not "to return". Furthermore, in the Greek of Paul's version of this verse, there is a difficult use of the word *ean*, the effect of which according to some scholars is that the sentence should be translated "Whenever someone turns to the Lord, the veil is removed." For such scholars, while Moses remains in the background of this verse, Paul is talking about the turning of some hypothetical person. It would not make much difference for the idea that Paul is now starting to express whether it was Moses or one of those children of Israel upon whose heart a veil has been laid who happened to be turning to the Lord: the real idea that Paul is building up to is that the Lord is the source for the gaining of glory, what worked once for Moses will work again now if one really turns to the Lord and not to some outmoded repository such as the old covenant.

Not only that: as Paul is about to show, there is now a way to gain permanent rather than intermittent glory, the time is ripe for a greater than Moses to have appeared. But first, almost as if he had thought of a possible objection or a possible question, he halts his argument for a moment. The question he seems to have thought of is this: "When you say 'whenever he returns to the Lord,' what or whom do you mean by 'the Lord'?" Paul's answer to such a question is "The Lord is the spirit," (3.17) meaning the spirit that he has described in so many places to the Corinthians (and in his letter to other churches), the animating principle of the body of Christ: if one turns to the spirit, the veil can be removed from a face on which the glory has faded and one can receive a re-infusion of that glory just as Moses did when he went in to talk with Yahweh. Having defined this term, Paul could then have returned to the argument which he had been building up, but instead he makes another statement: "But where the spirit of the Lord is, freedom is" (3.17). The intent of such a remark is to remind his readers that throughout his discussion of the veil and by means of it, he is suggesting an alternative to the death-dealing system of the old covenant. The codeword for that old covenant would be "law". The code-word for the new covenant which he is minister and servant of is "freedom": freedom from the death-threat which the law comprises, freedom from a code of prohibitions, but then this is to couch the meaning of freedom merely in negative terms. The new covenant not only frees us from certain old constraints, fetters, and threats, it also frees us up for certain new activities beneficial to the whole world, it frees us up for love and service.

We have already, in several places discussed how it is impossible to love when one is convinced of one's own failure and therefore unworthiness within a system of standards like the old covenant of law. Failure within the legal system leads to withdrawal and resentment. Furthermore, a system based on self-reliance and earned merit sooner or later shades over into a competitive system, and in a competitive system emulous and invidious feelings inevitably arise, hostility toward one's neighbors, the odium of comparisons, the desire to see my neighbor diminished so that I can grow, which kind of desire is antithetical to love: love is the privilege of recognizing in the need of another a claim on reality that is as valid as one's own. Response to such a recognized need in service of another human being is an ultimate expression of freedom. To discard one's self-importance as a mere trifle rather than to insist upon it bespeaks openness, release from the prison of embattled, suspicious selfhood, the outlook from within which other persons appear as threats, release from slavery to the imagined need of having to defend one's own little ego-stake at every moment. In the context of a discussion which began with the picture of Paul being led captive in every place with Christ, the freedom to serve would extend to suffering at the hand of hostile humans so as to purify them, so as to carry off the scum of all their anger and rage; to accomplish this task one cannot return evil for evil, one has to have advanced beyond the ego-need of revenge. Teachings of Jesus like those which enjoin his followers to turn the other cheek, to walk the extra mile, involve a kind of gamble. Jesus invites human beings to see what would happen if the chain of hostile action and re-action, the striking out from the siege-mentality of egocentric existense could for once be interrupted. The natural tendency is to think that if one does not defend oneself in the social-Darwinian struggle, one will simply be swallowed up, annihilated. Jesus had the audacity to suggest that such non-resistance is, on the contrary, the way to start to de-fuse the struggle.

Paul is reflecting his endorsement of Jesus' teaching in the passage we have been examining. The context must constantly be recalled: Paul has been faced with a challenge to his authority in the Corinthian church. The response of the "natural person" in such a situation is to strike out and defend his or her turf. As Konrad Lorenz and others have pointed out, such aggressive behavior constitutes a residue from a former ecological and existential phase: owing to a failure on the part of human beings to think through what real alterations the development of civilization has brought about in their status on this earth, what was good for primitive human beings and on beyond them for their primate forebears still tends to pass for good in a vastly altered situation. What the spirit enables human beings to intuit and to dare to move toward is a behavioral phase beyond the phase of highly organized and orchestrated aggression which so-called civilization constitutes. Civilization is about as far as the "natural person" can go, but there is a further phase which, as we saw Paul saying in Romans, the entire creation in its meaningless futility is eagerly awaiting: the revelation of the children of God. The first step into this next phase involves not automatically striking out to stick up for myself when I am attacked, and in this passage we see Paul taking such a step. Attacked, weighed in the balance with rival preachers and found wanting by part of the Corinthian congregation, he will not strike back by promoting himself as a better preacher than his rivals. Not that he is willing to abandon the field to the rival preachers who are attempting to seduce the Corinthian church — in fact he is sure that his glory is greater than their glory, but this fact is an instance of the rule that the one who gives up asserting his or her own ego, the one who loses his or her own life, will gain it back multiplied many times over, it illustrates the letting go that is necessary so that the new life can begin (or in Paul's case continue). Paul has a glory that surpasses that of his rivals because his works, to use the Johannine terminology which we have discussed previously, have been done in God (John 3.21), but he does not take credit for this glory, it is something which he has plugged into by becoming part of the body of Christ.

One gains this glory by turning to the lord, i.e. to the spirit, but turning to the spirit can only happen when one enters the divine society. Furthermore, the glory that Paul for instance gains by turning to the spirit is not something that distinguishes him from all the other Christians, such as those at Corinth — it is rather something that he shares with his Christian brothers and sisters: "But we all [i.e. everybody in the divine family] behold with unveiled face the glory of the Lord and are having our forms changing constantly into the same image from glory unto glory just as from the lord-spirit." (3.18) In this amazing image it almost seems as if Paul were anticipating some form of Whitehead's metaphysical theory, namely the idea of matter as a collection of sub-atomic flashes, on and off, disappearing instantaneously then coming back on as the same form (this all has to happen in random sequence of course — other-wise, if all the myriad atoms and other subatomic particles of which our bodies are formed all flashed off simultaneously, we would cease even to be there for an instant). Modern readers at least are in a position to appreciate Paul's figure, they have at their disposal from Whitehead a ready analogy to it, a means for imagining what Paul is picturing here: a perpetual renewal of the glow, an oscillation from glory unto glory. What Paul is trying to describe is the perpetual availability of the lord as spirit in the church, the possiblity of a society of many Moseses with ever-raying faces, a convenant the communicated glory of which is never in danger of fading, which will never have to be covered up in embarassment but will always be instinct with living knowledge of God. Paul is claiming to partake of this kind of glory insofar as he has to enter into competition with rival preachers, a glory which he could never have attained unto even as the ultimate Pharisee, the ultimate devotee of the religious life. This is a glory of the second, the adult phase of the new life into which a follower of Jesus is born, a glory which derives from the circulation of the spirit within the Christian group.

"Seek the kingdom of God and his righteousness first," Jesus had said, proposing one of his gambles, "and all these things shall be added unto you," (Matt. 6.33) meaning all those material things about which people tend to be anxious such as food and drink, but he also could have been talking about what Paul experiences here, namely that if you let yourself be subsumed in the kingdom, you will also have glory as (for instance) a preacher added unto you. The principle seems to be that the way to get what you have anxiously been striving for as your particular desiderated attainment is to let go in the manner of the followers of the kingdom of Jesus. Of course it is important to recall another occasion on which Jesus enunciates this same principal, an occasion which we examined in connection with Peter: "Peter started to speak to him [we might add: "not really knowing what he was talking about"]. 'Behold we have left all things and have been following you.' Jesus said, 'Truly I say to you, there is no one who has left house or brothers or sisters or mother or father or children or fields for my sake and for the gospel's sake who will not now therefore in this time receive a hundredfold houses and brothers and sisters and mothers and children and fields with persecutions, and life eternal in the coming age." (Mark 10.28-30) In dealing with Peter, we noted that he always wanted to suppress the warning proviso of persecutions, he preferred thinking of the inauguration of a glorious messianic age, the carefree spoils of which would be his.

Paul is under no such illusions. We have already shown how he began the discussion which culminates in the depiction of so much available glory with the picture of himself being led as a sweating slave in God's triumphal procession. In the next section of this second letter to the Corinthians he will return to suffering and persecution as part of the glory, interweaving this theme with responses to the attacks against him in Corinth. For instance, in the next sentence after he has talked about being changed into the same likeness from glory unto glory, he says "For this reason [i.e. because we are being constantly transformed into the image of the glory], having this ministry as we have had mercy shown unto us, we are not discouraged, but we renounce the hidden things of shame, not walking by craftiness or falsifying the word of God, but by displaying the truth plainly we recommend ourselves toward every conscience of persons in the presence of God." (4.1-2) The first fact to note here is that Paul considers it a mercy shown to him that he has this ministry (i.e. of the new covenant, as 3.6 shows us). By such a statement Paul may partly mean that as a former persecutor of the true church he feels it as an amazing mercy of God that he can now proclaim the good news of God's determination to save each human creature. But there may be more to this statement insofar as, in addition to his proclamation of this message, the service of the new covenant also involves a personal exhibition of himself: unlike Peter, who is repelled by the idea of suffering, Paul considers it a mercy shown unto him that he is allowed to suffer, that he is being led around as a fellow-slave of the despised and rejected suffering servant, placarded as God's prisoner. Paul not only endorses the Son of Man's need to suffer, but he considers it some kind of gift of God that he can sign on for similar suffering himself.

The next thing to remark is that in the midst of all the attacks he is undergoing in Corinth, he not only does not become discouraged but he also renounces the hidden things of shame. This phrase, "the hidden things of shame," may refer either to the tactics of his opponents or to the charges which they have brought against him or perhaps to both. The buck of aggressive or denigrating action is going to stop on Paul's desk so to speak (which does not mean of course that he will not with all necessary vigor discuss his reasons for thus opting out of the system which promotes self at the expense of others), nor will he walk in craftines or falsify the word of God. The falsification could arise equally from his words or from his behavior if he were to let it do so. In this case he may very well be referring to the kind of damage that would be done to the work of the Kingdom by his responding in kind to the attacks made upon him. In contrast to what his opponents are doing, though, Paul's tactic will be to recommend himself by manifestation of the truth to every conscience of persons in the presence of God. Here as always it is essential to remember that the Hebrew notion of truth is not so much intellectual, i.e. having to do with the presentation of true principals and endorsable propositions, as it is existential, i.e. having to do with faithful performance, reliable service: Paul probably means that he will recommend himself by remaining faithful to the role of suffering servant which he has been called to perform, bearing about in his body the marks of Christ's crucifixion.

At this point he reintroduces the idea of the crisis that his case constitutes or that his case precipitates, just as he did when he talked about the varying reactions to the odor which he and Christ as suffering servants emitted: "But if our good news has been veiled, it has been veiled among those who are perishing, among whom the god of this age has blinded the minds of disbelieving ones so that they cannot see the light of the good news of the gospel of the glory of Christ, who is the image of God." (4.3-4) Ringing further changes on Exodus 34, he here recognizes that even though the glory is available constantly to those within the society of the spirit with its mutual exchange of service so that the members of Christ's body are perpetually being transformed from glory unto glory into the image of that glory, nevertheless to people outside the body that glory may be muffled up, invisible, not because that glory has been extinguished as was the glory which Moses had received but rather because the minds of those who do not believe — the Greek word here is *apistos* and thus involves again the root *pist* which has to do with trust — are blinded. The group Paul is talking about is the group which cannot put their trust in the name Son of Man, the people to whom the thought of the servant of God having to suffer is anathema, to whom the glory of the Messiah would never consist of his being crucified as it does in the gospel of John. The eyes of this group are blinded so that they cannot see the light of the good news of the glory of Christ, who is the image of God, according to one way of translating the passage. The passage could also be translated to mean that their eyes are blinded so that the light of the good news of the glory of Christ, who is the image of God, cannot shine to them, i.e. so that for them effectively the gospel does become a dying ember even though, to those who can put their trust in the name, it is a neverending source of glory, an inexhaustible energy source. Either way, there is something which prevents this group from seeing glory in the kind of good news which the career of Christ communicates; for whatever reasons of conditioning or conviction they prefer remaining within or under the system of sin, Satan and so-called self-reliance.

In the context of this letter, as we have been saying over and over, their preference means that they expect Paul to respond to the attacks which have been mounted against his ministry. As he has done before, Paul at this point refuses again: "We are not proclaiming ourselves but rather Jesus Christ lord, and ourselves your servants on Christ's behalf." (4.5) The first element of his proclamation contains the three terms around which much of the controversy swirled wherever the church was established in its early days: Jesus is the name of a human being from the village of Nazareth; Christ is the title of the expected Jewish deliverer-king; lord is a general term for some form of rulership, whether earthly or cosmic. Just to show how arguments could arise concerning Jesus and his ministry: among whatever group or in the vicinity of whatever group the first epistle of John was sent to, the opponents of the writer are anxious to dissociate Jesus the mere human being from the office of cosmic messiah; the writer of that epistle by contrast insists upon bringing the human Jesus who had a body and who manifested the love of God by caring about the bodies of other human beings before the eyes of all his readers. In other places, in Jerusalem for instance, as we have seen in connection with Peter's speech in Acts 3, there were groups which were willing to recognize Jesus as Messiah-designate but which thought that he would have to come back later to really inaugurate his reign.

What Paul is doing is to insist on the linkage of all three elements: Jesus, the man from Nazareth who was killed on the cross but who is the Messiah nevertheless is also lord already, right now, even though the establishment of his reign is not yet complete, as Paul himself had told the Corinthians in a previous letter: "The last enemy death is being abolished" (1.Cor. 15.26), i.e. the definitive establishment of the Messiah's reign is still in progress. The proclamation of this fact, i.e. that Jesus = Messiah = Lord, as Paul has said before to the Corinthians, is either foolishness or stumblingblock (1 Cor. 1.18-25), but Paul refuses to dilute it in any way, and then as if further to offend or to challenge sensibilities among the Corinthians, who have evidently, after the advent of Paul's rivals, decided that a minister of theirs should emit a certain professional aura, he refuses to present himself as anything other than their servant on Christ's behalf — he will not assume the mantle of authority-figure which they seem now to want him to assume. To put this matter in contemporary terms (and to recall the role-model that, at the beginning of his career, a certain highly successful modern-day evangelist put all his efforts into shunning), Paul will do nothing to avoid the title of "baggy-pants preacher". In 1 Corinthians Paul talked about how the congregation had not advanced beyond the baby-stage. Their incapacity to see his glory when he insists on a single role for himself, namely that of the suffering servant, the role that the Messiah himself enacted, shows that they are still mired in this infantile stage. Paul proclaims and enacts for them (and also for us) just what that role and just what the second, the adult stage of Christian life ultimately entails.

He makes this uncompromising double proclamation, of Jesus = Christ = lord and of himself as servant, he now goes on to say, "because it is the God who says 'out of darkness light will shine' who shined in our hearts for there to be the illumination of the knowledge of the glory of God in the face of Jesus Christ." (4.6) In other words, it was God who had enabled him to make the double proclamation by giving him essential knowledge of what and where the true glory is. Once one has the knowledge of the glory of God in the face of Jesus Christ, one does not proclaim oneself. In a way, on both counts, this empowerment of Paul as the proper kind of herald seems to stand as an antitype to the charade of keeping up the old legal covenant, i.e. just as the veil had been over both the reading of the old covenant and over the hearts of the law-keepers who were still fixated on the extinguished ember of the old covenant as an efficacious repository of glory, so here by contrast there has to be a light both in the hearts of those who proclaim and embody the new covenant and also in the face of Jesus Christ. In another way, though, one has to admit that Paul is now not being stolidly consistent with his own earlier formulation of what has enabled him to be a servant and herald of the new covenant. Back at the end of chapter three he had claimed to gaze with unveiled face himself at the glory of God, i.e. in that chapter he himself and all the other members of the body of Christ were playing the role of Moses. Here Jesus Christ, in whose face the glory shines, seems to have assumed the role of Moses for himself, with Paul and other Christians now standing as the children of Israel before him. The general idea, however, seems to be the same as before, or rather a consistent application to the situation of Paul in Corinth can be derived from both figures (3.18 and 4.6), namely that Paul will not enter into competition with the rival preachers on the basis of any merits that he himself may possess.

The next verse makes this point completely clear: "We have this treasure in clay pots, in order that the surpassing quality of the power be of God and not from us." (4.7) Again, by using the metaphor of the commmonest household utensil, the clay pot used for everyday tasks (perhaps we are even supposed to think of a chamber pot here), by using this figure to describe himself, Paul is insisting on the common, cheap, cast-off or "baggy-pants" character of his ministry, doing nothing either to cosmeticize or to embellish it lest somehow he detract or distract from the main point, which is the message of the power and glory of God. He is by now rounding back to the idea with which he began, namely that of being led with Christ as a repulsive prisoner in God's triumphal procession, only now he gives certain more specific details of what it means to be thus paraded: "Afflicted in everything, yet not feeling that the walls are closing in around us, without resources and yet not despairing, pursued and yet not abandoned [i.e. to the enemy who is pursuing], cast down and yet not destroyed, at all times carrying around in our body the death of Christ, in order also that the life of Jesus might be revealed by our body. For we who are alive are always being handed over unto death for Jesus' sake, in order that the life of Jesus might be revealed by our mortal flesh. So that death is at work among us, but life among you." (4.8-12)

What Paul presents in a passage such as this one is a vision of the ultimate in Christian maturity, namely complete identification with Jesus in the role of suffering servant by whose stripes (in a way that is not always made perfectly clear) the benefit of healing and of new life devolves upon others. Of course in a skeptical age like our own we are driven to ask the question whether such behavior on the part of Paul (or for that matter on the part of Jesus) does not bespeak some form of psychopathology, the acting-out of what we like to call a martyr-complex. As we saw in a previous chapter Jesus had promised Peter and the others that there would be other rooms in his father's house, other opportunities to enact the role of Suffering Servant (John 14.1 ff. and John 21). For instance, when confronted with Jesus' prediction that he eventually would come to occupy one of those rooms, Peter had shown the normal human reaction of wanting to make sure that he was not receiving worse treatment than that of the other people around him: "Lord, what about this one?" (John 21.21) he had asked, meaning the beloved disciple. By contrast, Paul seems almost jealously eager to make sure that he will receive his fair or even more than his fair share of suffering. Paul speaks of a compulsion to preach and therefore suffer for the gospel (1 Cor. 9.16). Without doubt this compulsion was fueled in part by a desire to expiate for his past persecutions of the Hellenistic church and for his complicity in the murder of Stephen. It was also probably fueled by some profound understanding of and conviction about the need for reconciliation between Jewish monotheism and the Gentile world with its bewildering mixture of religious outlooks, which reconciliation could only have been accomplished by a Jew setting forth throughout the world and being buffeted so as to absorb the sepsis of hatred, on the one hand hatred from fellow Jews for the one who wanted to undermine the ramparts of their exclusive privileged system, and on the other hand hatred from Gentiles for the member of a religion which pretended to a status superior to that of any other human group. These compulsions on Paul's part could be delusions, the marks of a disturbed psyche, or they could be the insights of a religious genius, that kind of genius concerning which and by which we are driven to the sometimes baffled, sometimes awestruck concession that "Much madness is divinest sense."

If Paul is right though about death in him productive of life in others, then it is no wonder that he refuses to take time away from the kind of work that will continue producing such life in order to produce a dossier or to engage in the kinds of maneuvers that will make him look like a figure of fully certified religious authority. Furthermore he remains convinced that ultimately what he is doing will get through to the Corinthians, that (to speak in worldy terms) the course he is following will do more to commend him to them than any capitulation to the tactics of his rivals could ever do: "But having the same faithful spirit in keeping with what stands written, 'I evinced trust, therefore I began to speak', we also are evincing trust, we therefore are also speaking, knowing that the one who raised the lord Jesus will also with Jesus raise us and bring us into your presence." (4.13-14) Not that Paul would want to be brought into their presence as anything other than the sweating servant of God — he has not given up that idea of the role he must perform, it is in fact quite amazing how he holds fast to that idea throughout the anfractuosities of the passage we have been analysing. What Paul is really expressing is his confidence that eventually the God-spirit will shine in their hearts so that for them too there will be the illumination of the knowledge of the glory of God in the face of Jesus Christ and also in the face of Paul who accompanies him. To have this perception is to understand what one has been given by God. Paul at least wants to bring the Corinthians into this state of grateful babyhood: "All things are for your sake, in order that grace multiplying thanksgiving through a larger number might abound to the glory of God." (4.15)

But that is not all that Paul aims for, his hope for the Corinthians goes farther. In this same passage, after having contrasted the everlasting weight of glory that is accruing to him to the transitory afflictions which he is in the process of undergoing, having talked about the spiritual garment with which he can anticipate being "clothed upon" (4.16-5.10), Paul makes several final remarks about this matter of recommending himself. First of all he says that he hopes that they will eventually understand what he has really been doing, just as God does: "We then, knowing the fear of God, are seeking to convince human beings, but to God we have been made known. I hope also to have been made known in your consciences." (5.11) Seeking to persuade human beings is not the same as recommending himself: "We are not again recommending ourselves to you, but rather giving you an occasion to boast about us, in order that you might have something against those who boast in outward show and not in the heart." (5.12) He does not feel quite safe in boasting to human beings who may not yet understand him as well as God does, he checks himself in order not to be misunderstood: "For if we are out of our minds, it is to God. If we are within our right minds, it is to you. For the love of Christ constrains us so as to consider this fact, that one died for the sake of all, therefore all died." (5.13-14) Here Paul reintroduces his notion that in Christ's death all have died to the system of law, sin, and death. To repeat: it is one's comprehension of this fact that enables one to be born from above into Christian babyhood. But there is a farther calling, a farther goal of adulthood beyond this given baby-stage: "And he died for all, so that the ones who live might no longer live for themselves but rather for the one who died for all and was raised up." (5.15) To live for Christ in this sense is to become part of that enterprise that undertakes the redemption of the world.

v. LEVELS OF SERVICE FOR ALL

Paul exemplifies the ultimate in living for the members of Christ's body by sharing the form of the suffering servant. Not everyone is called to such an exalted level of Christian service, a fact which Paul acknowledges in one section of his first letter to the Corinthians: "For I think that God has set forth us apostles as the last [or least], verging on death, because we have become a spectacle to the world and to angels and to people." (4.9) In the passage that begins with this statement Paul seems to be setting the apostles apart as a separate category. The word "last" in this passage probably refers paradoxically to their status, meaning that it is no great thing to be an apostle as he conceives of that office, he is not under Peter's delusion that to be an apostle means reigning on some kind of throne with an ayatollah-type Messiah, he is convinced rather that to be an apostle means to perform the very lowest tasks, to become scum. He goes on to specify ways in which the apostles differ from the congregations which benefit from their work: "We are fools on behalf of Christ, but you are wise in Christ. We are weak, but you are strong. You have honor, we have none. Unto the present hour we hunger and thirst and go dressed in rags [worse than baggy pants] and are buffeted and go about homeless and labor, working with our hands." (4.10-12) What Paul has said thus far might only constitute the picture of a workaholic for Christ, someone who was almost frenzied for the cause, but in the next passage, which we have already looked at once, Paul interprets the meaning and the purpose of his labors: "When evil is spoken of us, we bless; when we are pursued, we patiently endure it; when we are slandered, we offer words of consolation. We have become as the garbage of the world, as the scum scoured off from all things until now." (4.13) The apostle is called to continue the work of the suffering servant, to drain off the (perhaps everlasting) abcess of the world's "torment, and loud lament, and furious rage."

Paul feels no resentment at the fact of his hardship as opposed to the relative comfort in Christ of his Corinthian congregation. "I'm not writing these things to chide you but as to instruct my beloved children. For if you have countless instructors in Christ, you do not have many fathers. For I begot you through the gospel in Jesus Christ." (4.14-15) This is extravagant language indeed, especially when one remembers the passage about birth from above in the prologue to the gospel of John (1.12-13), the passage which stated that the new family was generated from God rather than from any urging of a male. In some of the passages which we have looked at above, Paul seems to be equating himself with Christ, in this passage he might be said almost to be equating himself with God as a begetter of children in the divine family. One probably should not be too hard in pressing Paul's language here. What Paul is basically saying is that there is a group (the apostles) called to placard the office of redeemer that Jesus fulfilled. This group acts for the benefit of the more ordinary members of the body of Christ or rather it exists to keep generating such ordinary members (as Paul did in Corinth, i.e. he exhibited Christ to people there who were "pagans" and had never heard the gospel) and then, at least as Paul exemplifies it in his concern for the churches he has founded, the group of the apostles also exists to nurture, to bring up the babies in Christ whom it has begotten by its labors.

Paul seems to see a continuum connecting the supreme work of an apostle like himself and the tasks of more ordinary Christians, he uses the term "sacrifice" not just to apply to the kind of work he does but also to describe what more ordinary Christians need to undergo: "I therefore beseech you, brothers, by the mercies of God, to present your bodies a sacrifice, living, holy, pleasing to God, i.e. your rational worship." (Romans 12.1) No longer are we out of fear to present the bodies of dead animals to a fault-finding God, but in line with the merciful disposition of God which the Gospel makes known we are to present our own bodies, which have died to sin and been made alive to Christ, as a sacrifice to which our minds can subscribe, not one which is offered at some level of primitive or superstitious terror. "And don't be conformed to this age, but be changed in form by the renewal of the mind so that you can discover what the will of God is, the thing which is good and pleasing and perfect." (12.2) The latter part of the letter to the Romans contains an extended discussion of how this change can be carried out.

"This age", that is any age in which people must achieve status on the basis of their own efforts, tends to be characterized by self-centeredness. Paul, in describing what happens when a group of Christians help each other to move on to the second stage, is counseling the opposite outlook, i.e. he first cautions against any undue notions of one's own importance. In the first stage of the new life, the baby stage, there may be room for a little glorying in what God has done for "me" (cf. Raskolnikov in *Crime and Punishment*), but in the second stage, the ego must be put in proper perspective: "For I by the grace that was given to me say to everyone that is among you not to hold too high an opinion of himself but to set his mind so as to be sensible, to each one as God has measured the quantity of faith." (Romans 12.3) The rationale behind this piece of advice is that no one, whatever his or her gifts, is an independent entity, each person in the church contributes to the functioning of the body but could not exist apart from the body. It is the life of the body that matters most, not because individuality is unimportant but because by belonging to the group, individuals partake of an abundance of life which would be beyond any of them singly.

Having established the fact that the importance of the individual needs to be put in perspective, Paul then goes on to describe different kinds of desirable outlooks and qualities. "Let love be unfaked. Hating what is evil, clinging to the good, devoted to each other with the love of siblings, outdoing each other in honor, not lazy with respect to diligence, bubbling with spirit, serving the lord . . ." (12.9-12) It is always well, when dealing with lists of virtues in Paul, to remember that Jesus furnished him with his standard. When the lists of injunctions threaten to become too etiolated in one's mind as one reads them, one should try to picture Jesus as the exemplar of them; for instance, when Paul says "Live toward each other in harmony of mind, not having proud thoughts, but associating with the humble [or perhaps = performing humble tasks]," (12.16) one should picture Jesus performing the despised task of foot-washing, as an example to his disciples that they too should become servants and thereby show how really free they are. The church is that group which is committed to carrying on the life of the one whose "heart the lowliest burden on itself did lay".

The list goes on and at times does not seem to differ too much from what any group or society would prescribe as an ideal set of characteristics among its members. At other times, though, it startles with the kind of paradoxical precept that one can also find in the teachings of Jesus, whom Paul in fact is probably quoting directly when he says to the Roman church "Bless those who persecute you, bless and do not curse." (12.14) In precepts such as this one he is counseling more than masochism: he is urging the church to extend Jesus' work of condemning sin in the flesh, of not cooperating with evil. "Do not take revenge, beloved ones, but give place to the wrath, for it stands written, Revenge belongs to me, I will repay, says the lord. But if your enemy is ever hungry, feed him. If he is ever thirsty, give him something to drink. For by doing this, you heap coals of fire upon his head. Do not be overcome by evil but overcome evil with good." (12.19-21) The wrath to which Paul alludes here is that process which he has described in the first chapter of this same letter to the Romans, a process of progressive degradation in the human species, a process which results from a failure on the part of human beings to give thanks to God, a process which God gives rein to since he respects the freedom of human beings. In a startling formulation, Paul suggests that we should leave the working out of this process to God while in the meantime we human beings undertake the task of ministering to our enemies so as to purify them. It is almost as if we humans were to show more concern than God does inasmuch as the wrath constitutes on God's part a sort of indifference, a turning of his back. God lets those who fail to acknowledge and give thanks to him descend into further degradation according to what Paul says in the first chapter, but we purify them by giving them water or food; the burning coals which we heap on their head are to be associated with the coal which the angel uses to cleanse the unclean lips of the prophet in chapter 6 of Isaiah rather than with any burning sense of shame which an enemy might feel at being shown the rarer virtue of compassion as contrasted to revenge. That the model for this kind of behavior is again the career of Jesus is shown by the final summarizing verse. He was not overcome by evil because he forgave it, he overcame evil with good, he in fact transformed the evil that was directed against him into the greatest good, and Paul is telling his readers to do likewise.

It is clear then that in the second stage of the new life into which one is born from above, demands are made upon one, sometimes extraordinary demands such as that one should be so far beyond self-centeredness as to see and respond to need on the part of one's enemy. Paul is concerned that this demand be seen as something other than the demand which the law had made, as when he says in another place "If you are led by the spirit, you are not under the law." (Gal. 5.18) Not that Paul, any more than God, is unconcerned about seeing the fulfillment of the righteous deed of the law, but his point is that if one really enters into the viewpoint of the divine society, such things as the fulfillment of the law will be taken care of incidentally as part of a wider outlook and endeavor. Paul summarizes this conviction by saying "Don't owe anybody anything except to love one another, for the one who loves the other has fulfilled the law." (Rom. 13.8) Don't get caught in trying to work up from square one of the legal system, but rather love one another and all the things of the law shall be added unto you. This result will come about because the law is basically a system which exists to prevent injury to persons, and "Love does not work injury to the neighbor. Love therefore is the fulfilment of the law." (13.10)

But love is much more than that. It is the means by which we surpass the egocentricity which the law, as Paul has analyzed it, only seems to foster as part of a system in which status depends on striving for merit, in which each person tries to lay claim to his or her own standing before God or in the scale of human reckoning. As Paul goes on to discuss the new law, the law of love, in several places, he shows a way by which we can be released from limited egocentric outlooks: "For you were called for freedom, brothers. Only not for freedom to be an opportunity to the flesh [i.e. egocentric perspective], but rather serve one another through love." (Gal. 5.13) In two places (Romans and 1 Corinthians) he demonstrates the law of love in the context of certain squabbles over food. In Romans, unless Paul is only taking a hypothetical case, there are two groups that he has heard about, one that can eat meat, another that will eat only vegetables. He never makes clear what the basis for the position of the vegetarians is. Rome was a stew of many different kinds of religions and quasi-religions. There could have been, in the Christian church there, converts who had come in from some kind of religious sect, perhaps one that believed in metempsychosis, the transmigration of human souls into the bodies of animals. Another possibility, maybe even probability is that Judaizers carrying the food decree which, in our opinion had been agreed on after Peter had been granted his vision of the great tablecloth and had gone to Cornelius's house (Acts 10-11), had been active in Rome, and that certain super-scrupulous members of the Roman church, trying to observe this decree, were avoiding all meats so as to be sure that they would avoid the sub-set of meats prohibited by the decree, namely meats from which the blood had not been drained.

Either way, Paul is addressing himself to some sort of conflict in the Roman church, and he begins giving his advice by saying: "Receive the one who is weak in the faith, not so as to dispute opinions." (14.1) By "the one who is weak in the faith" he here means a vegetarian. One cannot from this passage conclude that Paul was against vegetarianism *per se* or in every case: what he is dealing with here is a kind of scrupulous or legalistic vegetarianism which, if sanctioned, would threaten to make the church fall from grace back into a system of do's and don't's, at least in the culinary sphere. It is for this reason that he says "The one who has a trusting attitude eats all things, the one who is weak eats vegetables." (14.2) Given the fact that there is this discrepancy within the church, Paul then goes on to say "Let the one who eats not treat the one who doesn't eat [i.e. meat] with contempt, let the one who doesn't eat not judge the one who does eat, for God has received him." (14.3) In thus cautioning his readers, Paul is being uncannily accurate and up-to-our-present-moment about human psychology as it manifests itself in many kinds of situations, including churches: the great danger for the one who is liberated is that he or she will show contempt for the backward (perhaps we can say the more conservative) brother or sister. The one who is weak in the faith will tend to judge the liberated ones (interestingly enough, in a Christian context trust seems to be strength, whereas judgmental vigilance equals weakness). Paul urges each side to avoid the reactions typical of it. By so doing, he is showing how love would work in this particular case.

By means of love the members of a church can achieve some of the objectives which Paul has already advocated, such as not ascribing an undue importance to oneself by acting as a judge: "Who are you to judge another's household servant? He stands and falls in reference to the same lord. And he will stand, for God is able to make him stand." (14.4) But Paul is asking for more too; in appealing for some kind of settlement, he is really asking each side to enter into the viewpoint of the other: "One person takes each day as it comes, another judges every day. Let each be fully assured in his own mind. The one who is concerned about the day is concerned in reference to the lord. And the one who eats eats in reference to the lord, for he give thanks to God. And the one who does not eat does not eat in reference to the lord and gives thanks to God." (14.5-6)

In this analysis of a way out of the squabble it is God who serves as the point of contact: if each one of us is doing what he or she does in reference to the same God, then nothing ought to divide us. "For none of us lives to himself and none dies to himself. For if we live, we live in reference to the lord, and if we die, we die in reference to the lord. Whether we live then or whether we die, we belong to the Lord." (14.7-8) It is this viewpoint that allows Paul so exquisitely to balance the claims of each side in this dispute; he enacts his own counsel. "We therefore ought no longer to judge one another. But rather decide on this, not to put a stumbling block or obstacle before your brother. I know and am convinced by the lord Jesus that nothing of itself is unclean, except to the one who thinks it to be unclean, to that one it is unclean. For if on account of food your brother is being saddened, you are no longer walking according to love. Do not by your food destroy the one on whose behalf Christ died." (14.14-15)

Paul on this occasion does not really explain how the sibling in Christ can be destroyed by someone else's food. He does seem to offer at least a partial explanation in 1 Corinthians when he deals with a similar dispute, although on this occasion the crux is eating food offered to idols rather than eating meat. There is for this controversy a completely enlightened and liberated positon, which Paul espouses: "We know that there is no idol in the world and that there is no god except one." (1 Corinthians 8.4) But not everybody has this knowledge (8.7) or not everybody is stable or assured in such knowledge as yet. "Some out of the habit of the idol until now are eating what is to them an idol-offering, and their conscience, since it is weak, is being polluted." (8.7) Not that this activity of theirs is really a problem, since "Food will not present us to God". (8.8) Just as earlier in this letter, where he is talking about another kind of taste, the church members' taste in apostles, Paul says that salvation does not hinge on the matter he is discussing. Perhaps the ultimate pettiness of this matter and matters that he has had to deal with in other churches is what distresses him, i.e. why should the body of Christ be split up over secondary matters (music programs might be an equivalent in many a contemporary church)? On the other hand, though, the people whom he is discussing, having come out of a pagan culture rife with idol-offerings, are like rehabilitated alcoholics who are forever at risk and must therefore deny themselves even a thimbleful of liquor: these people whom Paul is talking about here are not strong enough yet and may never be strong enough to resist falling back into their former outlook: "If someone sees you who have knowledge reclining at table in the place of the idol, will not his conscience, since it is weak, be encouraged to eat the idol-offering?" (9.10) The liberated person can handle the idol-offering with an enlighted outlook, but such free and easy eating would not be scatheless to the one for whom the idol once had numinous power, the old spell might overcome his or her psyche again, at which point there comes into effect the principle that "the one who doubts whether he should eat has already been condemned, because it is not out of an attitude of trust." (Rom. 14.23)

Paul goes on in 1 Corinthians to ask a series of resounding questions. "Am I not free? Am I not an apostle? Have I not seen the lord Jesus? Are you not my work by [or in] the lord?" (9.1) These questions seem to constitute his way of saying that he has certain rights and that he could exercise them if he so chose, or rather he could exercise them if he were not under the same precaution that he has laid upon the Romans: "Let not evil be said of your good thing", i.e. your freedom (14.16), don't use your freedom in such a way that evil could be said of it with justification because it has brought about the destruction of another. Paul presents an interesting relativism here: even the good is not good at all times. Love is not a series of precepts set in stone, either positive or negative precepts. The commandment to love is a commandment to use your imagination (cf. Shelley:

"The great instrument of moral good is the imagination"), to surmount your own little limited ego. The arguments concerning food in several of Paul's letters show how love meets all the requirements of the law in that it avoids injury to others, but what Paul is probably showing too is that it delivers the person who is able to live by it into another phase of existence and maturity, especially if in attaining unto an apprehension of another person's need we are really encountering Jesus ("Inasmuch as ye did it unto the least of these . . . "). Seen in this light, the imperative to love is more in the nature of a revelation, a gracious gift, than in the nature of an onerous obligation.

vi. LOVE THE TRUE MATURITY

Whatever its nature, love is, according to Paul, the mark of true Christian maturity in a person, no matter what function that person may have been gifted to perform or called upon to perform as part of the body of Christ. The abiding importance of love to the Christian life is the burden of the thirteenth chapter of 1 Corinthians, Paul's famous hymn to love's importance, which surpasses all else in the new life. Except perhaps for the twenty-third psalm, this chapter is probably the scriptural passage most familiar to the greatest number of people, and yet in the light of the categories that we have been looking at in Paul's letters above, it may not mean exactly what it has always been assumed to mean.

Paul begins this chapter, this hymn, with an assertion about the emptiness, apart from love, of the kinds of gifts which the Corinthian Christians have displayed in such abundance and which Paul has been talking about in his first letter to them. "If I speak with the tongues of people and of angels, but do not have love, I have become a noisy brass or a wailing cymbal. And if I have prophecy and know all mysteries and all knowledge and if I have all faith so as to remove mountains, but do not have love, I am nothing. And if I give away all my possessions and if I hand my body over so that I may boast [or in some manuscripts "so that I may be burned"], but do not have love, I am not profited in any way." (1 Cor. 13.1-3) Having said this much, he then goes on to try to define love or rather he discusses the traces, both positive and negative, left on the moral world by love, the ways in which it does or does not manifest itself — the thing itself is somewhat elusive, ungraspable, like God or certain sub-atomic particles — "Love is patient, love is kind, it is not jealous, love is not a braggart, it is not arrogant, it does not act disgracefully, it does not seek its own things, it is not exasperated, it does not keep tabs on evil, it does not rejoice in injustice, but it rejoices along with the truth. Love keeps all things in confidence [or "puts up with everything"], believes all things, hopes all things, endures all things." (13.4-7) This is Paul's working definition of the mature phase of the birth from above, this is a picture of the life into which the birth from above should issue.

Any person who presumes to have undergone the birth from above, or any group which presumes to be acting as the body of Christ, needs very carefully to check its behavior against the picture presented in these verses. At a moment in history when judgements are tending to be thrown about rather cavalierly, when certain groups are claiming to have their own kind of hammerlock on the "truth", it might be wise to single out some of the statements Paul has made in this passage to see what kind of standard they suggest.

"Love does not seek its own things": this means that love does not try to drive its own program through, does not insist on its own version of, say, the religious calling, as if no other person or group could possibly have received a scintilla of the truth, love does not roll a religious steamroller over the expression of other versions of the will and nature of God; this aspect of love is related to love's not being arrogant.

"Love does not keep tabs on evil": this assertion is related to Jesus' prohibition of judgment, but it goes farther, it recommends a sort of charitable amnesia, and it deprives any person or group of the license to act as an accusatory bookkeeper. "God does not need/Either man's works or his own gifts," especially not this kind of gift, this kind of kept ledger-book. Individuals or groups who pretend to carry out this function on God's behalf would do well to remember the remark that Paul makes in another place: "we must all appear before the judgement seat of Christ" (2 Cor. 5.10), there to receive in kind what we have given out in this life: if we have given out judgement, we will receive judgement, if we have given out mercy, we will receive mercy. If we start keeping records on others, then someone may be keeping records on us. The best policy would be to throw down the record-books: "Pull down thy vanity,/I say pull down."

"[Love] does not rejoice in injustice, but it rejoices along with the truth": In Greek the word which we have translated "injustice" comprises the root *dik*, on which such crucial New Testament terms as righteous, righteousness, and justification are built and some of the implications of which we have dicussed in previous chapters. The word which we have translated as "injustice" has to do with the opposite of the righteous state, but we need to remember that for God the righteous state obtains when inequities have been corrected, when wrongs have been righted, when the oppressed and the victimized have been restored to what they have coming to them as human beings, as the brothers and sisters of those who have enough (or maybe too much). "Injustice" does not refer to a state in which various so-called sins have gone unpunished: Paul is not saying here that love is long-faced until every last jot and tittle of punitive sentencing has been carried out but rather that love does not rejoice in any system of inequity or oppression. As for the "truth" which, according to Paul, love does rejoice together with: at the risk of repetitiveness, we will repeat that Hebrew truth does not involve the strict maintenance of some kind of repressive or fault-finding standard but rather the virtues of reliability and faithfulness; love rejoices when these virtues have been made manifest, when the church bodies forth the God the import of whose name (literally "I will be what I will be" or "I will cause to be what I will cause to be" — Exodus 3.14) might be phrased as "If you get it, I'll be there, if you need it, I'll make it".

Having tried to give some idea of what love is or rather some idea of how it does and does not act, Paul then proceeds to locate it along the line of growth in Christian existence. "Love does not fall away at any time. If there are prophecies, they will be done away with. If there are tongues, they shall cease. If there is knowledge, it will be done away with. When that which is mature comes, what is in part will pass away." (13.8) These verse and those which follow from them have usually been taken to refer to, on the one hand, the here and now in which we human creatures live, and, on the other hand, the afterlife, the eternal realm, i.e. Paul is thought to be talking about the impermanence of every kind of human gift, even those that are somehow divinely inspired. But if this were so, Paul would then be putting the climax, the perfection of the Christian life off into some future mode of existence, whereas we think that he is talking about love as the ultimate maturity available to members of the body of Christ here in this world. The phrase "when that which is mature comes" is the crux to any interpretation of Paul's meaning in this passage. The Greek word *teleios* is often translated by the English word "perfect", when the implication of the Greek word would be better reproduced by some such English word as "mature" or even "fully ripened". Hence the choice of the English word "mature" in our translation. But what kind of maturity? We think that Paul is talking about full growth within whatever Christian function a given person may have been called to perform. It does not matter what your particular gift is (as long as you realize that every gift has its supremely important function in the eyes of God); what does matter is that in your exercise of it you manifest love. In this passage Paul seems almost to be stating that all the splendid gifts that the Corinthian church has shown itself to be in possession of are part of an as yet immature phase, perhaps these gifts do not merit being placed as far back as the baby-stage of merely receiving the milk (although in a moment Paul is going to mention talking like a baby, as if in fact the stage of spiritual gifts such as speaking in tongues really was just part of being an infant), but still they are not totally ripe or mature, certainly not something to boast about or to rest content with. Paul has confidence that the Corinthian Christians will grow out of the infancy of such gifts into the maturity of love.

Such a reading would be more in keeping with Paul's use of the Greek word *nepios*, "baby," in this letter. All throughout this letter he has used it in connection with a stage of the Christian life which, although necessary as the portal to the new life, eventually needs to be gotten beyond: "When I was a baby, I was speaking like a baby, I was thinking like a baby, I was reckoning like a baby. When I became a man, I got rid of the things of a baby. For now in an obscure image we are seeing things by means of a mirror, but then face to face. Now I am knowing in part, then I shall know just as I have been known" (13.11-12) Paul could be using the adverbs "now" and "then" to refer to the present life and to the life to come. On the other hand, identifying himself with the Corinthian Christians, he could also be using them to refer to present stages of the Christian life, first the baby stage, then the stage of love that lies beyond that. The clue to this kind of interpretation comes in the allusion to seeing face to face, which takes us back to Exodus 34, to Moses removing the veil and talking face to face to God, receiving infusions of the divine glory. In 2 Corinthians, Paul shows how "we all", by whom, in context, he means the divine society in its mature phase through which the spirit circulates, and which the spirit sustains, "we all with unveiled face gazing at the glory of God are having our form changed into the same image from glory unto glory just as from the lord-spirit" (2 Cor. 3.18) — as we saw, the divine society here is shown to be surpassing Moses, the divine society has access to an "eterne in mutabilitie" infusion of the divine light, passing from glory unto glory, an infusion which will never fade.

If we connect the mention in 1 Corinthians of seeing face to face with this passage in 2 Corinthians, then Paul would seem to be talking, in the hymn to love, about the mature as opposed to the baby phase of the new life into which a person has to be born from above. In the baby phase, one does not look upon the divine light directly, with unveiled face — this kind of direct looking is the privilege of the mature phase. In the baby phase, even though it has been made possible by the spirit, one is still thinking of "me"; if he had been using imagery from Exodus 34 for both sides of the metaphoric divide at this point in his hymn to love in 1 Corinthians, Paul might have said that in the baby-phase some sort of veil remains over the faces or the hearts of persons, but instead he uses the metaphor of a cheap mirror of polished metal in which whatever image one happens to be looking at will appear imperfectly. The idea is evidently that as a Christian baby one is seeing God in this mirror, but that then, when one becomes mature, one turns around and looks at him directly. This two-step process bears a certain resemblance to Plato's parable of the cave in which one sees shadows being thrown by shapes, which stand for the eternal forms. We in this life, according to Plato, are not able to turn around and actually see what is casting the shadows (unless we are philosphers). In Paul's hymn to love, though, this privilege is available to those who move out of the baby stage with its spiritual "stunts" such as prophecy and "knowledge" into the mature stage of love.

vii. BACKSLIDINGS.

Paul eloquently presents this sort of vision of the divine society in its mature operation, but what he often has to deal with in the specific churches which he is addressing in his letter is something far less advanced, he often has to deal with various kinds of erosion and slippage back into infantile stages or into stages even farther back than these. For instance, to the same church at Corinth which is going to hear the hymn to love, to a church that is which prides itself on the possession of all kinds of spiritual gifts in addition to the one inexpressible gift of God's acceptance of them as children, we find Paul saying, "And I, brothers, was not able to speak to you as to spiritual persons but as to fleshy, as to babies in Christ. For I gave you milk to drink, not solid food. For you weren't able yet, nor are you able now. For you are still fleshly" (1 Cor. 3.1-3) Paul has a specific reason for thus characterizing them: "For where there is jealousy and strife among you, are you not fleshly and walking in a human way?" (1 Cor. 3.3) The strife which Paul has in mind concerns factionalism, the attachment of different groups to different leaders of the church, some to Paul, some to Apollos, some to Cephas, and some to Jesus as if he were just another one of the (in the modern sense) charismatic personalities to whom allegiance could be paid. Paul is disturbed at the undue importance that is being paid to mere servants in the garden which the Corinthian church constitutes ("neither is the one who planted anything nor the one who watered but rather God who gives the growth" — 3.7). He is also disturbed at the setting up of little rival colonies within what should be a united society, a society in which the members mutually serve and sustain each other; the energy given to sustaining one's own little faction is energy drained off from the work which the body as a whole could be performing.

In a change of metaphor he then re-describes his role in relation to the role that the church he has established must go on to play after he has finished his work: "According to the grace of God given to me, as a wise master builder I laid the foundation, but another will build upon it. No one can lay another foundation besides the one that is laid, which is Jesus Christ." (3.10-11) It is the job of the church members coming after Paul to build on the foundation which he has laid. There are of course various conceptions of what kind of building to raise upon this foundation, i.e. of what a church should do and be, and these conceptions will eventually be tested by surrounding elements and conditions, perhaps elements and conditions of an extreme type, as in times of crisis: "If someone builds upon the foundation gold, silver, precious stones, wood, grass, straw, of each one the work shall become revealed, for the day will make it known, because by fire it is being revealed. And of each person, the work such as it is the fire will test it." (3.13-13) Paul at this point makes it clear that one's standing before God does not depend upon how well one's chosen material weathers the ensuing conditions: "If someone's work which he will build will remain, he will receive a reward. If someone's work will be burned, he will suffer a loss, but he himself will be saved, in this way as by fire." (3.15)

In a formulation worthy of that same Stephen whose death by stoning he had once witnessed and approved of, i.e. evincing a conception of the place where God dwells as something other than a building in Jerusalem made by human hands, Paul now summarizes with a question what he has just been saying: "Do you not know that you [plural, i.e. the Christian group] are the temple of God and that the spirit of God dwells among you [plural again, i.e. the group is the locus of the spirit]?" (3.16) He asks this question so that the Corinthians will know what they are ruining if they engage in strife. He has said (in verse 15) that if one's building did not weather whatever trying conditions the time brought, then the builder himself or herself would be saved (being built upon the one foundation Jesus). His prediction is not so hopeful for the one who ruins the temple "If someone ruins the temple of God, God will ruin this one." (3.17) One wonders if this prediction is not, in Paul, roughly equivalent to Jesus' warnings about the unforgivable sin against the Holy Spirit, namely that of calling the work of the Holy Spirit satanic (Mark 3.29 and parallels). In the present passage from Paul, the Christian group is the temple of the Holy Spirit, to ruin the group would be another kind of attack on the Holy Spirit. It would be hard to decide for sure about any connection between the two sins; the penalty in both cases seems to be equally severe.

From the turn which Paul's thought now takes, one gathers that the threat from strife of ruination to the temple comes when someone thinks of himself or herself as knowing everything, when someone manifests the arrogance which is the opposite of love (1 Corinthians 13.4). Paul's antidote to this kind of stuck-up self-assurance is severe. "If in this age someone among you thinks he's wise, let him become a fool in order to become wise." (3.18) It is not that, in another sense, church members are not supremely lifted up, especially when one considers the message which Paul continues to reiterate: "All things are yours, all things are yours whether we're speaking of Paul or Apollos or Cephas or the world or life or death or present or future, you are Christ's and Christ is God's." (3.21-3) Church members never stop needing to receive infusions of this their original "baby food", the milk which they received, the message of their acceptance which allowed them to be born from above into the new life (just as, on the physical level, people never stop needing to receive milk or its equivalent in calcium-content so as to maintain the soundness of their bones); as in the popular hymn, they need to keep on hearing the old, old story of Jesus and his love, the scandalous message of the cross which is the basis of their salvation, but this milk is earmarked for them insofar as they belong to the body of Christ, it is not for individual consumption so as to puff people up.

The descent into dissent, as illustrated by this passage from 1 Corinthians, is one way in which the members of a church can fail to advance into the more mature stage of responsible love. In the letter to the Galatians, Paul is dealing with the tendency of Christians to regress even beyond the baby-stage clear back into what had been Paul's old "pre-natal" life under the law. It was not quite the old life of the Galatians inasmuch as they had been (from Paul's point of view) enslaved under another religious system, a system of homage to what Paul calls the elemental powers. The Galatians had been adherents of some sort of pagan religion (modern scholarship remains divided concerning the exact nature of it), then had become Christians, but then under the influence of Judaizers (who seemed to hound Paul wherever he went) they showed signs of wanting to assume the burden of the law, the earnest of which desire was for their males to undergo circumcision. Paul is so amazed at this development that he entertains the idea of their having been brought under a spell: "O foolish Galatians, who has bewitched you, to whom Jesus Christ was publicly displayed crucified. I only want to learn this from you: did you receive the spirit from works of the law or from the preaching of faithfulness? Are you foolish to this extent, that having started in the spirit you now end up in the flesh? Did you undergo such things in vain, if indeed it was in vain? The one who supplies you with the spirit and works with powers among you, was it from works of the law or from the preaching of faithfulness?" (Gal. 3.1-5) The faithfulness to which Paul is alluding is probably that of Jesus. It is by his faithfulness to the promises of God that Paul and the Galatians are being saved.

In a long and interesting argument based on scripture, Paul contrasts the system of the law, every adherent to which is under a curse, to the system of Christ's faithfulness by which people are redeemed: "Christ set us free from the curse of the law by becoming a curse on our behalf" (Gal. 3.13) Here again Paul is referring to the price which had to be paid so that God's forgiveness could be real: in some real way God had to be the victim of human hostility so as to forgive hostile humans. Paul then introduces the interesting notion that there was first a promise made to Abraham and to his seed (which, because the word for seed in both the Hebrew and Greek texts of Genesis is singular, Paul takes to mean one person, namely Jesus), the promise being that through Abraham and his seed all the nations would be blessed, and that the law which came four hundred thirty years later could not cancel this promise. (Gal. 3.8-18) For Paul in this passage the law is an interim expedient which sin necessitates; the law will only be in effect until the seed of Abraham, the heir of the promise, comes. (3.19) Not that the law is in contradiction to the promise: to the proposition that it might be in contradiction to the promise, Paul replies with his favorite expression of vehement disagreement: "May that thought never arise!" (3.21) He might than have gone on to give an analysis of what goes wrong within the legal system like the analysis which we have looked at already in Romans, but instead, in this case, he prefers simply to record how the failure of the law to effect righteousness and salvation has worked to the ultimate long-term benefit of the human race: "the law declared all things to be prisoners under sin so that from the faithfulness of Jesus Christ, the promise might be given to those who have trust." (3.22) The idea is basically the same as in Romans; those under the law always ends up being bankrupt, only in this case Paul argues that the law helps them to appreciate the gift; there is nothing to do but turn and accept the free gift of God.

The Colossian church constitutes another group that is threatening to fall from a system of grace back into a system in which people are expected to earn their own salvation by merit. In dealing with them, Paul gives an unusually vivid and revealing picture of the perils of the self-reliance situation, which can only end in failure; he also gives an eloquent description of the new life which has been made possible by Jesus. The signs of danger which Paul warns the Colossians against are like those he warns the "foolish Galatians" against: "Don't let anyone judge you by food and by drink and by respect of a feast or of a new moon or of a sabbath." (Col. 2.16; cf. Gal. 4.8-11) These signs of danger have to do with calendrical observances that supposedly can save or damn us depending on whether or not we keep them. Paul tells the Colossians not to fall into the trap of being judged on the basis of these things "which are a shadow of the things that are to be, i.e. the body of Christ." (2.17)

These observances are illusions compared to the reality of life within the Christian group, the divine family, therefore "let no one falsely enter into judgement against you, wishing to do so by 'humility' and 'angelic piety', claiming special powers on the basis of what he's seen, puffed up in vain by the mind of his flesh and not holding on to the head, from which the whole body supplied and brought together through the joints and ligaments grows with the growth which is from God." (2.18-19) These instructions are both painfully direct and painfully difficult to implement at any time. Paul is evidently being ironic (hence our quotations around the words "humility" and "angelic piety" in the text), caricaturing a kind of self-appointed religious-cum-inquistorial zeal embodied by a type of person who claims to have a special appointment "from above." The real kind of "from above" which Paul contrasts to such fanaticism of the Satan, seeking to undermine people's assurance with its spiritual nitpicking, is Christ as head of his body, which is the Christian group. He employs an idea of the head giving to the rest of the body which he has derived from contemporary medical thinking. [8] The test of any religious pronouncement is whether it is compatible with the structure of the somatic system which has Christ as its head and as its nourishing source; in terms of such a test, the harassment about observances to which the Colossians are being subjected derives from no true religious motive and should be ignored: "If with Christ you died from the elemental powers, why as if you were living in the world do you have decrees imposed upon you?" (2.20)

Paul goes on to enumerate some of the kinds of decrees they are consenting to have imposed upon them, he quotes some of the directives they have been following: "Don't touch or taste or handle, all which things [Paul then goes on to point out] are unto decay in the process of being used, according to the commandments and teachings of human beings, which things contain a teaching of wisdom by self-imposed piety and humility and unsparing severity toward the body, not of any use in subduing the flesh." (2.21-23) The modern world would provide some apt illustrations of the kinds of practices Paul seems to have in mind here, e.g, strenuous programs of exercise and meditation, none of which Paul is condemning *per ipsos*: what he does deplore is the pretence that by themselves such practices can save. The language he uses here is very compressed and sometimes a little confusing: for instance, he probably means that the things one touches and tastes rather than the actions of tasting and touching decay by the process of being used. Also there is some doubt as to the meaning of several terms in this passage. The Greek word which we have translated as "self-imposed piety" literally means "will-worship" — how apt such a term can seem to an age like ours in which we read about relationships being shipwrecked on the reef of one or the other partner's absorption in ascetic exercise-programs, will-worship at the expense of personal relationships, will-worship as a sort of pool of Narcissus, but the exact reference of Paul's meaning remains uncertain. With relatively little evidence to go on, i.e. long before the Dead Sea scrolls were discovered, Bishop Lightfoot, the great Nineteenth Century New Testament scholar, thought that Paul had the Essenes in mind when he wrote this passage, and with more evidence at hand about the severe practices of that idealistic sect, we can now marvel at the prescience of some of Lightfoot's intuitions, but there have been other suggestions since Lightfoot's time and the term "will-worship" remains *sub judice*. The final phrase of the sentence is also ambiguous: the Greek can mean either that the self-imposed practices which Paul is talking about are of no use in subduing the passion of the flesh or that they are of no good except to satisfy the passion of the flesh. Either way, if we remember that for Paul the flesh means the embattled egocentric outlook, the existential redoubt from within which we suppose that we are on our own, what Paul is leading up to in this passage is that unless it turns to receive the free gift of God, the self remains isolated and unfulfilled, that ultimately these practices of so-called self-help are futile.

Paul suggests an alternative for those who have been born from above into the new life: "If then you have been raised together with Christ, seek the above-things, where Christ is seated at the right hand of God. Think about the above-things, not the things which are on the earth. For you have died, and your life is hid with Christ in God. Whenever Christ, who is your life, is revealed, then you also are being revealed with him in glory." (3.1-4) This passage has usually been interpreted as recommending some sort of other-worldly eschatological outlook. In reference to such an interpretation it might be well to remember that when Jesus talked about heavenly as opposed to earthly things in chapter 3 of the Gospel of John, we saw that he was referring to the career of the Son of Man/Suffering Servant and its ultimate outcome. In other words, when Jesus made such a contrast between earthly and heavenly, the heavenly was not necessarily something refined out of any connection to things on this earth. But apart from any usage of these terms in John, we can say that when Paul uses the metaphor of dying and then being absorbed into the resurrection-life of Christ (here "hid" with him in God), he is usually referring to new life on this earth in the divine family. Furthermore, against those who see this passage as containing promises in its last sentence about the Second Coming, conventions of the aorist tense in Greek suggest that the revelation of Christ which is being talked about is something that happens at various points over and over again ("whenever") and not some great once-and-for-all eschatological appearance, or in terms of another Greek usage the revelation could also be the sum total of numerous successive appearances (constative aorist): Paul could, that is, be talking about successive manifestations of the Christ, who as head (to re-use Paul's medical metaphor) is what sends life out through his body; Paul could be saying that whenever the Christ is being revealed the members of his body are being revealed, he could be talking about the way in which Christ is now dependent upon his followers for whatever manifestation he will continue to enjoy in this world, in sum he could be talking about the way in which the head and its members are inextricably interinvolved and cannot exist without each other.

The next paragraphs support the idea that in this passage Paul is talking about the life of the church called to be the Son of Man, i.e. the righteous servants of Yahweh, about the church called to be such servants in this world and also called eventually to reign on high, to receive glory from the Ancient of Days as in the Book of Daniel. In contrast to the practices that have been imposed upon them, Paul talks about the kind of self-mortification which he would like to see the Colossians practice: "Mortify your members that are on the earth then, sexual immorality, uncleanness, passion, evil longing, and covetousness, which is to say idolatry, on account of which things the wrath of God comes upon the sons of disobedience." (3.5-6) It is safe at the outset to make one generalization, namely that a Twentieth Century reader, especially one who is reading passages such as this one only in an English translation, should not plunge in and assume that the meaning of each term in the list is immediately self-evident. For instance, we have translated the Greek word *porneia* as "sexual immorality" without being able to decide just how general or how specific the term's refernce may be. There is some reason to think that Paul may have been using it to refer only to prostitution, but if he were, one would then have to take into consideration the connection, in the ancient world, between prostitution and certain state-sponsored religions. In other words, *porneia* branches out into historical complications. By mentioning it in this list, though, Paul does not intend simply to supply a reader with moral buckshot whereby to spray any or all sexual practices which happen to offend him or her, he may have in mind a specific ancient practice for which there is no exact modern equivalent. The fact that Paul gives the term "covetousness" a special interpretation should also warn a modern reader that Paul might have intended special interpretations for some of the other terms in his lists. The statement about the wrath of God is still another sign that Paul may have especially deep or theologically charged meanings for the terms of this list in mind. The wrath of God, as Paul defines it in the first chapter of Romans, is a labefaction of the moral order which is set in motion by a failure on the part of human beings to acknowledge and give thanks to their creator. It is not some random sort of Jovian fire and brimstone set whirling around the cosmos in order to put "the fear of God" into people. God, after all, is for Paul primarily kind (Rom. 2.4); it is not likely that terrorization would be one of a such a divine being's tactics. At any rate this passage urging people to mortify their members is full of pitfalls and requires delicacy and caution on the part of would-be exegetes.

What Paul is probably talking about in this passage is the need for one's members to die to the sin/law/flesh nexus which we discussed in an earlier section. In order to make the nature of this nexus more clear, he has specified some of the ways by which the flesh, which we have interpreted to mean the egocentric perspective, expresses its governing convictions, namely that as an individual person *I* am the center and focus of all reality and that other people are objects or mere commodities for my use. One reaches such a conclusion about the passage quoted above partly because of the goal toward which the process of mortification which it describes is aimed, namely the renewal of the human family according to the image of its creator, a family which is not divided into groups that show contempt for each other: "But now you yourselves must put aside all such things as wrath, fury, hateful feelings, injurious speech, shameful utterance out of your mouth [i.e. these human characteristics are part of that flesh which needs to be mortified too — sexuality, even if it were the main subject of the list quoted above, would not be Paul's only concern]. Don't tell lies against each other, lay aside the old humanity with its practices and put on the new which is being renewed for full recognition as a result of the image of its creator, where there is not Greek or Jew, circumcision or uncircumcision, barbarian, Scythian, slave, free, but Christ is all things and in all people." (3.8-11) With a statement like this one by Paul in mind, with a set of admonitions like these, one would have to doubt that the kinds of preachers who hold up certain groups for constant cudgeling as examples of an extreme perfidy have really been born from above. Birth from above occurs so that the Balkanized human race can be subsumed in the divine family, which is the body which has Christ as its head conferring life upon the rest. The way to insure the birth from above of so-called outsiders ("so-called" because in God's mind there is no "out") is to grant them gracious invitation rather than to drive them away with condemnation — the condemnation of others may make the so-called inside group feel cozy, smug, snug, and secure, but it does nothing to forward God's plan for the redemption of the whole human race, the plan according to which those who love God are called (Rom. 8.28).

Snake-like, in the scenario which Paul would like to see implemented, the human race sheds the garment of its old manifestation and assumes the qualities of its new manifestation: "Put on then as chosen saints and beloved of God, inner feelings of compassion, kindness, humility [this time without the ironic offsetting quotation marks], meekness, patience, putting up with each other and forgiving yourselves if someone has cause for complaint against someone. And just as the lord has forgiven you, so you also forgive." (3.12-13) As with so many other general lists in Paul, perhaps the only way to understand this list to the fullness of its heights and depths is to meditate upon the life and the teachings of Jesus, he would be the model for the kind of life Paul is here propounding; lapses, regressions from the new life into things of the old "among which you walked at one time, when you lived among them" (2.7) could at all times be avoided by asking the question "Would Jesus feel the way I now am feeling?" Harsh judgmental attitudes, pseudo-prophetic invocations of the thunder of the divine wrath are almost sure signs of atavism into ways of the world: "The wrath of a man [interestingly enough the Greek word here can only refer to a male] does not bring about the justification of God." (James 1.20)

"Above all these things [let there be] love, which is the ligament of maturity." (Col. 3.14) Love is what binds people together into the mature stage of the new life. Paul is here couching the new life in terms of a society. Birth from above does not eventuate in solitude, one is born into the Christian group, the body of Christ. "And let the peace of Christ, into which you were called in one body, act as umpire among your hearts." (3.16) Paul had talked earlier about someone acting as a false umpire (*katabrabeuo*) by humility and angelic piety (both spurious). Here he nominates peace to act as true arbiter (*brabeuo*) among the members of the Christian body. "And become thankful" (3.15) Lack of thankfulness, as we recalled above from the first chapter of Romans, is what sets in motion the process which Paul refers to as the wrath of God, a process of moral deterioration on the part of human beings, a process which God does nothing to check since, like the ideal parent, he respects the autonomy of children. By contrast Paul urges the exercise of thankfulness upon the congregation in Colossae as one of the means by which they may be built up into mature adulthood.

viii. PAUL HIMSELF AS AN EXAMPLE OF SOMEONE BORN FROM ABOVE.

We have dealt so far, in our discussion of Paul, with his vision of what the birth from above might be and what it might lead on to and into. One would not exactly like to call these visions theoretical constructs, mainly because they arise as practical advice in specific church situations. They constitute glimpses of what a redeemed society might be, and they are often shot through with Paul's personal feelings and observations. Paul is not given to impersonal statements, he is always involved in his pronouncements. Nevertheless we in our discussions thus far have not exclusively focused on Paul himself as an example of the birth from above or of the new life. Perhaps one cannot focus exclusively on Paul, i.e. on Paul to the exclusion of all those church situations which concerned him, in a certain sense he did become those concerns, or as he himself said, for him to live was Christ (Philippians 1.21). Still it does seem that in propounding a vision of a new world, a moral theologian or an ethical philosopher should be held accountable for the standards he or she proposes. It is along this line that we would now like to train our focus on Paul, i.e. so as to assess his record and progress as we assessed Peter's.

We begin with passages from Acts, the problems of using which as a source of information about the life of Paul we have previously acknowledged. Despite all the difficulties which it presents (and in opposition to many modern scholars who see it as mostly contributing toward an understanding of the early church's theology rather than of its history), we see Acts as a source from which to quarry much valuable information. This being the case, it is interesting to read in Acts two stories about Paul's early career in the Christian ministry as an indication of how far he had to go even after he had been converted by the blinding light of the road.

In the thirteenth chapter of Acts an episode takes place on the island of Cyprus, to which Paul and Barnabas have gone on a mission perhaps a year or two after the conversion of Saul.[9] "They went through the whole island as far as Paphos and found a certain man, a sorcerer, a false Jewish prophet by the name of Barjesus who was with the proconsul Sergius Paulus, a man of understanding. This one summoned Barnabas and Saul and sought to hear the teaching of God." (13.6-7) So far, so good; Paul seems to be on the brink of an encounter with the semi-pagan world which is, as we have seen in connection with Cornelius, waiting to hear the gospel. "But Elymas the sorcerer (for this is the way his name is translated) withstood them, seeking to turn the proconsul away from the faith." (13.8) This kind of intervention was to be expected in the regions through which Paul was so sedulous to travel in his preaching of the word, Paul did pose threats to the vested religious interests, as his experience in an Ephesus devoted to the worship of Diana (Acts 19) shows. Up to this point the story on Cyprus is of great interest to students of anthropology and comparative religion. Where it becomes of interest to an understanding of birth from above is in its depiction of Paul's reaction to this sorcerer's interference: "But Saul, who is also Paul, was filled with the holy spirit and was looking hard at him [i.e. Elymas] and he said, 'O full of every guile and unscrupulousness, son of the devil, enemy of all righteousness, will you not cease from diverting the straight ways of the lord?" (13.9-10)

Even the fine fury, the righteous indignation of these words might be excusable except that, just as in Peter's dealing with Ananias and Sapphira, Paul's intent becomes minatory on more than the merely verbal level as he continues to speak: "And now behold, the hand of the lord is upon you and you shall be blind, not seeing the sun until the proper time. Suddenly a mist and a darkness fell upon him, and he was going around in search of someone to lead him by the hand." (13.11) It is true that this display of authority and power has certain results in these surroundings, i.e. "the proconsul then saw what had happened and he started to believe, being amazed at the teaching of the lord," (13.12) but the question might be asked whether God wants a flock of scared spiritual sheep who have been prodded into the fold by bolts of lightning called down from heaven as his worshippers, would such worshippers be capable of worshipping God "in spirit and truth" as Jesus conceived of those modalities, in his conversation with the woman at the well, and even if the new terrified worshippers were still capable of that kind of worship, would God want one group to be brought in at the expense of damage to even one person such as Elymas, does God ever look at any human being as an expendable thing to be used in forwarding the purpose of the kingdom?

It seems that Paul at the beginning of his career, like Peter, is prone to spiritual saber-rattling, has not yet attuned himself to the Jesus who rebuked his disciples when they proposed calling down fire upon the Samaritan villages. (Luke 9.51-56) In other words, birth from above does not result in instant spiritual adulthood for Paul.

It may not even result in spiritual adulthood after more than fourteen years. Again there are serious problems in precisely dating an episode which takes place at the end of the fifteenth chapter of Acts. From Galatians we can derive the fact that at least fourteen years have to have passed from the time of Paul's experience on the road to Damascus.[10] In Acts 15, after the Jerusalem conference (about which, as we have shown in our discussion of Peter, we feel that Paul in Galatians is a more reliable source than Luke is in Acts), Paul and Barnabas are shown settling down to preach in Antioch (Acts 15.35). It is to Antioch at this time that Peter and then the Judaizers come, and it is in Antioch that Peter, by his pusillanimity concerning table fellowship, corrupts even Barnabas (Galatians 2.11-14), so that Paul and Barnabas may have been somewhat at odds when, as Luke reports, "After a certain number of days Paul said to Barnabas, 'Let us return and throughout ever city see how the brothers are among whom we preached the word of the lord.'"(15.36) Barnabas must have responded favorably to this suggestion, but he had one request to make of Paul: "Barnabas also wanted to take along John called Mark." (15.37) Paul was not particularly pleased by this idea: "Paul did not consider it worthy to take along this one, the one who had gone away from them, from Pamphilia, and who had not come along into the work with them." (15.38. cf. Acts 13.13 for the so-called apostasy of John Mark)[11]

Reading between the lines, as one is driven to do with Acts, we think that in Acts 15 John Mark may have come down to Antioch with the delegation of Judaizers from Jerusalem and then been converted by Paul's arguments, by Paul's excoriation of Peter in the matter of table-fellowship which Paul describes in Galatians 2. Out of admiration for Paul, John Mark would then have wanted to sign on with Paul in his mission, and Barnabas, who is described as a good man and full of the holy spirit and faithfulness (11.24), and whose tendency is always to try to reconcile people, to try to re-introduce people into fellowships from which they may have been excluded (it is Barnabas who reconciles the apostles to Saul for instance in Acts 9.27), tries to act as an advocate for him with Paul. But Paul (in our interpretation of this episode) would still have tended to be suspicious of someone who had come down as part of a hostile delegation to Antioch, and so he refused to accept John Mark as part of the mission he was organizing, using the old Pamphilia episode as his ostensible excuse. The result, according to Luke, is that a "sharp disagreement" arose between Paul and Barnabas resulting in the divergence of their preaching paths. (15.39-40)

Here again, we can see Paul acting with less than full enlightenment, with less than full Christian maturity. Of course it is only a rare person who will agree to take someone whom he or she considers a potential traitor into his or her own retinue — Jesus was such a person in that he called Judas, whose tendencies he seems to have intuited in advance, as one of the twelve, but there are not many like him. On the other hand, if the scenario that we have drawn up is correct, then John Mark had repented of his old views and sincerely wanted to be taken into Paul's entourage. If this had been the case, then Paul's rejection of John Mark would have been somewhat less defensible, another sign that birth from above does not automatically or even after a long period of time extirpate harsh personality traits, unforgiving tendencies.

What the New Testament allows us to discover, however, is that Paul evidently came to have a change of heart concerning John Mark. In the personal greetings at the end of Paul's letter to the Colossians we read that "Aristarchus my fellow-prisoner greets you as does Mark, the cousin of Barnabas (concerning whom you received instructions, if he comes toward you receive him)" (4.10) This passage can be used to corroborate the stories which we have been looking at in Acts. John Mark might have been looked on as an enemy among certain followers of Paul, this reputation a residue of the old dispute in Antioch, so that in his letter to the Colossians Paul has to place special emphasis on the reinstatement of John Mark, but the fact is that now at least Paul wants such reinstatement, Paul has repented and matured. In 2 Timothy, which may not, in its present form, be entirely by Paul, but which in its personal sections does seem to reflect real information about the Pauline circle, we find John Mark described as "beneficial unto the service," (2 Tim. 4.11) i.e. from having been scorned, he has advanced so far as to be considered a valued colleague of Paul's.

There may be some who, in having been born from above, surmount immediately their old suspicions natures, their tendencies to judge and reject, to harbor grudges and suspicions, but if even the apostle Paul did not necessarily surmount such tendencies in himself right away, if even Paul had to grow, then perhaps birth from above needs to be regarded as a process which extends over a period of time rather than as a sudden miraculous blow completely altering a person.

And even relatively late in his career, in his dealings with the Corinthian church, Paul may still have been manifesting a certain unfortunate judgmental tendency, that is his birth may have had to go on even after some of his most significant apostolic accomplishments. Summarizing one of the Corinthian scandals which he has been asked to offer his opinion about in his first letter, Paul says "Actually there is news of sexual immorality among you, and sexual immorality of such a kind as is not among the heathens, so that someone has his father's wife." (5.1) The "incest" at issue here is evidently not what we would call the Oedipal kind, i.e. the man is not sleeping with his own mother. To continue couching the matter in Greek terms, one might call it incest as is threatened in the play *Hippolytus*, except that in Corinth the son is evidently a willing partner to sex with the perhaps divorced wife or maybe the widow of his father — the horror with which certain people greet the possibility of incest between a son and his stepmother in Euripides' play would give a basis for Paul's statement that the Corinthians are tolerating a form of behavior that is not even practiced among "the heathens". The Corinthians are evidently going a little farther than mere toleration too: "And you have been puffed up and have not rather started to mourn, so that the one performing this work might be removed from your midst." (5.2) Whatever the details of the case are, Paul by this characterization of their reaction to it intends to reprimand them for taking pride in their liberated outlook. It is hard to know just how fair or unfair Paul is being at this moment. There is such a thing as pardonable pride, and as long as it does not degenerate into smugness, i.e. as long as by its attempt to sympathize with all kinds of human situations and by its acceptance of the human beings involved in such situations, a church continues to earn the right to such pride, perhaps there are times when a church should be allowed to feel a little bit good about itself. One can imagine Paul's remark cutting rather cruelly against the corporate conscience of a group in Corinth that had been trying to be open-minded and non-judgmental.

Paul at any rate seems very anxious to put the clamps on what in Corinth has threatened to go beyond his own spiritual control: "For I for my part, being absent in body but present in spirit, have already decided as if present concerning the one who in such a fashion is doing this work, by the name of our lord Jesus when you and my spirit are gathered together with the power of our lord Jesus, to hand such a one over to the Satan for the destruction of the flesh, in order that the spirit might be saved in the day of the lord." (5.3-5) We can read in the history of our times about leaders who have nervously hovered over every phase of, say, a government's operation, unable to let go of even the smallest detail. Such leaders have at least been limited by the laws of time and space, but Paul here seems to be putting into effect a strange law whereby he can even extend his spirit so as to occupy and to offer judgement in a place from which he may be physically absent. He does seem to be evincing an almost frenetic concern with the maintenance of his own authority on this occasion as if he could not trust the Corinthians to make a decision on their own, he has to send his spirit so that it can make the decision with them. And what a decision! In terms of English legal tradition, Paul is denying the presumption of the man's innocence until the man can be proven guilty. On the basis of hearsay Paul says that he has already made a decision. And not to mention English tradition, even the Pharisees would not have been so peremptory, as the gospel of John shows us when it quotes Nicodemus as having said in defense of Jesus: "Our law doesn't judge a man unless it first hears from him and knows what he is doing, does it?" (John 7.51)

According to Matthew's gospel, Jesus had prescribed a procedure to the disciples who were not even at the stage of being able to forgive a brother's sins, i.e. the procedure represents a sort of second-best expedient in the absence of the disposition to forgive, but at least it offers some hope for a somewhat fair trial: "If your brother sins against you, go, convince him of his fault between you and him alone. If he listens to you, you have gained a brother. But if he doesn't listen to you, take in addition one or two with you, so that on the evidence of two or three witnesses every saying may stand. But if he refuses to listen to them, speak to the assembly. But if he refuses to listen to the assembly, let him be to you like the gentile or toll-collector." (Matt. 18.15-18) The provenance of this passage has been debated by modern Biblical scholars, many of whom point out that the word *ekklesia,* which we have rendered "assembly" but which could also mean "church", gives this passage away as a construct which later Christians have cast back into the mouth of Jesus, and it may be that Jesus himself would have been likely to hold his followers more strictly to the idea of forgiveness, not wishing to give them any judicial procedures to fall back on. If so, then Paul moves even farther away from having the mind of Christ when he hands down his verdict about the Corinthian so-called offender, i.e. in offering his own summary judgment, he would be at two removes rather than just one from what Jesus had prescribed.

Even more disturbing, however, is the idea of turning someone over to the Satan for the destruction of his flesh so that his spirt may be saved. There have been various interpretations of this prescription. The term "Satan" in this passage may refer to the cosmic adversary of God's purpose (i.e. *the* Satan) or it may refer to some sort of public prosecutor,[12] although in decreeing that a member of the Corinthian congregation be handed over to such an official, Paul would then seem to be contradicting his own subsequent advice in this same letter against taking disputes involving members of the Christian fellowship before secular courts of law. (6.19) But "the Satan" must refer to some kind of accusatory force, to some person or group who will bring charges against the so-called offender.

Some have thought that "flesh" in this passage stands for the man's physical existence and that in handing him over to the Satan, the Corinthians would be putting him beyond the church's protective pale, exposing him to elemental powers which would then kill him. On the other hand, one could interpret "flesh" to mean the man's egocentric perspective as it does elsewhere in Paul, or even some sort of glorying by the man in his advanced outlook, a glorying similar to that which Paul accuses the church of, but then Paul would be suggesting weirdly that the way to cure a man's fleshy outlook is to hand him over to Satan whose whole operation is to encourage reliance on the flesh, to encourage egocentric enterprises:

Satan promotes failure, and the way to insure that human beings will fail ultimately is to isolate them within the boundaries of their own egos and their own resources.

It is true that Satan is a master at pulling people down a peg or two in their own conceptions of themselves; we will examine this aspect of Satan's power later, in connection with the thorn in the flesh which Satan uses as his messenger to buffet Paul, but Paul is not proposing Satan or his emissary (who again, as we suggested above, may in this case be some official of the judicial system) as merely a reminder or an admonition to the man in Corinth, but rather he is proposing that the man be handed over utterly to the Satan. And while it is true that flesh and spirit are often viewed as contrarieties in Paul, it is still strange to see Paul falling back upon what in this passage sounds like the Greek notion of a spirit which can be separated off from its dispensable fleshly counterpart or even worse, husk. The New Testament offers various correctives to the sometimes convenient, sometimes self-exculpating or self-serving, the almost always self-deluding notion that one can do damage to the body so as ultimately to do good to the soul. Several New Testament passages (e.g. 1 John 3.17, James 2.16) suggest that if you claim to love a person's soul, then you should demonstrate that love by doing good to the body on which that soul, according to the Hebrew notion, depends. In the light of this New Testament strain, Paul's directives here look rather ill-judged and unfortunate.

By itself this passage reveals that even at a fairly advanced stage of the new life, a person may exhibit deeply rooted character-traits, the character-trait in Paul's case c. 56 A.D. being a tendency toward judgmental authoritarianism. Birth from above, that is, does not immediately eliminate every element of a person's make-up that is contrary to the message of the gospel and to the will of God, does not turn a person into some sort of euphoric robot remote-controlled in all things by God. There is, however, more to be seen about Paul's dealings with this case, and it is this additional material that reveals certain possibilities inside the new life, which is, after all, the life within a society and not a life of isolated spiritual endeavor.

In the first chapter and a half of 2 Corinthians Paul refers to events that have taken place after the writing of 1 Corinthians. The talk is of a visit or of visits that Paul has promised to make but then has not made to Corinth. Paul defends himself for having changed his plans. He makes implied reference to but does not elaborate on the nature of one visit that he has paid to Corinth already: "For I decided this thing for myself, not to come toward you again in grief." (2.1) To wish not to come to them again in grief implies that he has come to them in grief at least once before, hence the need on the part of Biblical scholars to posit some sort of visit to Corinth, probably after the writing of 1 Corinthians, that did not go well: "For if I grieve you, who is the one who will cheer me up except the one who has been grieved by me? And I wrote this very thing so that I might not come and have grief from those whom I needed to cheer me, convinced about all of you that my joy derives from all of you." (2.2-3) The experience of alienation from the Corinthian church has evidently been so traumatic to Paul that he does not wish to repeat it even though he feels that his motives have been less than perfectly understood among that group: "For out of great suffering and distress of heart I wrote to you through many tears, not so that you would be grieved but so that you might know the love I have for you to such a great degree." (2.4) But still, at this point Paul would rather make peace than see another controversy break out.

This last verse quoted points to one of the difficulties in understanding the circumstances of 2 Corinthians. What document did Paul produce when he wrote out of great suffering and through tears? Scholars have not always agreed on an answer to this question. Some have said that Paul is here referring to 1 Corinthians or at least to some part of it (such as 5.1-11, the part about the "incest" case). Others have said that the document being alluded to has not survived. Others have said that it is different from 1 Corinthians but that it has survived spliced in as a part or as parts of 2 Corinthians. We cannot adjudicate among these various scholarly claims in a book such as this one, although we do have to mention them.[13] Our position is that during the visit that went so badly, that in fact turned into a fiasco, one of the main issues must have been Paul's attempt to enforce his own decision concerning the man who had been living with his father's wife. Paul must have come under sharp attack, and what he is doing in verse four quoted above is to defend his motives, telling how hard it was for him to write about the case of so-called sexual immorality, for whatever reasons and at whatever time (i.e. in 1 Corinthians 5 or in some other document). But there remained the attack to be dealt with.

Evidently the accused man himself had attacked Paul, even though Paul does not consider this an attack solely upon himself: "But if someone has caused giref, he has not caused it to me, but in part (so as not to exaggerate) to all of you." (2 Cor. 2.5) After Paul's visit the Corinthians had evidently seen the attack in a similar light and had gone on to censure the man. It is at this point that Paul wants the process of accusation to stop. "For such a one this punishment by the majority is sufficient so that on the contrary you may the more forgive and console him, lest such a one be swallowed down somehow by excessive grief. Therefore I urge you to put love toward him into effect." (2.6-8) Paul still seems to manifest certain signs of the nervous, hovering authority-figure afraid to let go of his church: "Because for this very reason I wrote [or perhaps here = am writing] to you in order that I might know your character, whether you are obedient unto all things." (2.9) He is afraid, that is, that they will not put into effect this new phase of dealing with the man when it is very important for him that they do so: "But to whom you are forgiving something, so am I. For what I also have forgiven, if I have forgiven anything, I have done so for your sake in the presence of Christ . . ." (2.10)

Perhaps we can point to this episode as one of the best examples of the necessary sociality of the more mature phases of the new life: people acting together, helping each other. It is in fact hard to tell from the verse just quoted above whether it is Paul or the Corinthian Christians who have taken the initiative in forgiveness, so interinvolved has this forgiveness become. Paul and the Corinthian church can re-accept someone whom they have treated as an erring brother. Whether they were correct in so treating him at any time, in so ostracizing him, is another question. This case raises all over again the question of how Jesus might have dealth with a "sinner" such as this one in Corinth, but given the fact that Paul first and then the Corinthians, evidently in response to his frenzied visit, had pretty much made a mess out of the case of this man accused of sexual immorality, the two parties manage to rescue themselves at last from the designs of Satan, whom Paul had originally designated to dispose of the case. Paul says that insofar as he has forgiven anyone anything, he has done so for the Corinthians' sake in the presence of Christ "in order that we might not be taken advantage of by Satan, for we are not ignorant of his designs." (2.11) The designs of Satan involve branding people as worthless and isolating them from the fellowship of the divine society. Paul, by his own admission (Acts 26.18), had once belonged to Satan's party or had been in Satan's power. Even after having been born from above into the new life, he is threatened by relapses into his old Satanic outlook, the conviction that a certain kind of sinner needs to be thrown out. But inasmuch as the new life includes fellowship within a society, and the support of the Paraclete (which name literally means "called to one's side," thus suggesting that the Holy Spirit calls us by means of the person beside us, that our access to the Spirit is not solipsistic), it offers opportunities for continued growth and antidotes to atavistic behavior.

ix. PAUL'S RECORD OF DEALING WITH HIS OPPONENTS: AN EXAMPLE OF HIS GROWTH.

As we see Paul's career, the need to deal in Corinth with this man who had been living with his father's wife may have represented a real turning point. The clue to the importance of this episode lies in the remarks about Satan which we have just quoted above. In lashing out against the man, in attempting to enforce his own authority, Paul may suddenly have seen an abyss opening underneath him, the abyss of the insatiability of the Satanic mechanism once it is put into motion, the self-proliferating endlessness of judgement once it is allowed to manifest itself within a church situation (or within the world for that matter). A passage from Philippians may point to how Paul has been changed by dealing with this man in Corinth, and we will examine that passage eventually, but first, for purposes of comparison, it will be helpful to go back and show Paul at less advanced stages, to review some of the attitudes which he had evinced earlier whenever he had to deal with opponents.

In Galatia, as we saw when we were dealing with the ways in which Christians could backslide from the life into which they were born from above, Paul was facing opposition from a group of Judaizers, i.e. Jewish Christians who wanted to enforce the whole range of traditional Jewish legal observances among a new group of Gentile converts. In his letter, Paul is trying to show why the Galatians are under no obligation to the Jewish law and how they are called to something far less restrictive in the Christian faith. Paul goes to almost vehement lengths to defend his vision of what God wants the gospel to the Gentiles to be. In fact he insists that his vision is based on divine revelation rather than on consultation with any fellow human followers of Jesus: "For I, brothers, am making known to you, the gospel that was preached by me, that it is not according to a human being. For I did not receive it from a human being nor was I taught it but through a revelation of Jesus Christ." (Galatians 1.10-11) Paul counters what may have been some implication on the part of Judaizers in Galatia that he was ready to sever Christianity from its roots in God's Old Testament revelation with a reminder of his own past record of having been loyal to that revelation, perhaps too loyal in fact: "For you heard of my behavior at one time in Judaism, that I was persecuting the church of God excessively and trying to destroy it, and I was advanced in Judaism beyond many contemporaries in my generation, being an even greater zealot for the traditions of my fathers." (2.13-14) It is not that Paul at any time conceived a desire to abandon this intense attachment to Judaism — in fact chapters 9-11 of his letter to the Romans testify eloquently to his continuing concern that the emerging divine family be understood to include his brothers and sisters in the flesh — but rather that at some point he received a special appointment from God which made him an advocate for the viewpoint of the Gentiles too. He describes this special appointment at that same time that he insists on its absolute freedom from any admixture of human consultation or advice, the untainted divinity of its origins: "But when it pleased the one who set me apart [or in some manuscripts "when it pleased God who set me apart"] from my mother's womb and who called me through his grace to reveal his son by me, so that I might proclaim the good news of him among the Gentiles, immediately I did not go to flesh and blood for advice nor did I go up to Jerusalem toward those who were apostles before me, but I went away into Arabia and returned again to Damascus." (1.15-17)

Paul then talks about how after three years he at last went up to Jerusalem and held conversations mostly with Cephas (Peter) but also part of the time with James. The point of this information is that those two apostles did not see fit on this occasion to correct him in any course of gospel-preaching which he had embarked on already, there remained only the one guiding force to his endeavors, namely the divine revelation which he had received. On the other hand, Paul did not think that he could just go ahead and constantly flout or ignore the apostles and their authority. He makes this point explicitly when he discusses another visit which he paid to Jerusalem fourteen years after this first one; he says "I went up according to revelation. And I set before them the gospel which I am proclaiming among the Gentiles, privately to those who have a reputation [i.e. James, Peter, and John], lest in some way I be running or should have been running in vain." (2.2) He would have been running in vain if his mission had split the church off into two rival groups, Paul felt the need to touch base from time to time with the apostles, to receive some blessing, however implicit, from them; for instance, in connection with this second trip to Jerusalem, even though he is under attack from certain "false brothers brought in under false pretenses, who slipped in to spy on our freedom which we have in Christ Jesus so that they might enslave us", (2.4) he still is able to make the significant point that "to me the ones who had a reputation added nothing, but on the contrary, seeing that I had been entrusted with the gospel of the uncircumcision, just as Peter with that of the circumcision, [and that] the one who was at work in Peter unto the mission of the circumcision was at work also in me unto the Gentiles, and knowing the grace given to me, James and Cephas and John, who are reputed to be pillars, gave to me and Barnabas the right hand of fellowship, in order that we might be unto the gentiles and they unto the circumcision." (2.6-9) Again the pillars contributed nothing to the gospel or to the mission of Paul, they only seemed to confirm him in his divinely-appointed labors.

Here then was the dispensation that Paul was at greatest pains to preserve: one mission (his) offering unconditional admission (i.e. no legal observances) to the Gentiles, another mission (under the supervision of the "pillars") to Jews, who would keep their own traditions within the Christian church. It was with great justification that Paul resented any implications that he was anti-Jewish in his bias; in fact he seems to have envisaged what a disaster it would be for the church to reject its Jewish element, and subsequent history has borne him out in such an intuition. The Christian church tacitly accepted the Roman persecutions of the Jews, starting with the Jewish Wars in 66 A.D. Eventually the church tied in with the Roman Empire and continued or extended the policy of attacking "Oriental infidels" in the form of Crusades. In the meantime, as Schoeps in his *Judenchristentum* has shown, the rejected Jewish element of Christianity influenced Mohammed and therefore the whole history of Islam. Islam inherited hostility toward Western Christianity from the start, it inherited it from these Jewish Christians, that hostility was exacerbated by the Crusades . . . Obviously there is no space here for a rehearsal of the religious history of humanity during the last two thousand years, but there is a sense in which Paul was laboring to avert a schism the effects of which are still with us down to the present moment in our violently divided world, three hostile cultures at war where there should have been one human family.

It is important to do maximum justice to the grandeur and the profundity of Paul's vision in respect of the need to have at least a two-track church; one says at least a two-track church since Paul felt that even the Jew who did *not* become Christians were going to be saved ("all Israel will be saved" — Romans 9.26), so that a mere two tracks do not quite represent what he saw as the determination of God to gather human creatures together into one kindred group. It is important to do justice to the scope of Paul's vision lest he be seen on this occasion, i.e. in writing to the Galatians, as merely obsessed with his own authority. Paul did have a vision which, whether or not one wants to ascribe it to divine revelation, was aiming at a radical cure for the splintered condition of the human family, he had in mind a program which he was desperately and, in the main, disinterestedly intent on implementing. But at the stage of his career when he was writing to the Galatians, he tended to identify the needs of this program with himself, he seemed to think that the progress of the divine plan depended solely on him, he held implementation rather desperately in his clutch. One bases such remarks on the warning he issues to the Galatians almost at the very beginning of this letter; he works himself up to a perfervid pitch of agitation concerning the dangers to which the Galatian church is being exposed: "I am amazed that you thus quickly have turned away from the one who called you by the grace of Christ into another gospel, which is not another, unless there are some stirring you up and wishing to distort the gospel of Christ. But even if we or an angel from heaven preaches to you a gospel besides the one which we have preached to you, let that one be accursed. Just as we have said I now say it: if someone preaches a gospel besides the one that you have received, let that one be accursed." (1.6-9) The seriousness of this imprecation may not come across in an English translation; what Paul is putting the hypothetical preacher of another gospel under is a curse from God, in modern colloquial terms he is asking God to zap this kind of rival gospel preacher.

Now of course one could say that Paul is engaging in a little flamboyant rhetoric here as a way of alerting his Galatian readers to the importance of the issues he means to discuss with them; one could say that he has not really called a curse down upon a specific person, but only on a hypothetical someone. But since we have to assume that he is dealing with real opponents in Galatia, sooner or later someone is going to preach a different gospel again and thus fall under the curse that Paul has asked God to deliver. Therefore this threatening posture of Paul's must be taken seriously and as a Christian leader, one of the fountains of the faith, he has to be judged by the standard which we have continued to hold up at many places in this account, namely the life and the attitudes of Jesus. No gospel contains any record of Jesus ever calling down on another person the kind of curse (Greek = *anathema*) which Paul calls down upon the rival preachers in Galatia. All three Gospels do record prophetic woes (Greek = *ouai*), which are cries of indignation or pain and somewhat akin to curses, issuing forth from Jesus' mouth. Matthew groups a number of these together to form an impressive jeremiad delivered against the Pharisees (chapter 23), and he is not the only reporter of such a strain in Jesus' preaching: Luke's gospel contains many of the same statements that Matthew groups together in one place; Luke scatters them to different sections of his gospel, but the fact that he also records them removes from them the possible limitation of reflecting only Matthew's biases. Furthermore Mark, who presumably did not draw from one great tradition about the preaching of Jesus which Matthew and Luke both utilized, the hypothetical document referred to by scholars as Q, also depicts Jesus as uttering woes of this kind. Therefore there is good reason to believe that Jesus did at times break into denunciations of evils, denunciations mostly of hypocritical behavior on the part of self-styled "religious" types. It is important to remember that Jesus did not spend his time attacking so-called sinners who fell outside the pale of supposedly pious norms, i.e. he did not pick on groups such as "secular humanists" or homosexuals to pillory; what angered him was judgmentalism parading as pious virtue when in his view God was the loving parent who had gotten rid of Satan, his onetime prosecuting attorney.

If Jesus be the standard, then Paul may not be missing the mark completely, he at least has some justification, some precedent when he denounces those who preach a gospel other than his, at least if we assume that it was God's will that the Gentiles be brought without conditions, by a free gift, into the divine family that was being formed: there may be times when those who are in possession of ultimate truths may have to insist upon them with the utmost vehemence. On the other hand, by further examining the career of Jesus for clues, we are made aware of what is perhaps a still more excellent way, the way of what we might call divine disengagement. Jesus exemplified this way when, according to the Gospel of John, he said to his disciples at the Last Supper "it is better for you that I go away, for unless I go away the paraclete will not come." (John 16.7) At this point in his career, Jesus evidently did not think that the advancement of the cause for which he had labored depended solely on him, he did not think that without him the cause could not go forward. He in fact had made the amazing promise to his disciples that without him present (although it was to be with his help somehow) they would go on to do greater works than he himself had ever done. (John 14.12) He showed himself willing that is to let his own cause go free. One does not sense the existence of a similar willingness in the Paul who wrote to the Galatians and insisted on his message and no other as the authentic embodiment of God's purposes for the Gentiles.

Now of course Paul is not the only human being ever to have confounded himself with a cause or ever to have thought that only he or she could continue to carry forward a cause. It is strange that the French Nineteenth Century poet Gérard de Nerval, in a poem about the Mount of Olives, has Jesus say "Et si je meurs, c'est que tout va mourir" (and if I die it is that everything is going to die). Jesus, as we have just seen, is conspicuously free of such an attitude, at least as the Gospel of John depicts him at the Last Supper. Nerval's words would have been much more germane to Paul at the stage of his career when he was writing his letter to the Galations and thinking that only he saw how important it was to let the Gentiles in with no conditions attached, when he was thinking that the whole enterprise of the establishment of the divine society throughout the world depended on the truths which he had been granted by revelation. By contrast to an anxious insistent attitude such as this one of Paul's, being born from above involves coming to understand that you are part of a body and that the body does not rise or fall with your performance, that there are other cells that will contribute. As we have said before, being born from above is in part learning to let go.

It seems that by the time he comes to write the last part of his second letter to the Corinthians Paul has made some progress toward a more enlightened evaluation of his own position in the divine scheme. One reaches this conclusion by following Paul's thoughts through a rather complicated apology which comes at the end of this letter.[14] The situation in these last chapters seems to be similar to the one which led to his remarks about being led around as an odorous prisoner in God's triumphal procession (chapters 2-5), remarks which included his assertions about the true glory of an apostle. He may even be here resuming the defense which he had conducted in that other extended discussion. His apology at any rate has some of the same paradoxical qualities, at least in reference to what people might expect an apostle to be. Paul has evidently been attacked from a number of standpoints, some of them of a rather pettily personal nature having to do perhaps with his appearance, or with appearances, so that Paul first tries to lay it down as a premise of the self-defense he is willing to make that "we are walking in the flesh but we do not do battle according to the flesh for the weapons of our warfare are not fleshly but rather powerful in God toward the tearing down of strongholds, tearing down false arguments and every proud obstacle piled up against the knowledge of God, and leading prisoner every thought into obeying Christ, and being ready to avenge every disobedience, whenever your obedience is fullfilled." (2 Cor. 10.3-6) This all sounds like more authoritarianism of the kind he was trying to enforce among the Galatians and such an impression is not dispelled by what follows, where Paul seems to be on the verge of making claims for himself after the manner of those who, to use his vivid term, were "huckstering" the gospel: "If anyone has convinced himself, that he is of Christ, let him take this into account, that just as he is Christ's, so also are we." (10.7)

But again, as we soon see, Paul is not basing his defense on any claims that he can muster up out of his own person, or at least in comparing his position here to his position as he was writing to the Galatians, one can say that he is not insisting here on his own authority as an apodictic dispenser of propositions about the purposes of God. It is true that, in what seems to be a response to some kind of charge that he has gone beyond his apostolic jurisdiction, he falls back on divine allotments which he feels sure that he received: "But we will not boast beyond limits but according to the measure of area which the God of measure has measured out to us, so as to reach as far as you. For just as, having reached as far as you, we are not overextending ourselves, for we reached even as far as you by the gospel of Christ, without boasting beyond limits in the labors of someone else, but having hope as your faith grows to be magnified among you according to our much greater sphere so as to preach the good news to parts beyond you so as not in the sphere of another to boast about things that are already prepared. But let the one who boasts boast in the lord. For it's not the one who recommends himself, not that one who passes the test, but the one whom the lord recommends." (10.13-17) In the somewhat garbled prose of this passage (the translation reflects the difficulties of the Greek), Paul may be appealing to the counsels of God, but here the appeal is not for the purpose of building up his own authority.

Furthermore, having pulled this much rank in regard to his rivals in Corinth, Paul then seems slightly embarrassed, he pulls back a little (although not completely) by giving his reasons for concern: "You ought to put up with my foolishness a little bit. But also put up with me. For I am jealous of you with the jealousy of God, for I gave you in marriage a holy virgin to one man to stand before Christ. But I fear lest, just as the serpent led Eve astray by his guile, your minds may be seduced from the sincerity and holiness which are of Christ." (11.1-3) It sounds as if he fears the Corinthians are in a plight similar to that which was plaguing the Galatians, and Paul corroborates this impression by stating a condition which almost sounds like a re-run of the condition which he stated in his letter to the Galatians: "For if the one who comes proclaims another Jesus whom we did not proclaim, or you receive another spirit which you did not receive or another gospel which you were not taught, you do a good job of giving patient attention to him." (11.4) Almost the same conditions as with the Galatians, yes, but what a different conclusion! "You do a good job of giving patient attention to him." Now of course, Paul is to a large extent being ironic here; he isn't really commending the Corinthians for the attention which they devote to any rival preacher, but the mere fact that he can now be ironic in regard to a situation which once prompted him to call down curses from God suggests that he is making some sort of progress in letting go of an insistence on only *his* particular message.

Not that he is willing to capitulate completely, to cave in before these rival preachers or before the ones who may have sent them: "For I suppose myself to have fallen short of the extra-special apostles in no way. But even if I am unskilled in speech, I am not so in knowledge . . ." (11.5-6) But in this passage, as he returns to dealing with some of the charges that have been brought against him he does not resort to the highhanded expedient of invoking his divine authority. He seems willing to be judged on the same level as the others just so long as his true motives have been understood. For instance, he has evidently been criticized for not taking payment from the Corinthian church even though he has let other churches support him financially in his endeavors. Paul does not explain why he will not take payment from the Corinthians although he dismisses the implication that he is refusing payment from them because he does not love them (11.11); what he does do is evoke the sort of accusation-charged atmosphere in which he has been forced to work, suggesting that it is this atmosphere which has driven him to refuse payment from the Corinthians: "What I am doing I also will do, in order that I may cut off occasion from those who want an occasion, in order that by what they boast they may be found exactly as we are." (11.12) Then he goes on to characterize this group that has driven him to refuse payment: "For ones of that kind are false apostles, guileful workers, disguising themselves as Christ's apostles. And it's no wonder. For Satan himself was disguised as an angel of light. Therefore it's no great thing if his servants disguise themselves also as servants of justification. Whose end will be according to their deeds." (11.12-15) That is to a Corinthian church that may have been impressed with the rival preachers, Paul tries to point out the self-contradictions in their message: it is play-acting for such people to preach justification; as Judaizers preaching obedience to the law, they don't really believe in justification but rather in salvation that is earned; they are advocates of the system that Satan is so adept at using to his advantage and toward the promotion of his ends (condemnation). The comment that their end will be according to their deeds probably reflects the key New Testament idea that "with what measure you measure out it will be measured out to you," (Matthew 7.1) so that if you preach justification by merit, then in the end you will be judged by that standard, the idea that one picks one's own kind of treatment before the judgment seat of Christ.

The situation which Paul finds himself in as he writes these chapters is evidently the same one he had been in earlier when he wrote about himself as the sweating fellow-prisoner of Christ. He finds it distasteful to have to defend himself again, he even makes excuses for doing so, but he has been driven to such a position, he can no longer refrain: "Again I say, let no one think me foolish. Or otherwise, at least bear with me as foolish, in order that I also might boast a little. What I am saying I am not saying according to the Lord but as by foolishness, in this assurance of boasting. Since many boast according to the flesh, I also will boast. Being wise, you gladly put up with those who are foolish. For you put up with it if someone enslaves you, if someone swallows you down, if someone takes you in, if someone puts on airs, if someone beats you in the face. I speak in shameful fashion, as if because we have been weak." (11.16-21) On a superficial level, Paul here seems to be reversing his earlier refusal not to advertise himself, but on closer examination, the boasting in which he now engages is really consistent with that earlier refusal, for as Paul at one point puts it, remarking on the services to the gospel which he has started to recite, "If it is necessary to boast, I will boast of the things of my weakness" (11.30), that is the things he shows himself to be proud of are things that most people would be ashamed of, namely beatings, lashings, persecutions, the life of a public outcast: "Five times under the Jews I received the 'forty minus one' [this refers to lashes of the whip], I was beaten with a stick three times, I was stoned once, three times I suffered shipwreck, I passed a night and a day in the deep. Many times in journeys, in dangers from rivers, in dangers from robbers, in dangers from kinfolk, in dangers from pagans, in dangers in the city, in dangers in the wilderness, in dangers in the ocean, in dangers among false brothers, in labor and hardship, in sleepless nights many times, in famine and thirst, in fasting many times, in cold and nakedness. Apart from these external things, the daily pressure on me, the anxiety for all the churches. Who is weak and I am not weak? Who is offended and I am not set on fire?" (11.24-29)

He also goes on to set forth mystical experiences, which someone, whom he refers to in the third person, has had — this someone is probably himself, and he would be willing to boast of this someone's special access to the divine dimension (just as he had once boasted to the Galatians of his divine revelation): "I will boast concerning such a one, but I will not boast about mysef except in my weaknesses." (12.5) But then he tells how even if he is the one who has had the mystical experiences, he nevertheless seems to carry around inside his body a sort of safeguard against the putting on of airs, against the tendency to boast about the wrong things: "Lest I be puffed up with pride, a stake in the flesh was given to me, a messenger of Satan so that he might buffet me, in order that I not be puffed up with pride." (12.7) This stake probably refers to some region of extreme self-doubt which Paul continued to harbor, some psychic point at which he was vulnerable to accusatory inner voices, to voices calling his career as an apostle in question (perhaps over the issue of his persecution of the Hellenistic church). The impact of the work of Satan, whether we think of him as some specific spiritual agent or whether we think of him as a force at work throughout the human race, some collective tendency of judgement to which the human race is unhappily subject, is to hamper the free self-fulfillment of persons. The idea of neurosis eating away at most individuals, preventing them from reaching their potential, may be a modern clinical way of describing Satan's work, or the effect of Satan's work. Paul's way of describing Satan's inroads has its own vividness of course; he says that the pain of the stake was such that three times Paul petitioned God for relief from it, but God evidently saw a use to which the inroads of Satan could be put (just as neurosis can sometimes be a spur to certain great kinds of achievement): "And he has said to me, My grace is enough for you, for by weakness power is made perfect." (12.9) This oracular pronouncement might be taken as a gloss upon the career of the suffering servant, upon the mysterious way in which God brings about the redemption of the world (how different from the way of secular rulers, who have a horror of appearing weak in any way — among nations no one will ever take the first step of standing back and saying that the chain of aggressive action and re-action has to stop somewhere, and so aggression continues escalating toward Armageddon).

Paul seems to be talking here, however cryptically, about the way he came into a deeper understanding of the career he was called to fulfill. In the immediate context of this passage, he is explaining why he does not boast about the things that most people trying to win adherents from among a group of people like the Corinthian church would tend to boast about. "Most gladly all the more then I will boast in my weaknesses, in order that the power of Christ may rest upon me." (12.9) Here we can see that at this stage Paul has learned or is in the process of learning how to let go, a lesson which we have cited several times as one of the most important ones to learn in connection with the birth from above. Jesus told the rich young ruler that he had to let go of his wealth (the supposed source of his power). He also told his disciples that in order to gain one's life one had to lose it. It is this kind of outlook which Paul seems to have advanced to here so as to embrace the office of buffeted suffering servant: "I delight therefore in weaknesses, in insolences, in necessities, in persecutions and tight squeezes on Christ's behalf, for when I am weak, then I am strong." (12.10) It is this kind of outlook therefore which colors any boasts he now may be making, as when he says "For I in no way fell short of the extra special apostles even if I am nothing." (12.11) In the divine family, one becomes preëminent by agreeing to become nothing first, one has to surrender the usual trappings and tricks by which we tend to build up self-esteem.

At this point in Paul's discussion, the subject of Paul's not taking any payment from the Corinthian church arises again, this time in connection with two different responses that this refusal of his prompts. It is ironic that Paul should have just shown himself so enlightened in view of the role of the suffering servant only to remain perhaps at a less advanced stage in respect of the exchange of resources and gifts which is also an essential part of the new life. When we discussed the encounter between Jesus and the woman at the well, we showed how, as soon as the woman revealed her openness to Jesus' searching concern, as soon as she revealed her willingness to stand in the light of his understanding and love, a circulating system started to operate in which the one who had conferred benefits also started to receive benefits back. The one who is truly born from above will be ready to let such a circulating system work. Jesus was willing to accept gifts during his career — he accepted for instance the costly gift of myrrh that was being used to anoint him in his encounter with Mary of Bethany. It may be that in his refusal to accept gifts from the Corinthians Paul continued to be motivated by guilt concerning the role he had once played as persecutor of the Hellenistic church (even though such an analysis would not explain why by contrast he was to accept gifts from the Macedonians — 2 Cor. 11.9). Nevertheless at this point he seems still to have been closed to one aspect of the new life, not perfectly mature, unable to acknowledge his dependence, which dependence is no disgrace inside the divine family.

Furthermore, as far as his maturity is concerned, he still seems to be exhibiting some of the old authoritarian nervousness when he says "I am afraid lest I come and not find you such as I want you to be." (12.20) It should be added that to this statement he adds the fear that he will not be found as they want him to be, that is he recognizes that there are responsibilities on both sides if the relationship between him and the church at Corinth is going to be mended, but he still seems a little bit like the Paul whom we saw in Galatians (or like Talus, the iron man with the flail in the fifth book of Spenser's *Faerie Queene*) when he rattles the power of Jesus as a kind of threat: "I have said before and I am saying before, just as being present a second time so being absent now, to those who have sinned before and to all the rest, that if I come again I will not spare, since you seek attestation of the Christ who speaks in me, who will not be weak to you but will be powerful among you." (13.3) But behind this threat there now lies a willingness to sacrifice himself for the cause of his congregation: "But we pray toward God that you not do anything evil, not in order that we might appear to have passed the test, but in order that you might be doing the good, and we be as having failed the test." (13.7) This is the same sort of willingness to throw away his own standing before God that Paul manifests when in regard to the apparent rejection of Israel he says "For I have prayed to be accursed (*anathema*) from Christ on behalf of my brothers, my kinsmen according to the flesh" (Romans 9.3). Whatever residues of immaturity we can find in Paul's attitudes at this juncture, we must still admit that it is quite a change from his having once called down curses upon rival preachers for him to now wish to have the curses light upon him (as in Romans) or for him to now be willing to be the one rejected, found wanting for the sake of some group which he cares about.

But Paul matures still farther before he disappears from historical sight. The last letter of his which we have was written from some prison to the church at Philippi; scholars are divided as to where the prison was, but one can at least say that when Paul was in this prison, he had been through all the crises at Corinth, he had perhaps had some sort of profound insight about the overreaching designs of Satan to swallow the churches down into the sump of strife and accusation. The letter to the Philippian church shows Paul having pulled back from his former readiness to engage in controversies into a new willingness to let God work things out in a way that maybe no human being is completely able to understand. Near the beginning of this letter he writes, "I want you, brothers, to know that in what concerns me the things that result in the gospel's advance have come about all the more powerfully, so that by Christ my chains are becoming known in the whole praetorium and to all the rest, and a greater number of the brothers in the Lord are having confidence by my chains to dare to a greater degree to speak the word fearlessly." (Philippians 1.12-14) In this situation perhaps Paul is at last enjoying the type of publicity that truly befits one who wants to act as a suffering servant, and interestingly enough, what Paul has talked about in previous letters is actually happening here: his situation of weakness does impart power to others around him, perhaps more power than a situation of strength could ever have imparted.

The motives of those who now have more courage to preach the gospel are of a mixed sort: "Some on account of envy and strife, some on account of good will are proclaiming Christ. Some out of love, knowing that I am laid up for the gospel's defense, some from selfish ambition are proclaiming Christ, not with pure motive, supposing to raise up affliction to my chains." (1.16-17) This sort of contradictory situation is not new in a career that has coincided with the ferment of the early days of Christianity. What is new and quite extraordinary is Paul's reaction to it; all he says about the various motivations of the gospel preachers is "What of it? Only that in every way, whether by false motive or by truth, Christ is being proclaimed and in this I rejoice." (1.18) No longer do we find him angrily insisting on only the correct (meaning his) doctrine's being preached. It seems to be enough that Christ is being made known in some way, that Christ is being introduced into various minds. Paul himself almost seems no longer to matter.

Of course by now, for such a famous apostle, anonymity or invisibility is not quite feasible and he does have to consider what his own options are. But again, in so doing, he seems to want to be nothing but a clear medium through which the glory of Christ can shine. "For I know that for me this will result in salvation through your prayer and the support of the spirit of Jesus Christ according to my eager expectation and hope that I will not be ashamed by anything but that with all boldness as always even now Christ will be magnified by my body, either through life or through death." (1.19-20) He then goes on to discuss how his own preference at this point would be to die, "for to me to live is Christ and to die a gain" (1.21). But he also recognizes that it might help other people if he were to go on living: "But if to live, this to me is the gain of the work, and I don't know what I will choose. I am under tension between the two, having the wish to depart and be with Christ, for it is much better. But to remain in the flesh is more necessary for your sakes." (1.23-24) What Paul may mean by this last remark is that the faith of his readers will be strengthened if they see him being delivered from prison. He is probably not propounding a theory of his own indispensability, but at the same time the remembrance of the Philippians' needs seems to pull him away from his own preference for death back toward a willingness to live for the sake of others: "And being convinced of this, I know that I will remain and stand by all of you for your advancement and enjoyment of the faith, in order that your boast might abound in Christ Jesus by me through my presence again toward you." (1.25-26) Still the lack of any ego-insistence is what seems most conspicuous in this passage.

There is also a new spirit in the admonitions which he delivers to this congregation: "Only conduct yourselves in a way worthy of the gospel of Christ, so that whether I come and see or am away and hear things about you, you stand in one spirit, that you work together as one self by the faithfulness of the gospel, not being frightened by any of those who oppose, which is a demonstration to them of destruction, but of your salvation, and this from God. For the things concerning Christ were given to you, not only to believe in him but also to suffer on his behalf, having the same struggle such as you see in me and now hear to be in me." (1.27-30) Opposition is no longer something to lash out against or to obliterate, nor is it something to be feared; it is first of all something to be looked at as the tares are looked at in Jesus' parable, i.e. as something for God to take care of; it is also to be endured as one of the sufferings which Jesus' fellow servants must undergo. How far such an attitude is from that of the old Paul who seemed intent on extirpating every last piece of faulty doctrine wherever he encountered it. In a way the wisdom which by now he has attained resembles that of his teacher Gamaliel when faced with what the leaders of Israel were regarding as the Christian heresy in its early days. Gamaliel had said to his fellow religious leaders concerning the Christian movement "If this purpose or this work is from human beings, it will come to nothing. But if it is from God, you cannot destroy it lest you also be found to be opposing God." (Acts 5.38-9) In a negative sense Paul now sees that one can wait confidently to see the purposes of God being accomplished in time. But in a positive sense, he is also ready to suffer in order to bring those purpose about. In this sense he has truly developed since the time of writing his letter to the Galatians from being one who wanted to pronounce the word from on high to being one who was willing to present it by enacting and embodying its message, namely that God had taken upon himself the brunt of all the destructive energies of the world so as to convert them into good.

EPILOGUE

Perhaps like unthrifty stewards, or virgins failing to trim their lamps, we have reserved very little for our conclusion. Nor are we, as literary strategists, overly fond of that tactic whereby an author or authors simply repeat all the points which they have already made, as if the reader had not retained them or could not, if he or she were interested, go find them again in the text. Still, it may be wise to look once more at birth from above under the assumption that such a process will look different to us now because of our having examined four people who experienced it.

Four emotionally charged people who had led morally dubious lives underwent encounters with Jesus and thus the transformation of their lives began. This is perhaps the first generalization we can make about the New Testament characters whom we have examined. The generalization holds even in the case of Paul who claimed to have been blameless with reference to righteousness by law (Philippians 3.6): perfection in his case had led to the moral catastrophe of fanatacism and persecution. It is interesting to speculate, as we have done at several points, about a possible preference on God's part for moral failures and failures of all kinds, rejects, outcasts, as chosen vessels and instruments for the advancement of his kingdom, a preference which Paul has formulated memorably in his first letter to the Corinthians: "God has chosen the foolish things of the world, in order that he might put to shame the wise, and God has chosen the weak things of the world in order that he might put to shame the strong things, and God has chosen the world's unpedigreed ones and those treated by it with contempt, the things which are not in order that he might nullify the things which are, in order that no flesh might boast before God." (1 Cor. 1.27-29) Not that God wants personality-ciphers. The people we have dealt with in this study all seem to have had strongly formed personalities when they met Jesus. From their cases one could conclude that in order to induce birth from above, God needs something to work with that will offer real resistance, not inert lumps of human matter. Perhaps the most relevant Biblical image here would be that of Jacob who wrestled all night with his mysterious adversary, the conclusion to be drawn being that God welcomes a live adversary, just as he wants to hear from human beings in prayer what is really on their minds, not the perpetual "After you Alphonse" of a "Thy will be done." Relationships between human beings depend on people being forthright; a relationship can be destroyed when one person will not make his or her true wishes or feelings known. So it would seem to be in a relationship with God. The woman at the well in her willingness to stand before Jesus as she really is exemplifies one important factor in any birth from above.

Not that she in her strength of personality, with her emotional charge, is necessarily oriented in a productive or fruitful direction. Except for Paul, who was organized too much, the people whom we have looked at were more like diffuse energy fields waiting to be properly organized or integrated, pulled together to use a modern phrase. But there has to be something there if God is going to pull it together in what we have been calling the birth from above. Luther had an insight related to our concept of what is requisite beforehand for the birth from above when he counseled bold sinning. Better some sort of strength of conviction than that lukewarmness which, as Revelation suggests, God has little use for. Better assertion toward something than the "tumid apathy" which T.S. Eliot saw afflicting spiritually stagnant Londoners in one of his *Four Quartets*.

So much by way of last summarizing remark about the pre-natal phase. But what about after birth from above? First of all, the new life out into which the birth from above issues is not a panacea. We made this point as often as we could in the chapters above or at least we made it about the two men whose careers we analyzed; the New Testament did not provide us with enough material about the long-term born-from-above condition of the two women. In the case of Peter and Paul, however, we saw how personality traits which had marked them before their births from above continued to manifest themselves in their new lives and had to be gradually transformed. Secondly, as the career of Paul shows, in being born from above, a person does not suddenly, miraculously come into complete possession of all spiritual and doctrinal truth. One only has to follow in chronological order the formulations of Paul concerning resurrection to see how, concerning a matter so fundamental to the Christian faith as this one, Paul had to grow out of handed-down dogmas into his own far bolder intuituions about the transfer from a state of life in this world to a state of life in another. In 1 Thessalonians (4.15-18) he is still propounding traditional Jewish inter-Testamental eschatology; even in 1 Corinthians 15 he retains some features of a traditional Day of Judgment although here his originality starts taking shape too; in 2 Corinthians (5.1-10) and Philippians (1.23) he has arrived at an original doctrine of his own. But this sort of evolution is to be expected in a state which Paul had finally come to understand and to describe by the time he wrote the last letter of his which has been preserved: "It is not that I have already received or been brought to maturity already, but I am seeking whether I might obtain, in that I also have been obtained by Christ Jesus. Brothers, I do not reckon myself to have obtained. But one thing, having forgotten the things behind, but stretching toward those that are ahead, I am pursuing toward the goal unto the prize of the higher calling of God in Christ Jesus." (Phil. 3.12-14) If we think of the entire span of Paul's career, we can say that he had a long way to go and that he went it, or that he was going it, because as he himself seems to suggest in this passage, there is a sense in which one never reaches the goal — just as, in the case of knowledge, the rule is that the more one obtains, the more one sees that there is to obtain, so in the Christian life, the more one matures, the more one is aware of the need to mature still further.

The above remarks refer to the implications, both personal and spiritual, of birth from above for an individual. There is also an outward-looking societal aspect to this process, a world-orientation, a concern for the redemption of the human race and not just for one's own personal salvation. The Samaritans point to this aspect of the birth from above when they recognize Jesus as the "savior of the world". (John 4.42) The woman who washed Jesus' feet suggests by her action (in the Lucan version of it) that this outlook, this aspect of the birth from above may require a willingness to take risks. There was a certain reckless courage in her action if it really did take place at the house of a Pharisee that was full of other Pharisees. In untrammeling her hair, i.e. her own sexuality, out of love for Jesus, she presented a group of pious men with the image of their own inmost buried fears, the image of their own desires which men have always expected women to keep under control for them, and if any man's desires ever break forth in actual enactment, then the man naturally projects all blame for this débacle out onto the the supposedly seductive woman. For her action, for her pains, the woman in this story receives the obloquy of those pious types, she probably knew enough, as someone beyond the pale of respectability, to expect such obloquy beforehand, and yet she proceeds fearlessly anyway. At some point such fearlessness may be a required step toward this world-orientation of the more mature phase of the new birth. Not that it is always or ever very easy to take such a step — one only needs to examine the careers of many of the prophets starting with Moses to see how even some of the most inspired servants of God were reluctant to commit themselves to paths of resistance. As we have pointed out in this study, it may be hardest of all for those who already have some stake (however small) in the established order to commit themselves to making it more just.

We have found Paul glorying in the obloquy he receives, counting every lash and every insult as gain. Birth from above is not a ticket to a comfortable place on the settee of society as it may be constituted at any particular epoch but rather an impetus to change the world. Peter furnishes a good example of the way this impetus works. He has been a parochial legalist all his life in his outlook and yet he is compelled by various means into extending the kingdom which he preaches out toward the so-called sinful world of Gentiles. He encounters fierce resistance within his own psyche ("no way Lord") and from his own complacent group of religious haves, the other "pillars" who lack Peter's burgeoning sense of concern for the world of the "pagan" have-nots. Thus in some sense to really be born from above is to court opposition from those who like the world the way it is already established. A person who is truly born from above is likely to be at odds with society out of a desire to see realized some of the reversals envisioned in Mary's Magnificat. At the same time to have taken up one's place with concerned outsiders or outcasts committed to change is to be fulfilled in some higher sense as Jesus to one's amazement and maybe also to one's disbelief proclaims in the Sermon on the Mount: "The ones who have been persecuted [or the sense of the perfect tense of the Greek participle may almost = who bear the wounds of persecution] for the sake of righteousness [which, as we have said often enough before, = the correction of society's wrongs] are happy, because theirs is the kingdom of the heavens." (Matthew 5.10-11). Jesus is probably thinking here of a group working together, not of some aggregate of Lone Rangers or Don Quixotes (however loveable) tilting at windmills. Part of the happiness of the persecuted ones arises from the context of the group effort (cf. Paul and Silas singing in jail — Acts 16.23), in such a context one's hope is living because the hour is not only coming, it also now is: Jesus does not say that the kingdom of heaven *will* be theirs when he talks about those who have suffered the wounds of persecution for righteousness' sake, he says that it is theirs *now*.

As we have said at several points above, being born from above involves a gamble. One needs the kind of optimism Dwight L. Moody evinced when he said "Make big plans, God is your partner", and yet it is reasonable to wonder how much difference one's own little protest can make in the face of so much that is contrary to the will of God. At the same time, the last point to be made about the four Biblical characters whom we have studied above is that they did make a difference, they had an impact on world history even though, before the fact, they would have had no reason to expect important results from any of their actions. Paul was evidently the one person of some prominence in the group or at least he says that he was conspicuously successful as an observer of the law, a kind of religious celebrity (although not of course to the extent that he became afterwards). But as for the other three: one was a Samaritan woman who had botched her personal life, and yet she ended up being the first preacher of the Gospel and she set in motion or somehow prepared for the conversion of a whole region — the successful preaching in Samaria in the eighth chapter of Acts has to be seen as an outgrowth of the woman at the well's mission; another was a prostitute, a social outcast, and yet she alone was willing to prepare Jesus for an ordeal the effects of which, in the Christian view, have changed the nature of reality, have given us "living hope" (1 Peter 1.3), and as Jesus foretold, she herself has become a part of his place in world history, her story has been intertwined with his; a third was a simple Galilean fisherman who was probably pulled in beyond his depth in many senses but who never gave up thrashing, never gave up trying to swim and whose failures and successes, for better or for worse, established a pattern for behavior on the part of the followers of Jesus which is still influential today. The exfoliating significance of the lives of our characters is no guarantee that any other lives will exfoliate, the person being born from above is in the position of the King of Nineveh in the book of Jonah (3.9) when, concerning the effect of the mass repentance which he is instituting, he says "Who knows?" Jonah had already predicted mass destruction for the Ninevites, the king could have acceded to such a gloomy prediction, but he took the chance, he gambled that it was not too late. Does one dare disturb the universe? The Bible suggest that the answer to this question is yes, one does dare and should dare. Birth from above requires a willingness to offer contributions with a mind open to the possibility that they may actually produce results.

FOOTNOTES

Chapter 1

(1) Hermann Strack and Paul Billerbeck, *Kommentar Zum Neuen Testament* (München, 1924), vol. 2, pp. 421-1.
(2) Raymond E. Brown, *The Gospel According to John* (Garden City, 1966), The Anchor Bible, vol. 29A, pp. 1022-3, 1036-9.
(3) See *ibid., passim.* for apparent problems of historicity created by the "timelessness" of Jesus' remarks in the Gospel of John, i.e. by Jesus seeming to know too much too soon in his career.
(4) For a profound and eloquent discussion of this sort of fluidity on Jacob's part, see Francis I. Andersen and David Noel Freedman, *Hosea* (Garden City, 1980), the Anchor Bible, vol. 24, pp. 594-615.
(5) Perhaps an unidentified king in the text; the Hebrew of this passage in Isaiah is extraordinarily difficult, nor have we tried to produce a smooth translation which might gloss over these difficulties.
(6) There are many ambiguities in the Greek of the prologue of the Gospel of John. Translation involves choices. See Brown, *op. cit.* for discussion.
(7) There is some scholarly debate as to where the exact diving line is between Jesus' words and those of the writer of this Gospel — see Raymond Brown, *op. cit.*, p. 149 for discussion.
(8) For a succinct though magisterial discussion of the Hebrew idea of righteousness, see C.H. Dodd, *The Epistle of Paul to the Romans,* (New York, n.d.), The Moffatt New Testament Commentary, pp. 51-3.

Chapter 2

(1) There are ambiguities in the Greek of this text, about which the authors of this study have had to make some decisions in order to arrive at our interpretation. For a discussion of all possible translations, and for a decision about the ambiguities which differs from ours, see Brown, *op. cit.*, pp. 320-4. Brown also discusses the fact that although Jesus claims to be quoting scripture, there really is no clear-cut scriptural passage from which one can derive this statement of his.

(2) The woman takes Jesus' mind-reading, or we might call it life-reading ability as a sign that he is a prophet, i.e. as a sign that Jesus speaks with some sort of supernatural authority. It may very well be some sort of superhuman gift to have the veils covering a person's life thus fall away, to receive this sudden access of knowledge about someone, although Jesus is not the only one to have ever received such a gift. Jung talks in his autobiographical writings about a similar gift which he possessed.

(3) When the woman leaves her water jar behind, one is reminded of the water jars at the wedding in Cana, since the same Greek word is used to denote both vessels. At the wedding in Cana, Jesus had performed a sign, the meaning of which was that the old system of purification (another product of religious anxiety) was being replaced by the wine of joy. One cannot help thinking that by word-echo the episode of the woman at the well is somehow reiterating or reinforcing the message already made by the scene of the wedding at Cana, that the writer of the Gospel is accumulating evidence by which to make his case for a *novo ordo saeclorum*, a new understanding of the divine dispensation.

(4) Brown, *op. cit.*, pp. 273-4.

(5) The authors would like to acknowledge that the orgins of this theory are to be found in David Smith, *The Days of His Flesh*.

Chapter 3

(1) Brown *op. cit.*, p. 76
(2) cf. Ernest Haenchen, *The Acts of the Apostles* (Philadelphia, 1971), p. 150.
(3) cf. Bruce Metzger, *Textual Commentary on the Greek New Testament.* (United Bible Societies, 1971), pp. 429-34 for arguments for and against its inclusion.
(4) There is a problem with the text of Acts here: some manuscripts call the group being preached to "Hellenes", others call them "Hellenists", but then according to scholars both words may very well refer to Greek-speaking Gentiles, so that whatever the text-reading is, what Luke is depicting is the preaching of the Gospel to non-Jews.

Chapter 4

(1) Paul is known as Saul down to Acts 13.9, which refers to "Saul, whose name is Paul."
(2) Haenchen, *op. cit.*, p. 292.
(3) *ibid.*, pp. 295-7.
(4) In the light of the possibilities which we have posited for Paul's state of mind before the Damascus road encounter there would be two ways to interpret this phrase, namely against the name of Jesus Christ period, i.e. as that name would have been anathema to Paul in any form; or against the name of Jesus Christ as it was embodied by certain Hellenist Jewish Christian groups whom at that time he deplored but whose positions, in a sad irony given that fact that Stephen had to be sacrificed along the way, Paul then later came to adopt.
(5) Unfortunately for those who admire Paul and/or for those who take seriously the need for inclusive language in the church, there is no getting around Paul's lapses into sexist language. These lapses reflect habit built up within a sexist religious system. Buy the grace of God Paul had been

liberated from the sexist Hebrew outlook (and from other parochialisms as well), as he reveals in his dealings with female colleagues, as he reveals when he says "There is neither Jew nor Greek, neither slave nor free, neither male nor female, for you are all one in Christ Jesus," (Gal. 3.28) or as he reveals in his long discussion of the need of husband and wives to be subject *to one another* (Ephesians 5.21 ff.), but the linguistic habits of a lifetime were not easily eradicated, hence Paul's reference here to sons rather than children.

(6) Here we encounter the same paradox which we encountered and discussed in connection with John 1.12-13 in our first chapter, namely the paradox of somehow receiving the authority to become natural children of God; Paul uses the same Greek word that the writer of John does: *tekna,* meaning "natural children". In Paul's thought we are adopted, and yet God has made us like natural children.

(7) John A.T. Robinson in his *Wrestling with Romans* (Philadelphia, 1979), pp. 105-5, interestingly argues for the Spirit as the subject of this verse. This identification works well except for the fact that the spirit would then have to continue on as subject of verses 29 and 30, which are given no new subject explicitly. These following verses, however, seems to require God as their subject, and therefore one tends to prefer God as the subject of verse 28 also.

(8) See Markus Barth, *Ephesians*, (Garden City, N.Y., 1974), The Anchor Bible, vol. 34, pp. 183-192, for an exhaustive treatment of the literature on this subject.

(9) Chronological difficulties arise in dealing with this phase of Paul's career; cf. William F. Orr and James Arthur Walther, *1 Corinthians* (Garden City, N.Y. 1976), The Anchor Bible, vol. 32, pp. 59-61.

(10) cf. Orr/Walther, *op. cit.*, pp. 6-10.

(11) Luke's Greek is somewhat garbled here, perhaps because of faulty transmission, although the basic meaning is clear; the text is hard to render into smooth English.

(12) cf. Orr/Walther, *op. cit.*, pp. 186, 188

(13) For compendious treatment of all of them, and for one solution to the problem see Victor Paul Furnish, *II Corinthians* (Garden City, N.Y. 1984) The Anchor Bible, vol. 32A, pp. 153-168.

(14) Some scholars think that the material in these chapters (10-13) is foreign to the rest of the letter and constitutes some part or perhaps even the whole of another document in a sequence of letters to Corinth; the arguments over this issue do not really affect the point that we are making here; whatever relationship the closing chapters of 2 Corinthians may bear to the other letters Paul wrote to this church, they still show him at a different stage from the one he had reached when he wrote the letter to the Galatians.